INSIDERS' GUIDE®

OFF THE BEATEN PATH® SERIES

Off the Beaten Path®

NINTH EDITION

illinois

A GUIDE TO UNIQUE PLACES

BOB PUHALA

Revised and updated by
Lyndee Jobe Henderson

The prices, rates, and hours listed in this guidebook were confirmed at press time. We recommend, however, that you call establishments to obtain current information before traveling.

To buy books in quantity for corporate use or incentives, call **(800) 962–0973** or e-mail **premiums@GlobePequot.com.**

INSIDERS' GUIDE®

Text design by Linda R. Loiewski
Maps by Equator Graphics © Morris Book Publishing, LLC
Illustrations by Carole Drong
Spot photography throughout © Jason Lindsey/Alamy

ISSN 1540-871X
ISBN 978-0-7627-4413-8

Manufactured in the United States of America
Ninth Edition/First Printing

To the wife and young'un . . .

Contents

Introduction

Blue lakes, stunning, tree-covered bluffs, vast, open prairies, and marshy wet-lands . . . colonial French forts, mysterious Indian mounds, abandoned lead mines . . . quiet, picturesque villages and towns, sprawling suburbs, and one of the most storied, populous cities in the nation. Where do you find all these? Illinois, of course, though you may be forgiven for thinking otherwise. After all, for many non-Midwesterners, Illinois is notable solely for the fact that it is one of those three flat, treeless "I" states that you have to drive through to get to the exciting part of the country. I grew up in a suburb of Chicago and must admit that, as a boy, I myself wasn't all that thrilled about the place. Our family vacations were spent elsewhere, with Wisconsin generally fulfilling any weekend getaway needs, so I never had a chance to experience the state. As a budding young history buff, I was also aware that there were no cowboys, no Revolutionary or Civil War battles, and no big American Indian wars in the history of the state. It was just one very boring place, indeed.

Needless to say I eventually came to discover that my perceptions were wildly incorrect. No, there may not be any cowboys or Civil War battles lurking in Illinois's past, but there's still plenty to capture the military fancies of a young boy—not the least of which is George Rogers Clark's campaign in southern Illinois during the Revolutionary War. More intriguing yet was Chicago's rapid development from a trading post to the nation's most innovative nineteenth-century city. Or the role the Illinois-Michigan Canal played in extending an inland waterway from the Atlantic Ocean to the Gulf of Mexico. As for Native American and frontier history, Illinois is as rich as any state, from the days of the French explorers and powerful Illini Confederacy to the Black Hawk War of 1832.

So if it's history you're interested in, Illinois is chock full of it. But if you're just looking to take in the sights or enjoy nature, the state has just as much to offer. Go boating or fishing on Lake Michigan; spend a night on the town in Chicago; hike through the rugged, forested hills and canyons of the Shawnee National Forest in southern Illinois; take a tour of Abraham Lincoln's home in the capital city of Springfield; explore the craggy bluffs and lead mines of Galena near the Mississippi River; lounge in a cozy bed-and-breakfast in Lake County. Whatever your pleasure—whether you're looking to relax or work up a sweat, itching to spend money or pinch pennies—Illinois will not disappoint. But enough talk, let's get going!

Illinois Facts

TOURISM CONTACT

Illinois Bureau of Tourism: (800) 2–CONNECT;
www.enjoyillinois.com

MAJOR DAILY NEWSPAPERS

Chicago Sun-Times; Chicago Tribune; Daily Herald, Arlington Heights; *Wall Street Journal,* Midwest Edition, Naperville; *Journal Star,* Peoria; *Register Star,* Rockford; *State Journal-Register,* Springfield; *News-Gazette,* Champaign; *The Daily Chronicle,* De Kalb; *Clinton Daily Journal,* Clinton; *Effingham Daily-News,* Effingham; *Southern Illinoian,* Carbondale; *The Beacon News,* Aurora; *The Register Mail,* Galesburg; *The Daily Journal,* Kankakee; *LaSalle News-Tribune,* LaSalle; *The Pantagraph,* Bloomington; *Herald & Review,* Decatur; *The Telegraph,* Alton; *Daily Dispatch,* Moline; *Belleville News-Democrat,* Belleville; *Freeport Journal-Standard,* Freeport; *Commercial-News,* Danville; *Herald-News,* Joliet.

READING

Illinois State Parks: A Guide to Illinois State Parks, Bill Bailey, Glovebox Guidebooks of America, Saginaw, Michigan; *52 Illinois Weekends,* Bob Puhala, McGraw-Hill, New York, New York; *Canoeing Adventures in Northern Illinois: Apple River to Zuma Creek,* Bob Tyler, iUniverse, Incorporated; *Guidebook to Illinois Nature Centers and Interpretive Trails,* Walter Zyznieuski and George Zyznieuski, Southern Illinois University Press, Carbondale, Illinois.

READING FOR KIDS

Dragon of Navy Pier, Kate Noble, Silver Seahorse Press, Chicago, Illinois.

PUBLIC TRANSPORTATION

Chicago: Regional Transit Authority (bus, subway, and elevated trains), (312) 836–7000, CTA buses require exact change ($2.00 one way, no transfers issued when paying with cash); Metra commuter train service to Chicago and suburbs, (312) 322–6777; Amtrak train service to various parts of the state, (800) 872–7245; O'Hare International Airport, (800) 832–6352; Midway International Airport, (773) 838–0600. For all public transportation in the Chicago area, log on to www.rtachicago.com.

CLIMATE OVERVIEW

If you don't like the weather, just wait a minute, and it'll change. Chicago's weather can be quite mercurial, and the rest of the state can offer dramatic changes almost overnight, too. Remember that the state's length is equal to that of an area stretching from New England to Virginia, so geography explains some of the variation.

The southern portion of the state also gets, on average, more precipitation than the north, with means of 48 inches and 35 inches, respectively. And tornadoes can occur frequently in the spring.

POPULATION

- Illinois (state)—12,763,371
- Chicago—2,842,518
- Chicago and its Primary Metropolitan Statistical Area—8,192,579

FAMOUS PEOPLE

- Carl Sandburg, poet
- Everett M. Dirksen, senator
- Wyatt Earp, lawman
- Ronald Reagan, president
- Wild Bill Hickok, lawman
- Ernest Hemingway, writer
- Edgar Lee Masters, writer
- Studs Terkel, writer
- Nelson Algren, writer
- Charlton Heston, actor
- Chris Chelios, hockey player
- Jesse Jackson, civil rights leader
- Jack Benny, comedian
- William Jennings Bryan, politician and lawyer
- Clarence Darrow, lawyer
- Mahalia Jackson, gospel singer
- John Hope Franklin, historian
- Bill Murray, comedian

QUICK FUN FACTS ON ILLINOIS' STATE WEB SITE

- The name *Illinois* comes from a Native American word meaning "tribe of superior men."
- Illinois became a state on December 3, 1818. Illinois was the twenty-first state to enter the Union.
- When Illinois became a state in 1818, it had a population of 34,620 people. Illinois is now the fifth most populous state in the country, with over 12.5 million people.

- Illinois' favorite son is Abraham Lincoln. The Lincoln sites in Springfield are among the best-known tourist sites in the world.
- The state slogan, "Land of Lincoln," was adopted by the General Assembly in 1955. The State of Illinois has a copyright for the exclusive use of the slogan.
- The Sears Tower, located in Chicago, was the world's tallest building from 1973 until 1996. The Sears Tower is still the tallest building in North America. It covers 2 city blocks and rises 0.25 mile above the ground.
- Illinois ranks third in the nation in the number of interstate highway miles.
- Illinois was the home of President Ulysses S. Grant, whose home is preserved in Galena.

Chicago

Why not start your Illinois off-the-beaten-path adventures in Chicago? Okay, I can hear you saying, "What is he talking about? I'm in search of the undiscovered gems lurking in the Land of Lincoln, and he's sending me to the Windy City—second-largest (or third-, depending on which government statistics sheet you use) city in the country."

Are you loopy?

Funny you should say that. Because the "Loop," and its environs in the downtown Chicago area, is a great place to begin looking for "off-the-beaten-path" Chicago.

In fact, there's lots more to Chicago than the Sears Tower and Wrigley Field. For example . . .

To set the tone for undiscovered Chicago, head to the **International Museum of Surgical Science,** 1524 North Lake Shore Drive. While you take a time-travel tour through the history of surgical science (more than thirty "rooms"), you'll see everything from ancient medical instruments dating back to Roman times to true oddities.

Survey the postmortem plaster cast of the right (writing) hand of English novelist William Makepeace Thackeray, encased

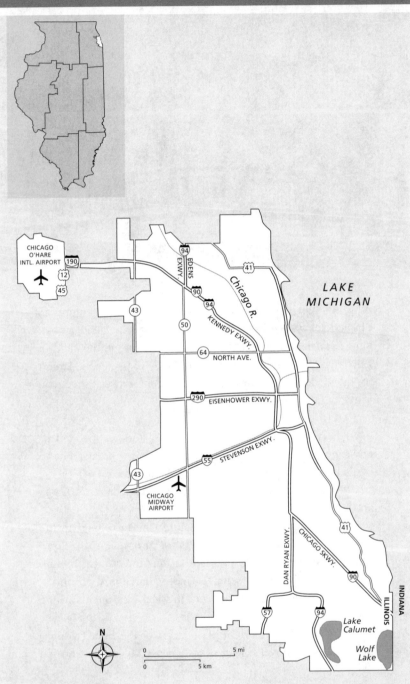

in a red Moroccan leather folding case, or the 4,000-year-old Peruvian trepanned skulls; (312) 642–6502, extension 3130 for reservations.

Get the idea? Chicago is filled with such often overlooked surprises.

Now that I've pointed the finger at one of Chicago's less-traveled but quite interesting side trips, let's wander the city for some more off-the-beaten-path pleasures. These can be either places that are brand-new to you or familiar favorites that hold some kind of lesser-known enticement.

The Magnificent Seven

Perhaps we'll start at the north end of Michigan Avenue, dubbed the *"Magnificent Mile,"* to see what we can see. This portion of the "mile" is home to some of the swankiest, chicest hotels and haute couture stores in the world. In fact this strip of unbridled capitalism has been compared to New York's Madison Avenue, and even to Ocean Drive in Miami and Rodeo Drive in Beverly Hills.

Nike Town Chicago, near Michigan and Erie, is certainly not one of those locations unknown to Chicagoans or out of towners. This paean to the "house that Jordan built" is 58,000 square feet of shoes, shoes, and more shoes. Okay, so there's more to the store than those popular swoosh-decorated must-haves. Besides footwear, browsers and buyers can peruse the hottest trends in exercise fashion and accessories. If you're visiting on Thursday evening, you're welcome to join in a store-sponsored running club that traverses 3-, 5-, or 8-mile courses throughout the city. Nike Town is located at 669 North Michigan Avenue, (312) 642–6363.

Be like Mike!

Although Michael Jordan retired from the Chicago Bulls in January 1999, the memories of "His Airness" linger, not only in the hearts and memories of Bulls fans, but also in the form of an extraordinary statue that memorializes Jordan's trademark "dunk in flight." Designed by Highland Park, Illinois, sculptors Omri and Julie Rotblatt-Amrany, the 12-foot-tall bronze image of #23 incredibly connects with its black granite base by just one knee, providing an uncanny air-borne realism with its human subject. An inscription carved into the granite reads, "The best there ever was. The best there ever will be."

Tourists, fans, and the curious make the pilgrimage to the front entrance of the United Center sports arena, at 1901 West Madison Street, to have their photograph taken with the statue. For most, it's the only way to commune with the former basketball superstar who helped lead the Chicago Bulls to a remarkable string of six NBA championships and thrilled a grateful city. Call (312) 455–4500.

Continuing south, the *John Hancock Center,* 875 N. Michigan Avenue, plays second fiddle to its skyscraping, bigger, more tourist-popular brother, the Sears Tower. But that doesn't mean you should pass by a chance to take the tower elevators up to the all new, completely renovated Hancock Observatory. You'll travel at a speed of 1,800 feet per minute and, before your ears can finish popping, be more than 1,000 feet above the ground. It's said that on a clear day, you can see four states from up here; (888) 875–8439.

chicagotrivia

It takes only forty seconds to travel ninety-four stories up to the Observation Deck of the John Hancock Center.

If you're still proud as a peacock to watch *Saturday Night Live,* you can purchase a T-shirt bearing the show's logo at the NBC Tower, located off Michigan Avenue almost directly behind Tribune Tower; (312) 836–5760.

At the **Tribune Tower,** walk to the side of the building into Pioneer Court where you'll see an interesting collection of stones cemented into the walls of the main building edifice, labeled as parts of the Alamo, Great Wall of China, Pompeii Baths, Hamlet's castle, and so on. Correspondents collected these 136 historically important relics at the behest of *Chicago Tribune* owner Colonel Robert McCormick.

You'll have to take the stairs down from Michigan Avenue to Rush Street and on to Hubbard for lunch at the **Billy Goat Tavern.** Remember this is the place made famous by John Belushi of *Saturday Night Live,* who as cook barked out the orders, "Cheezborger, cheezborger, no Pepsi, Coke." You can sample your own Billy Goat cheezborger, then get hip to Billy Goat's curse that has gotten the goat of the Chicago Cubs for more than fifty years.

AUTHOR'S TOP TEN PICKS

Wicker Park/Bucktown
Neighborhoods,
(773) 384–2672

Supernatural Tours,
includes summer boat tours,
(708) 499–0300

Untouchables Tours,
(773) 881–1195

Lincoln Park Zoo,
(312) 742–2000

Mexican Fine Arts Center,
(312) 738–1503

Green Mill Lounge,
(773) 878–5552

International Museum of Surgical
Science,
(312) 642–6502, ext. 3130

Lincoln Park/Lakeview
Neighborhoods,
(773) 880–5200 and (773) 472–7171

Buckingham Fountain,
(312) 747–2474

Second City Theatre,
(312) 337–3992

Popcorn

No trip to downtown Chicago is complete without a stop at one of the five **Garrett Popcorn Shops** sprinkled throughout the Magnificent Mile and the Loop. This heavenly concoction of freshly made gourmet popcorn has been a Chicago favorite since 1949.

It's good at any time. But when you're waiting in line for a bag of goodies, and the CaramelCrisp corn is piping hot, just popping out of the roaster, and the counter person scoops it into your waxed-paper bag, and you reach down inside and pull out some of those caramel-drenched hot kernels . . . umm, umm, it is heavenly.

For a special treat, try Garrett's "Downtown Mix"—a combination of CaramelCrisp and CheeseCorn. It has been called "addictive"; it also has been rated "the best in the world" by food critics.

At Michigan and Wacker, note the lines on the pavement signifying the structure that stood here until August 15, 1812—Fort Dearborn, which gave name to the Fort Dearborn Massacre. The incident was, in reality, a battle—though with overwhelmingly lopsided odds. Due to U.S. setbacks in the War of 1812, the fort's commander had been ordered to abandon his post and retreat toward Fort Wayne, Indiana. Only a little over a mile south of the fort, past the sand dunes along the banks of Lake Michigan, sixty-eight men, nine women, and eighteen children from the garrison were engulfed by a force of about five hundred Potawatomis. The most brutal episode of the encounter took place among the supply wagons, which had become separated from the main body of troops when the latter charged a cluster of Potawatomis firing upon them from a high dune. All the men escorting the wagons were killed along with most of the children—tomahawked by Potawatomis who had jumped into the wagon in which they were riding. The women fought back desperately with swords and whatever other weapons they could grab, but two were killed. In the end, the Potawatomis killed or captured every single individual from the fort. Of those taken prisoner, some were put to death, but the majority survived and were eventually ransomed off, returning to white society.

chicagotrivia

The site of Mrs. O'Leary's barn, where legend says the Chicago Fire started, is now occupied by the Chicago Fire Academy—the city's training school for new firefighters!

Continue far south on Michigan Avenue to Grant Park. The object of your attention here is **Buckingham Fountain,** built in 1927 to resemble the Latona Basin at Louis XIV's Versailles palace. The massive fountain shoots water nearly

Rock On

Wanna party like a rock star in Chi-Town? Head to the like-named suite in the *Hotel Monaco Chicago.* It's a one-of-a-kind crib that has hosted the likes of Britney Spears, *NSYNC, Matchbox Twenty, the Black Crowes, and others.

What's so special? Well, the plush digs celebrate the rock 'n' roll lifestyle in high fashion. For example, open the room's door to this interactive rock 'n' roll shrine, and you can't miss the archetypal rock star suite signature: There's a 19-inch television sailing through the picture window overlooking downtown Chicago. At least it looks like there's a huge TV heading south (thanks to the prop shop of Chicago's renowned Steppenwolf Theatre).

Plush red velvet is the main focus of the sitting room, resplendent with its regal couch that folds down into a comfy sleeper. Note the room's zebra-striped rug as decor counterpoint. There's also a fully loaded digital jukebox with tunes from all the top bands. And you can take an up-close peek of gold records from the likes of Smashing Pumpkins, Bare Naked Ladies, and others.

The master bedroom is huge, with a cavernous king bed and deep double whirlpool in the bath. You'll never run out of music with the room's fifty-two-disc CD player; you'll marvel at the autographed handwritten lyrics of Beatle John Lennon's "Imagine" and "Day Tripper." And there's lots of the band Chicago's rock memorabilia.

Perhaps the best decadent rock star touch in the master bedroom is the little glass "room" built out, overhanging the street. There's a twin-size red velvet cushion that you can recline upon, with nothing but three walls of glass separating you from the elements—and people busying themselves six stories below.

One can only imagine what kind of rock 'n' roll shenanigans might go on here.

For more information, contact the Hotel Monaco Chicago, 225 North Wabash; (312) 960–8500, or check out the Web site at www.monaco-chicago.com.

150 feet into the air, and for an hour before its 10:00 P.M. summertime shutdown boasts a fantastical color-and-water display. Watch the fountain, feel its cooling spray, stare at the stars, walk across Lake Shore Drive, and gaze at the boats harbored in Lake Michigan as the blue waters stretch to the night horizon and disappear into a silky blackness.

It won't feel like Chicago. It'll feel like paradise.

State Street/The Loop

State Street is the heart of Chicago's Loop—named for the elevated train that encircles this area. You can browse the street and its environs yourself to conjure up the latest discoveries.

Open-Air Sculptures

Walking around Chicago's **Loop** is like visiting a museum without walls. That's because when it comes to open air sculptures by the greatest artists of the twentieth century, Chicago is second to none—a factoid little realized by visitors to the City of Big Shoulders.

To glimpse the grandeur of five of these magnificent works, some of which are often overlooked by the public, let's start with the **"Chicago Picasso,"** located on the plaza grounds of the Richard J. Daley Civic Center, 50 West Washington, in the heart of downtown Chicago. When it was unveiled here in 1967, the untitled monumental contemporary by famed artist Pablo Picasso caused quite a stir—and lots of head scratching, too. What was it? A giant bird with wings? The profile of the mayor?

Picasso never revealed just what his piece represented. We do know that it is a 50-foot-high work of Cor-Ten steel. It kind of looks like a double exposure of one of Picasso's famous depictions of women, a head with an akimbo body. What do you think?

Marc Chagall's **The Four Seasons** often can be overlooked because of its location in a busy sunken deck of the First National Plaza at the crazed intersection of Dearborn and Monroe. Made of thousands of pastel-hued chips of more than 250 colors, the work (also adorned with hand-chipped stone and glass) depicts Chagall's images of flowers, birds, suns, lovers, and so on.

Much less viewed by visitors is a controversial sculpture by Frank Stella called **The Town Ho's Story.** Located at 77 West Jackson Boulevard, in front of the Ralph H. Metcalfe Federal Building, it has been denigrated for both its name (which refers to a chapter in Herman Melville's *Moby Dick*) and its aesthetic. In fact, some critics simply called it a pile of junk.

chicagotrivia

Chicago, nicknamed the "Windy City" for its blowhard politicians rather than its lake breezes, actually ranks fifteenth in terms of windiest U.S. cities, with an average wind speed of a 14.9 mph.

Whatever, the 18-foot-high amalgam composed of several smaller structures made of steel and aluminum evokes Stella's abstract bent.

Another overlooked work is **Reading Cones** by Richard Serra, resting in Grant Park at 301 East Monroe Street between Columbus Drive and Lake Shore Drive. Two austere arcs of steel sit like ancient monuments, with a slight opening between them that only one person can squeeze through at a time. The minimalist work is worth a peek.

You have to go inside the plaza of the Cook County Administration Building at 69 West Washington to see Joan Miró's **Mystical Force of a Great Earth**

TOP ANNUAL EVENTS

Lincoln Park Zoo's
Caroling to the Animals,
early December,
(312) 742–2293

Winterbreak,
early December–early January,
(312) 744–3315

Chicago Cubs Convention,
mid-January,
(800) 843–2827

St. Patrick's Day Parade,
mid-March,
(312) 744–3315

South Side Irish St. Patrick's
Day parade,
mid-March,
(773) 393–8687

Printer's Row Book Fair,
early June,
(312) 222–3986

Chicago Blues Festival,
early to mid-June,
(312) 744–3315

Taste of Chicago,
late June–early July,
(312) 744–2400

Venetian Night,
late July,
(312) 744–3315

Chicago Air & Water Show,
late August,
(312) 744–3315

Chicago Jazz Festival,
early September,
(312) 427–1676

Celtic Fest Chicago,
mid-September,
(312) 744–3315

Chicago International Children's
Film Festival,
mid-October,
(773) 281–9075

Mother. It was cast in the artist's hometown of Barcelona, then shipped and finished here. It stands 39 feet tall and is made of steel, wire mesh, concrete, bronze, and ceramic tiles.

Neighborhood Discoveries

One of Chicago's most intriguing characteristics is its neighborhoods. It might even be said that the city more resembles a "city of neighborhoods" than a typical metropolitan area. So let's head out of the downtown area and explore some of Chicago's less-trod neighborhoods while revisiting a few favorites.

The heart of the Mexican community in Chicago—and maybe the entire Midwest—can be found in the adjoining neighborhoods of **Little Village** and **Pilsen.** You can experience a little bit of "old Mexico" in the area around

Twenty-sixth Street and Kedzie Avenue, with all the sights, sounds, and aromas of the old country mixing here in a festive atmosphere. (In this neighborhood, Twenty-sixth Street actually goes by the name "Avenida-Mexicana.") Note the handpainted murals on neighborhood walls depicting Mexican heroes (like Emiliano Zapata), history, culture, politics, and religion, especially between Eighteenth and Twenty-sixth Streets.

There may be no finer Hispanic museum in the Midwest than the often overlooked *Mexican Fine Arts Center,* 1852 West Nineteenth Street. Showcasing the finest of Mexico from both sides of the border, the museum boasts more than 1,000 art works in its permanent collection, by such Mexican masters as Orozco and Siqueiros, as well as Linares family folk art and contemporary pieces by the likes of Carmen Lomas Garza; (312) 738–1503.

And if you're looking to sample an authentic Mexican meal, try *Los Dos Laredos,* 3120 West Twenty-sixth Street. Steak gorditas and fajitas are among the sumptuous traditional dishes; (773) 376–3218. Another neighborhood favorite is *Nuevo Leon,* 1515 West Eighteenth Street, an upscale taqueria serving everything from taco plates to huge guisado de puerco platters; (312) 421–1517.

Walk through the colorful gate into *Chinatown,* which arches across Wentworth Avenue just south of Cermak Road, and you'll be entering a world of Asian culture and history. Forget the shops that cater to tourists; venture inside some of the smaller neighborhood stores that residents frequent (keep your eyes open). You can get your fortune told at tea shops, buy cures for what ails you at herbal shops, purchase rare Chinese silks and other arts, eat treats at authentic Chinese bakeries, and sample Chinese cuisine.

Chinatown Arch, Chicago

The best restaurants in the neighborhood are in Chinatown Square—an open-air mall north of the Cermak Road/Archer Avenue intersection. Unlike the more tourist-oriented eateries on Wentworth, here you'll find a variety of restaurants that would make any Hong Kong native feel at home. *Ken Kee Restaurant,* 2129 South China Place; (312) 326–2088, is well worth a visit. Their congee with "ghost bones" is particularly good. Afterward you can satisfy your sweet tooth at *Aji Ichiban,* 2117 South China Place; (312) 328–9998,

Ancient Chinese Secret

Have you ever wondered if Chinese herbal remedies actually work? Well, I got a chance to put one to the test. My wife had always suffered from seasonal bouts of eczema that no medicines could adequately relieve. A friend with the same problem told her about *Chiang Ying Ginseng Hong, Inc.,* a shop on 2314 Wentworth Avenue. After consulting with the resident herbalist, she came home with an oddly shaped clay pot and seven small packages wrapped in heavy, white paper. She had been told to boil the contents of one package each day in the clay pot for twenty minutes, which would produce a mugful of "remedy."

Simple enough—except for the fact that my wife was too squeamish to actually look inside that first package. I had to prepare it for her, and wasn't allowed to tell her what I saw. This was best, for mixed among many unidentifiable roots, twigs, and shoots were about a dozen dried, whole cicadas—little curled up legs and all. *I'm glad I'm not drinking this,* I thought. But when I presented her with that first mugful, she kept chickening out.

"Just drink it," I told her. "It's not that bad."

"Then you drink it first," she shot back.

No way, I thought, but then I quickly realized that the only way to convince her she wasn't drinking cicada juice was to go right ahead and take a gulp. It tasted very bitter, and, well, green—but very healthy also, as if I'd just swallowed a dozen brussels sprouts or some equally wretched vegetable that's supposed to be good for you. Outstanding husband that I am, I fought back an urge to grimace. Instead I simply smiled and said, "See, it's not that bad—it's not like there's dried bugs in there."

This convinced her to drink it, though she continued making me prepare it each day and never did take a peek at the contents. After only six days her eczema was gone and has returned only in very mild forms over the past couple of years. Which makes me wonder: would something like this cure as common an affliction as acne? I mean think of all the money shelled out on acne medication—isn't it possible that some sort of cheap dried cockroach compound could be just as effective? Hmm, me and the good herbalist need to talk—there's money to be made with these bugs and herbs! Call (312) 791–1525.

Gourmet Dining—Chicago Style

Forget about haute cuisine. Chicago is most notable for its meat-and-potatoes approach to dining. After all, this is the town that invented deep dish pizza—the very best of which can be sampled at **Pizzeria Uno** on Ohio and Wabash, in the heart of downtown. Be forewarned that it takes about forty-five minutes to make one of these culinary delights, but it's well worth the wait.

If you're not in the mood for pizza, chow down on a Chicago-style hot dog. The classic Chicago hot dog is an all-beef wiener smothered in mustard, tomatoes, relish, onions, and celery salt, with a slice of dill pickle added for emphasis. Hot peppers can be included without compromising the integrity of the dog, but ketchup is a no-no. Such a dog can be had at most hot dog joints in the Chicago area, of which there are literally hundreds to choose from. My personal favorite is **Parky's** on Harlem Avenue in the nearby western suburb of Forest Park. Along with the dog comes a greasy bag full of exquisite, fresh cut fries. These are so tasty you can make a meal of them alone.

The Chicago-style Polish sausage, however, should be sampled only at **Jim's.** Located on O'Brien in what used to be known as the historic Maxwell Street neighborhood, but is now chi-chi University Village, Jim's will not serve you a fat hot dog on a bun like most joints. What you get instead is a genuine length of red, mottled, angry sausage. After simmering, this bad boy is charred, heaped with fried onions, and served on a bun with mustard. After a late night of barhopping, there's nothing better.

Ever had an Italian breaded steak sandwich? You're not alone if you haven't, for as far as I can tell, this is a unique, southside Chicago invention—unknown even to many northsiders. What exactly is it? Well, I'm glad you asked, for this is a treat you won't want to miss. The Italian breaded steak sandwich consists of tender, paper-thin, breaded steak cutlets heaped on a thick Italian roll. Red sauce, hot peppers, and mozzarella cheese are then slathered over it. It's one of the best, most filling sandwiches you'll ever eat. **Ricobene's,** on Twenty-sixth Street near Wentworth in the blue-collar Bridgeport neighborhood, is the place to go for this monster. Just don't forget to grab extra napkins.

which carries scads of Chinese and Japanese candies. **Hit Music,** 2105 South China Place; (312) 326–3222, is a must for music lovers who also happen to be in the market for a new oven range hood. You're guaranteed to find the right match for your kitchen along with all your favorite Asian pop CDs and Chinese-language DVDs. Now that's concept retailing!

Greektown, on Halsted between Adams and Van Buren, is all that remains of what was once among the largest Hellenic communities in the country. So populous was this ethnic neighborhood that the area was called "Delta" (the triangular letter in the Greek alphabet). Today, it's mainly a gourmet's delight,

Don't Forget to Say Grace

Did you ever think of combining attendance at Sunday morning service with a good meal?

It's not a sacrilege at Chicago's **House of Blues,** located at the foot of downtown's futuristic Marina Towers, huddled against the Chicago River at State Street. Sacred music combines with exotic Sunday brunch (two seatings, 9:00 A.M. and noon) at this eye-popping music venue, whose decor alone (a mixture of American folk art, African American and Caribbean influences, and exuberant colors and textures) causes heads to shake with amazement and wonder.

More than a dozen serving tables provide all kinds of brunch specialties: smoked turkey, jambalaya, smoked catfish, peanut noodle salad—even brandy-laced Bananas Foster, flambéed in front of your eyes.

Then music begins, music that has been called "the best gospel this side of heaven." You'll be raising the roof in no time. And if the heavenly strains so inspire you, saunter up to the front of the stage where a handheld microphone allows you to join in with the morning's featured choir, selected from some of the finest African American local and regional church choirs in the Midwest. Call (312) 923–2000 or visit the Web site at www.hob.com.

with restaurants such as Athena, Greek Islands, Pegasus, the Parthenon, and Rodity's serving up authentic Greek favorites—all washed down with generous swallows of ouzo. And you must try the flaming cheese appetizer—saganaki—concocted not in Greece but here in Chicago.

More overlooked is the specialty shopping here. For example, **Athens Grocery** at 324 South Halsted, (312) 332–6737, offers those plump Greek olives, and baklava is the treat at the **Pan Hellenic Bakery,** 322 South Halsted, (312) 454–1886.

The **Athenian Candle Company** at 300 South Halsted, is also worth a visit. They make the candles in the back room, and the variety and prices are amazing. You can actually buy candles as long as your arm for only six bucks. Along with the candles you can stock up on incense, icons, prayer cards, and other spiritual items.

Taylor Street is the epicenter for one of my favorite neighborhoods, **Little Italy,** located just west of the University of Illinois at Chicago near Racine and Harrison. It's a tiny slice of Italy tossed into a spaghetti-bowl mixture of tall university buildings, expensive new townhomes, and old ethnic enclaves.

One comes here for the ambience, starting with "A Touch of Italy" posters hanging from area lampposts. And, of course, the food. Not many people realize that the **Tufano's Vernon Park Tap,** at 1073 West Vernon Park Place right across the street from the university's Behavioral Science Building (the one that looks as if it's been disassembled by a recent earthquake), was a favorite of Frank Sinatra's. It's also a hangout for Chicago Blackhawk hockey players, who often grab a bite to eat before or after games.

Gennaro's, 1352 West Taylor Street, serves up homemade gnocchi, eggplant, veal dishes, and more. **The Rosebud Cafe,** 1500 West Taylor Street, has offered some of the best Italian food for almost a quarter century; in fact, it was named one of the fifteen best pasta restaurants in the country. You often can spot Hollywood stars eating here when they pass through town.

chicagotrivia

Did you know that Chicago boasts more than half of the state's entire population?

For a more casual approach to dining, try **Al's No. 1 Italian Beef,** another Taylor Street eatery, offering a mammoth sandwich of steaming hot beef smothered in hot and sweet peppers. And there's no better place for old-fashioned Italian ice than Taylor Street's **Mario's Italian Lemonade,** open from May to September.

One of the city's "newest" neighborhoods is the **South Loop.** A once-dilapidated area, the region's renaissance (spearheaded by urban pioneers: stores and lots of yuppies) includes a plethora of landmark buildings, expensive lofts, condominiums and town homes, art galleries, bookstores, and jazz and blues clubs. Even Mayor Daley moved near here a few years ago from his family's historic enclave in Bridgeport.

If you're looking for the hip part of town, you'll find it in the **Wicker Park/Bucktown** area. A Polish ghetto back in the 1940s (as chronicled by writer Nelson Algren), the neighborhood gave way to a large influx of Mexicans, as whites left for the suburbs in the '70s. By the '90s, however, artists seeking cheap rents began filtering into the area, followed by a slew of hipsters and yuppies. The neighborhood began gentrifying rapidly and is now quite expensive, yet it's still the place to go to get in touch with your "inner bohemian." Coffeehouses, vintage shops, low-profile art galleries and studios are everywhere—

chicagotrivia

Baggage tags for Chicago's O'Hare International Airport are marked "ORD" because the airport was originally named Orchard Field.

not to mention restaurants and nightclubs, which range in style from swank to grungy, avant-garde to no-nonsense. And there are still plenty of taquerias and even a few Polish and Ukrainian restaurants for good measure.

I moved to the area right out of college in the early '90s, when, yes, I had pretensions of hipness. Congestion and escalating housing costs prompted the wife and me to leave, but I still have a sentimental attachment to the place.

chicagotrivia

Chicagoans generally hate the nickname "Second City," which comes from years of trailing only New York City in terms of population.

Though my days of barhopping appear to be over (parenthood will do that to you), this is still my neighborhood of choice. There are clubs and bars for every budget and taste, and the people watching is first-rate. The **Rainbo Club,** 1150 North Damen Avenue, is a favorite of the old-timer artist crowd, while the **Club Foot Lounge,** 1824 West Augusta Boulevard, is a fun, laid-back place to down a few and dance to old punk rock and new wave standards. **The Empty Bottle,** 1035 North Western Avenue, is the city's best, independently owned live music venue, while **Earwax Café,** 1561 North Milwaukee Avenue, is a great place to go for a cup of joe and a light meal.

Finally let's not forget one of Chicago's most famous neighborhoods, at least during the April through October baseball season—Wrigleyville. This upscale enclave owes most of its joie de vivre to **Wrigley Field,** the venerable home ballpark of the Chicago Cubs, which is located at Clark and Addison. It is a happening place that should be experienced even by nonbaseball fans.

The excitement builds outside the ballpark as crowds swirl around the Harry Caray statue (a tribute to the Hall of Fame Cubs' broadcaster who passed on in 1998). As you make your way through the bowels of the old stadium and finally emerge to the playing field, you'll be overcome by a sense of nostalgia. This is the way baseball should be played—on a sea of green grass, with brick outfield walls covered with ivy (which occasionally turn a triple into a ground-rule double when the ball disappears into the vines), and seating right on top of the action.

Night baseball is another twist to the Wrigley Field experience. The atmosphere for these games more resembles Mardi Gras than an ordinary baseball game, and tickets are nearly impossible to get.

If you are lucky enough to get Cubs tickets for any game, make sure to look over the outfield walls, past the bleachers (home of the Cubs' infamous Bleacher Bums, who yell all kinds of quaint names at opposing ball players, in addition to throwing opponents' home runs back onto the field). You'll notice tall three-flat apartment buildings across the street (Waveland Avenue on the left field side, Sheffield on the right field side) from Wrigley. Note that several of these buildings have their own bleachers on their roofs, so that residents can view the action without ever having to set foot inside the ballpark.

Go Cubbies!

The Chicago Cubs haven't appeared in the World Series since 1945—a league record. They haven't won a World Series since 1908—a world record. Yet the drought almost ended in the 2003 season. Once the Cubs secured a play-off spot, Chicagoans were convinced those infamous records would finally be forgotten, for the Cubs were a cinch to win the series. This notion was reflected everywhere, from people on the street to local media. Now though I've always been aware of the Cubs' history of choking down the stretch, I haven't closely followed baseball in years and therefore can be excused for buying into this hype—which I ingested on a daily basis through my local newspaper. The fact that my local newspaper, the Tribune Company, actually owns the Cubs didn't have anything to do with this, did it?

The first play-off opponent faced by the Cubs—the Atlanta Braves—were dismissed out of hand, so I paid little attention to that series. By the next round against the Florida Marlins, I was sitting up and taking notice, still thoroughly convinced the Cubs would ultimately be successful. It wasn't until about the seventh inning of the seventh game—with the Cubs down—that it finally hit me. "Hey," I announced out loud to myself in shocked disbelief, "I don't think they're gonna be able to pull this out!"

Sure enough, they didn't. No World Series appearance—no World Series victory. I felt betrayed and confused. I mean, as a very casual fan, it was only natural that I might fall prey to the hype—but what about all those hard-core fans? They've followed this team for decades, and they, too, were convinced of victory. When it comes to the Cubs, however, Chicago just can't help itself. It's as if pixie dust fills the Wrigleyville sky and gleaming white unicorns prance and frolic about Addison Avenue. As hard-nosed and cynical as Chicagoans like to believe themselves to be, the Cubs prove they can still believe in fairy tales. After all, there's always next year . . .

Never mind that those crosstown rivals, the Chicago White Sox, managed to secure the World Series crown in 2005, their first since 1917. As far as Cubbie fans are concerned, those Southside American League batcrackers at their "new" Comiskey Park (renamed U.S. Cellular Field in 2003, but loyal Sox fans won't admit to that) can just keep their trophy to themselves.

Wrigley Field, Chicago

Go Wild in the City

Okay so the Lincoln Park neighborhood may be one of the best-known sections of the city, with its beautiful Lake Michigan shorefront parks, tony high-rises, and bike paths galore. But a book about Illinois can't fail to mention the **Lincoln Park Zoo.**

And it's not just because admission is free—remarkable in this day—but because this is one of the most accessible wildlife retreats in the country, with spectacular animal displays in natural habitats that put you almost face-to-face with beautiful creatures.

The zoo got its start back in 1868, when New York's Central Park Zoo gave the Windy City two swans. Acreage was taken near the lakefront for these animals, and the collection continued to grow. Today Lincoln Park Zoo is the second-oldest zoo in America, as well as the smallest "major" zoo, covering little more than thirty-five acres but including more than 1,600 animals.

It boasts a spectacular Great Ape House, where you can watch 400-pound gorillas swing on heavy ropes from station to station. There is also a Lion House, Reptile House, Sea Lion Pool (these guys are real hams), Penguin and Seabird House (it's cold in here and a great spot for summer cool downs), walk-through Rookery, Children's Zoo, and more.

For kids, Farm-in-the-Zoo, is a must-visit. This is a minifarm where you can pet a horse, tend to sheep, see chicks being hatched, watch cows being milked, and more. All in all, a real moo-ving experience. The parking lot is at Cannon Drive and Fullerto Avenue. Call for hours, (312) 742–2000.

All in all, you haven't really seen a baseball game until you've seen the Cubs in action (or inaction) at Wrigley Field. For more information about Wrigley Field, contact the Chicago Cubs at (773) 404–2827.

Other neighborhoods worth checking out on your own include the **Lincoln Park/Lakeview** area, featuring the widest array of shops, eateries, and clubs in the city; **Heart of Italy,** one of the oldest sections of the city, located ten minutes west of the Loop, where most of the residents come from Tuscany; **River North,** an art lover's delight; and **Andersonville,** filled with bakeries, stores, shops, and restaurants featuring Scandinavian crafts and food.

Tour Tales

It seems as though everyone who comes to the Windy City takes some kind of tour to get a better feel for the area. But why sign up for a bus tour that will take you to all the usual haunts when you could do some tours that are much more fun—and unusual?

Hop aboard the **Supernatural Tour,** which leaves in darkness and searches for things that go bump in the night. Led by Chicago's most notable professional ghostbusters, who claim to have seen all kinds of spooky spirits, you will visit some of the allegedly most haunted sights in Chicago—including creepy cemeteries and doppelganger-filled houses. You might even see "Resurrection Mary," one of the city's most famous ghosts; (708) 499–0300.

For more of the city's ghoulish history, take an **Untouchables Tour,** which centers on the gangster-related historic sites made famous during the city's Prohibition Era; (773) 881–1195.

Weather permitting, you might consider gliding along Chicago's waterways aboard one of the **Wendella Sightseeing Boats.** Board at the northwest corner of the Michigan Avenue Bridge, at 400 North Michigan Avenue next to the Wrigley Building. There's also an in-depth River Architecture tour that allows passengers to view many of Chicago's remarkable buildings from a rather novel angle; (312) 337–1446.

Chicago's Ethnic Museums

If some cities are a melting pot for nationalities, Chicago is a thick ethnic stew. And it seems each ethnic group boasts its own museum, often well off the beaten path. More than 1,000 years of Lithuanian art is featured at the **Balzekas**

Spook-tacular Fun

Since 1973, Richard Crowe has been Chicago's premier ghostbuster. His Supernatural Tour explores the legend and lore of Windy City spirits, everything from the curse of Cap Streeter on the world-famous Boul Mich (Michigan Boulevard) to the hanged man ghost of the Water Tower—both in the heart of downtown.

But for an even more spectacular way of exploring Chicago's spooky haunts, try one of Crowe's Supernatural Cruises. Join the ghostbuster, himself, on a two-hour cruise of Chicago's waterways, riverfront, and lakefront. It's the only tour of its kind in the world!

You'll learn about jinx ships, the haunts of the skyline, tales of organized crime "cement overshoes," the "Lake Michigan Triangle," and more. Maybe you'll see ghostly images in the water and hear banshee screams at the site of the *Eastland* boat tragedy, where 835 people lost their lives in 1915 when an excursion boat capsized.

Or maybe you'll see one of two ghost ships that sail the waters of Lake Michigan. Yikes! Lake tours run from early July to Labor Day weekend; (708) 499–0300.

Mary

"Resurrection Mary" is perhaps Chicago's most enduring (and endearing) apparition. For decades the tales of encounters with this ghost, a beautiful young woman with blue eyes and flaxen hair, haven't changed.

She takes her name from her ultimate destination, **Resurrection Cemetery,** 7201 Archer Road, in nearby suburban Justice. Is Mary her real name? No one knows for sure, but there is a girl of Polish descent named Mary about the same age interred in the cemetery, according to burial records there.

Mary is always seen wearing a long, off-white ballroom gown and dancing shoes . . . in which she died in 1934. Legend says she met her end upon returning from the O. Henry Ballroom (now called the Willowbrook).

How do appearances occur? She is most often seen coatless and in her gown on the side of a road (especially in bad weather) near Resurrection. A kindly Good Samaritan, most often a male driver, pulls over to give the beautiful lady in distress a ride to her home. She gets in and drivers note that the car suddenly seems icy cold inside. Then as the car passes the cemetery, she either simply disappears from inside the car . . . or asks the driver to pull over in front of the cemetery, jumps out of the car, and runs right through the cemetery's closed gates!

Museum of Lithuanian Culture, 6500 South Pulaski Road. Antiquities and artifacts include suits of medieval armor, crossbows, rare books, and maps; there's also an extensive collection of ornamental, designed clothing, weaving, and even Easter eggs; (773) 582–6500.

Home to the largest population of ethnic Poles outside of Warsaw, Chicago's residents of Polish descent can point proudly to the *Copernicus Cultural and Civic Center,* 5216 West Lawrence Avenue. It features artifacts, tapestries, and paintings, and hosts cultural events, plays, and exhibits—and a huge annual summer festival called Taste of Polonia; (773) 777–8898.

You also can visit the *Polish Museum of America,* 984 North Milwaukee Avenue, which claims to be one of the largest and oldest ethnic museums in the country—but because of its location, it remains largely a well-kept secret; (773) 384–3352.

The *DuSable Museum of African American History,* 740 East 56th Place, has become one of the country's finest repositories of black history and culture; (773) 947–0600. The November 2007 reopening of the *Spertus Museum of Judaica* will unveil over 155,000 square feet of exhibit and educational space for study of Jewish history and culture; (312) 322–1747.

Greeks have the *Hellenic Museum and Cultural Center,* 801 West Adams Street, #400; (312) 655–1234. Irish herald the *Irish American Heritage Center,*

4626 North Knox, which has undergone an extensive renovation (including a depiction of designs from the ancient *Book of Kells* stenciled on walls throughout the center) and hosts a massive annual St. Patrick's Day bash complete with live bands, Irish step dancers, and Guinness on tap; (773) 282–7035.

Two more worth noting: the **Swedish American Museum Center,** 5211 North Clark, which features an annual traditional family Christmas dinner; (773) 728–8111; and the **Ukrainian National Museum,** 2249 West Superior Street, with beadwork, costumes, dolls, jewelry, and Easter eggs from twenty-six different Ukrainian regions; (312) 421–8020.

Shopping and Nightlife

I am always very hesitant to recommend any off-the-beaten-path shops or clubs because of the nature of those businesses—more than 90 percent of them fail within the first year. But there are a precious few of these kinds of discoveries I can note, ones that have shown at least some staying power.

The **Abraham Lincoln Book Shop,** 357 West Chicago Avenue, is a gem specializing in Civil War history and Lincoln memorabilia; (312) 944–3085. *Joy of Ireland,* 700 North Michigan Avenue, level three of the Chicago Place Shopping Center, is an unlikely location for this bastion of all things Irish, from handknit Aran wool sweaters and traditional grandfather's shirts to Claddagh jewelry and Irish christening gowns; (312) 664–7290. **Gigi's Dolls and Sherry's Teddy Bears,** 6029 North Northwest Highway, has one of Chicago's finest selections of antique and collectible dolls, bears, miniatures, and more; (773) 594–1540.

chicagotrivia

Did you know that in the late 1800s the Chicago River spewed so much raw sewage into Lake Michigan that engineers "reversed" its course so that it doesn't flow into the lake any longer. Instead, they built the Chicago Sanitary and Ship Canal, and connected it to the Des Plaines River so that the sewage flowed away from the city. Where it went, you don't want to know.

For nightlife fans, hear authentic Chicago blues at the "new" **Checkerboard Lounge,** 5201 South Harper Court in Hyde Park's Harper Court Mall. The Checkerboard's storied history began in Chicago's Bronzeville neighborhood where it thrived for over thirty-one years until city inspectors discovered structural defects in the crumbling building. Although many were disappointed over the Hyde Park move, true fans are forgiving now that the delicious music has returned; (773) 624–3240. *Rosa's,* in the out-of-the-way Humboldt Park area (3420 West Armitage Avenue), offers all kinds of topflight (and adventuresome) bookings; (773) 342–0452. *The*

Wild Hare, 3530 North Clark Street, is a great place to enjoy live reggae; (773) 327–4273. And the *Abbey Pub,* 3420 West Grace, is an authentic Irish haven that regularly books acts from the Auld Sod; (773) 478–4408.

Places to Stay in Chicago

Chicago Marriott Downtown,
540 North Michigan Avenue,
(312) 836–0100

Conrad Chicago Hotel,
521 North Rush at Michigan Avenue,
(312) 645–1500

The Fairmont Hotel,
200 North Columbus Drive,
(312) 565–8000

Four Seasons Hotel,
120 East Delaware Place,
(312) 280–8800

Hilton Chicago,
720 South Michigan Avenue,
(312) 922–4400

Holiday Inn
Chicago City Centre,
300 East Ohio Street,
(312) 787–6100

Hotel Inter-Continental Chicago,
505 North Michigan Avenue,
(312) 944–4100

OTHER ATTRACTIONS WORTH SEEING IN CHICAGO

Art Institute

Field Museum of Natural History

Chicago Board of Trade

John G. Shedd Aquarium and Oceanarium

Museum of Contemporary Art

Museum of Science and Industry

Navy Pier

Dave & Buster's

Water Tower Place

Adler Planetarium and Astronomy Museum

Chicago Academy of Sciences

Chicago Historical Society

Chicago Children's Museum

Museum of Broadcast Communications

Peace Museum

Pullman Historic District

University of Chicago

University of Illinois at Chicago

Robie House

Chicago Fire Academy

Lincoln Park and Garfield Park Conservatories

Bergen Garden

North Pier

Haymarket Monument

Museum of Holography

SELECTED VISITORS BUREAUS AND CHAMBERS OF COMMERCE

Chicago Office of Tourism,
78 East Washington Boulevard, 60602
(312) 744–2400

Chicago Convention and
Tourism Bureau,
2301 South Lake Shore Drive, 60616
(312) 567–8500

Mayor's Office of Special
Events Hotline,
(312) 744–3370

Chicago Fine Arts Hotline,
(312) 346–3278

Illinois Bureau of Tourism—
Travel Information,
(800) 2–CONNECT

WEB SITES

Illinois Tourism,
www.enjoyillinois.com

Chicago Convention and
Tourism Bureau,
www.chicago.il.org

Hyatt Regency Chicago,
151 East Wacker Drive,
(312) 565–1234

The Inn Lincoln Park,
601 West Diversey Parkway,
(773) 348–2810

Marriott Chicago Down-
town Medical District/UIC,
625 South Ashland Avenue,
(312) 491–1234

Palmer House Hilton,
17 East Monroe Street,
(312) 726–7500

Radisson Hotel and
Suites Chicago,
160 East Huron Street,
(312) 787–2900

The Raphael,
201 East Delaware Place,
(312) 943–5000

Ritz-Carlton Chicago,
160 East Pearson Street,
(312) 266–1000

Sutton Place Hotel,
21 East Bellevue Place,
(312) 266–2100

Swissôtel,
323 East Wacker Drive,
(312) 565–0565

The Tremont,
100 East Chestnut Street,
(312) 751–1900

The Westin Hotel,
320 North Dearborn,
(312) 744–1900

Places to Eat in Chicago

Ann Sather's,
929 West Belmont,
(773) 348–2378

Berghoff's,
17 West Adams Street,
(312) 427–3170

Charlie Trotter's,
816 West Armitage Avenue,
(773) 248–6228

Chicago Diner,
3411 North Halsted Street,
(773) 935–6696

Ed Debevic's,
640 North Wells Street,
(312) 664–1707

Frontera Grill,
445 North Clark Street,
(312) 661–1434

Gino's East,
633 North Wells Street,
(312) 943–1124

Green Door Tavern,
678 North Orleans,
(312) 664–5496

Healthy Food
Lithuanian Restaurant,
3236 South Halsted Street,
(312) 326–2724

Heartland Cafe,
7000 North Glenwood
Avenue,
(773) 465–8005

Leona's
3215 North Sheffield Avenue,
(773) 327–8861

Lou Mitchell's,
565 West Jackson
Boulevard,
(312) 939–3111

Orbit Restaurant,
2954 North Milwaukee
Avenue,
(773) 276–1355

Pump Room,
1301 North State Parkway,
(312) 266–0360

Reza's,
5255 North Clark Street,
(773) 561–1898

Tucci Benucch,
900 North Michigan Avenue,
(312) 266–2500

Wishbone,
1001 West Washington
Boulevard,
(312) 850–2663

Northeastern Illinois

North Suburban Chicagoland

Lake County seems to possess the best of both worlds, at least in the eyes of those who live there—and the rest of us from the outside looking in. At its lower edge are some of the Chicago area's most affluent suburbs, such as Lake Bluff, Lake Forest, Kenilworth, Glencoe, and Winnetka. The county even claims the tenth greatest buying power in the United States at $67,675 per household average. At its northern border lies Wisconsin, and to the east, Lake Michigan. Other lakes, too, are never far away; there are more than 120 fishing and boating lakes in the county, including **Chain O'Lakes State Park.** Open year-round, the park, which also expands into McHenry County, has 238 campsites—some with electric hookup—showers, boat rental, fishing, and a playground. Go horseback riding from May through October; snowmobiling and cross-country skiing are popular during the winter months. At 8916 Wilmot Road, Spring Grove; (847) 587–5512.

Illinois Beach State Park, only 20 miles east of Chain O'Lakes on Lake Michigan at Zion, is a 7-mile stretch of beach with Illinois' last and best natural lakeshore dunes area; (847) 662–4811.

WISCONSIN
ILLINOIS
Spring Grove
Zion
Woodstock
Wadsworth
Waukegan
NORTHWEST
SUBURBAN
CHICAGOLAND
Gurnee
Libertyville
Fox R.
NORTH
SUBURBAN
CHICAGOLAND
Long Grove
Lake
Michigan
Evanston
Elgin
St. Charles
WEST SUBURBAN
CHICAGOLAND
Chicago
Wheaton
Aurora
Naperville
Joliet
Morris
SOUTH ENVIRONS OF
CHICAGOLAND
Kankakee R.
ILLINOIS
INDIANA
Kankakee

N

0   20 mi
0   20 km

Appropriate to its name, *Zion* hosts the *Zion Passion Play* each year at the Christian Arts Auditorium. Performances coincide yearly with the Easter holiday; (847) 746–2221.

In Libertyville is a very special place called *Lambs Farm* (Route 176, east of I–94), a nonprofit organization dedicated to helping mentally handicapped adults. Lambs Farm is both a residence and a workplace, where vocational training and employment are provided. More than 250 residents work here in ten businesses at the seventy-two-acre campus. Each year, 300,000 people visit Lambs Farm for special events and to sample the products made by residents. Shop at the pet shop, housed in an early 1900s barn, for some cuddly puppies or furry cats. The thrift shop and the country store have a wide variety of items. Indulge your sweet tooth at Aunt Mary's Bakery. Younger visitors can entertain themselves at the petting farm or the minigolf course. The possibilities for fun are endless: an ice cream parlor, carousel, and

strangebuttrue

Zion was founded as a utopian religious community. The city plat was designed to resemble the British Union Jack, and most of the original streets were named after Biblical references.

AUTHOR'S TOP TEN PICKS

Goose Lake Prairie State Nature Park,
Morris,
(815) 942–2899

Six Flags Great America,
Gurnee,
(847) 249–4636

Garfield Farm Museum,
LaFox,
(630) 584–8485

Morton Arboretum,
Lisle,
(630) 968–0074

St. Charles,
(630) 377–6161 or (800) 777–4373

Kane County Flea Market,
St. Charles,
(630) 377–2252

Fermi National Accelerator Laboratory,
Batavia,
(630) 840–5588

Illinois and Michigan Canal National Heritage Corridor,
Lockport,
(815) 588–1100

Naper Settlement,
Naperville,
(630) 420–6010

Waukegan Boat Association Charter,
Waukegan,
(847) 244–3474

miniature train rides. One of the most popular Lambs Farm offerings is *The Country Inn,* a wonderful old-fashioned restaurant with hearty home cooking. Open weekly for lunch at 11:00 A.M., Saturday 8:00 A.M. to 9:00 P.M., and Sunday 8:00 A.M. to 3:00 P.M. For reservations call (847) 362–5050.

While in Libertyville tour the *David Adler Cultural Center,* at 1700 North Milwaukee; (847) 367–0707. The estate of noted Chicago architect David Adler (1882–1949) features many period furnishings, circa 1920–1930, and extensive landscape design.

The property also houses the David Adler Music and Arts Center where Lake County residents of all ages study music, art, and drama. Open year-round. Tours Monday through Friday 9:00 A.M. to 9:00 P.M. and Saturday 9:00 A.M. to 4:00 P.M. Free admission.

What was formerly the farm of Illinois' most political family, the Adlai Stevensons, is here in Libertyville as well, now part of the *Lake County Forest Preserve.*

Bigger than the herd at Vienna's famous Spanish Riding School, the handsome Lipizzan stallions at *Tempel Farms* are housed in the country's largest stable, right here in Wadsworth. Catch a rare demonstration of equine talent at the 6,000-acre farm. Performances are held from mid-June to early September. Dates and times vary, so call for information. Performances last an hour and ten minutes and are held regardless of the weather. Stick around after the show for a tour of the stables, a "can't miss" delight. No reserved seating, adults, $17.00; seniors, $14.00; children four to fourteen, $9.00; under four, free. At 17000 Wadsworth Road; (847) 623–7272.

For nature lovers, the *Des Plaines River Wetlands Demonstration Project* in Wadsworth is a show of its own. A joint undertaking of the Lake County Forest Preserve District and the conservation organization Wetlands Research, Inc., it protects 550 acres of restored and newly created marshes. Project Director Donald Hey calls it a "living laboratory" where botanists, water quality experts, and environmental engineers from universities across the country come to conduct research. It's open to the public as well for hiking, bird-watching, and nature study. Watch for beaver, muskrat, and the rare yellow-head blackbird, in addition to migrating waterfowl. The project is at U.S. Highway 41 at Wadsworth Road.

Cleopatra's ghost! Also in Wadsworth, at 37921 Dilley's Road, is the unique and kind of downright weird *Gold Pyramid House.* Built by contractor James Onan, the 55-foot, 24K-gold-plated pyramid is probably one of the most unusual residences in the country. With a 200-ton statue of Ramses II standing guard, the structure is protected, too, by a spring-fed moat. It's oriented to true north, as is its model, the Great Pyramid of Cheops in Egypt. The home is no

Gold Pyramid House

longer open for tours and the Egyptian Bazaar retail shop is now an Internet-only enterprise. Suppress the temptation to enter the fenced yard. This is a private residence best viewed from the car.

Another family entertainment spot—one with plenty of "show biz"—is *Six Flags Great America* in Gurnee, the most popular amusement theme park in Illinois. Bugs Bunny, musical stage reviews, and the American Eagle—the world's biggest and fastest double, racing, wooden roller coaster, featuring a 147-foot drop on its first hill that speeds passengers to thrills at 66 mph—bring families by the thousands each summer. Theme villages, 150 attractions, and plenty of entertainment and food make it a sure bet for a Lake County outing. Open daily May through August, and on weekends only September through October. Opens 10:00 A.M., closes at varying times. Guests 54 inches and taller, $54.99; under 54 inches (and seniors 60 years plus) pay $34.99; three and under, free. Parking is $10.00. At *Gurnee,* on Grand Avenue (Route 132), 1 mile east of I–94. Just west of Great America is bargain central, *Gurnee Mills,* one of the country's largest outlet malls. Bring your walking shoes to this behemoth at 6170 West Grand Avenue; Monday through Friday 10:00 A.M. to 9:00 P.M., Saturday 10:00 A.M. to 9:30 P.M., and Sunday 11:00 A.M. to 7:00 P.M.

Or bring your skates! *Rink Side Sports* is an NHL-size ice-skating arena located in the Gurnee Mills Mall; the entrance is between the TJ Maxx and JCPenney stores. For a mind-blowing extravaganza, check out Cosmic Skating on Saturday night. Skate rental is $4.00 per pair; $6.00 admission for adults, $5.00 for ages four–twelve; free three and under. The facility also has a game and video arcade; a 2,000-square-foot laser tag room; and a restaurant. Call for schedules, which vary with season; (847) 856–1064.

TOP ANNUAL EVENTS

Lilac Festival,
Lombard, early May,
(630) 620-7322

Kane County Flea Market,
St. Charles, first weekend of
every month,
(630) 377-2252

Swedish Days Festival,
Geneva, late June,
(630) 232-6060

Alpine Fest,
Lake Zurich, mid-July,
(847) 438-5141

DuPage County Fair,
Wheaton, late July,
(630) 668-6636

Momence Gladiolus Festival,
Momence, mid-August,
(815) 472-6353

Apple Festival,
Long Grove, late September,
(847) 634-0888

Garfield Farm Harvest Days,
LaFox, early October,
(630) 584-8485

The Gurnee Park District sponsors *Gurnee Days,* a festival held annually in Viking Park during the second weekend of August. The theme changes every year, adding to the fun. You can count on a parade, amusement rides, concerts, fireworks, and great food. Call for schedule; (847) 623-7788.

Long Grove (at Route 83 and Route 53 in the southern part of the county) invites you to turn your watch back to yesteryear. The historic village was settled in the 1830s by a group of German farmers who found it much like their own Alsatian homeland. Even after World War I, they continued to speak Plattdeutsch and tend their farms. The village grew up as a place for farmers to buy their supplies, weigh their milk, make their cheese at the cooperative, and have their horses shod. In 1847 they built a tiny church on a hill near town, where services are still held today.

Antiques seem to be everywhere you look in Long Grove now, with one of the better collections of shops anywhere. The *Long Grove Apple Haus* (847-634-0730) presses its own cider, makes heavenly apple butter and jam, and should be a definite stop. *Long Grove Confectionery* (847-634-0080), on the other hand, is famous for hand-dipped chocolates. Try a fat (the size of a child's fist), juicy, chocolate-covered strawberry on for size.

Each summer, the acclaimed Chicago Symphony Orchestra migrates north to Highland Park, taking up residence in their summer home, *Ravinia Park.* Since 1916 its outdoor music festival has featured a wide variety of classical and popular programs—even soft rock like James Taylor and Jackson Browne—

as well as renowned guest artists, ballet, and chamber music. For a more relaxed atmosphere, forsake seats under the roofed pavilion, take a picnic, and lie on the lawn for music under the stars. Call (847) 266–5100 for reservations and prices. Early June through mid-September.

Settled in 1835, *Waukegan* has a rich history well worth exploring. Originally a Native American village and then a French trading post, its name means "Little Fort" in Potawatomi. In 1860 Lincoln, interrupted by fire, delivered what came to be known as his "unfinished speech" here. Today a bit of that past remains in *Old Waukegan*, a designated historic district along North Avenue and Franklin Street. The *Waukegan Historical Society* maintains a restored home and research library at 1917 North Sheridan Road. Free tours of the *Haines House Museum* run Monday through Friday and the first two Saturdays of the month from 1:00 to 3:00 P.M.; (847) 336–1859. The *John L. Raymond Research Library* conserves thousands of documents and welcomes researchers and genealogists to inquire about the collection. Open Wednesday to Friday from 10:00 A.M. to 2:30 P.M., and Saturday by appointment; (847) 360–4772.

If fishing is more to your taste, Waukegan is one of the two main Illinois ports for charter boats. (The massive $51 million, 2,000-boat marina at Winthrop Harbor, just to the north, is the other.) Call (847) BIG–FISH for information on day trips for chinook and coho salmon. In June the city sponsors a *Coho Fishing Derby* with daily prizes.

strangebuttrue

Those Golden Arches seem to be everywhere, right? Yep, even on the water. Seems that McDonald's of Fox Lake is one of the only Mickey D's in the country with "drive-up" service for boats. That's right—you can tie your boat right up to the pier and stroll to the counter to order some of that famous McDonald's grub—a Big Mac, fries, Coke. Hey, let's supersize this one. We've got a long stretch of road . . . er, water ahead of us.

In the Lakewood Forest Preserve, at 27277 Forest Preserve Drive in Wauconda, you'll find the *Lake County Discovery Museum.* This is a great place to bring kids, as many of the exhibits are interactive. You can sit in a sightseeing skiff, walk on an old plank road, and ride the "Vortex Roller Coaster" into prehistoric Illinois and back again. The museum also has a surprising postcard collection. Numbering 1.5 million pieces from 1878 to 1975, the collection documents a century's worth of popular American history. Call for details. Open 11:00 A.M. to 4:30 P.M. Monday through Saturday and 1:00 to 4:30 P.M. Sunday. Admission is $6.00 for adults and $2.50 for ages four to seventeen. Discount Tuesdays adults pay $3.00 and children under seventeen are free. Call (847) 968–3400.

Spontaneous Combustion

If you're looking for something to do on the spur of the moment on a weekend afternoon, Lake County has plenty to offer. If you're looking to spend a weekend in the county, however, I would recommend planning ahead. I had this forcibly brought home to me a couple of summers back. It was a Friday afternoon in mid-June, and I had a sudden brainstorm: the wife and I would go camping that weekend. Now I'm not exactly a spontaneous kind of guy, but I figured this would be a great way to appear that way. No extensive plans were necessary. On Saturday morning we could simply drive someplace nearby and hike and loll about for a day, then leave early the next morning. The wife—impressed that I was actually willing to do something without at least two weeks' notice—was enthusiastic. We would head north into Lake County rather than attempt to wrangle a campsite at a place like Starved Rock State Park, which I figured would be way too crowded. The Chain O' Lakes State Park near the Wisconsin border would be our destination.

Well, as luck would have it, our plans weren't unique. Though we arrived before noon, all the campsites were taken. Since the Bong State Recreation Area in Wisconsin was fairly close, we headed there next. Plenty of our fellow Illinoisians had already beaten us to it, as the license plates of their cars attested. Shut out once again, we returned to Illinois, figuring we had one last possibility—Illinois Beach State Park.

Lo and behold, we managed to grab one of the last remaining campsites. This could have been because it was drizzling by now, but we didn't care. We happily set up the tent then drove into town to buy cheap rain ponchos, determined to enjoy ourselves. Unfortunately, the rain had picked up by the time we got back, and the wind had also shifted. The rain was now solidly peppering the front of our tent, which had no fly to protect it. Though we had closed the flaps, rain had poured in through the zipper, leaving a mini-quagmire in the tent.

Needless to say, we'd had enough. It was now early evening, and since Chicago was only a short drive away, we packed up and hit the road. We made it home with plenty of time to enjoy what was left of the evening. Or would have, I should say, if we hadn't been immediately engulfed in a massive traffic jam, which kept us in the car for well over two hours. The lesson of this story? Lake County is a populous place, full of families with kids looking to maximize their weekends. So please, don't make the same mistake—plan ahead if you're looking to stay overnight somewhere. As for myself, the stolid German side of me became even more convinced that spontaneity just ain't worth it. One more adventure like that and the wife will finally be convinced too.

At the western edge of the county, in the little town of Volo, U.S. Highway 12 and Route 120, the **Antique Auto Museum** at 27582 Volo Village Road, has on display nearly 300 classic motor cars. And if you're souvenir minded, the showroom has mint-condition, classic autos for sale; (815) 385–3644. Hours are 10:00 A.M. to 5:00 P.M. daily. Admission is $8.95 for adults, $6.95 for seniors, and $4.95 for children ages six through thirteen.

Northwest Suburban Chicagoland

The lucky people of Union—all 600 or so—have more to see and do than many in much larger towns. Fairly close to almost nothing, Union boasts three major museums, each with a busy calendar of special events, and a collection of antiques shops to suit every taste.

To start with, the **McHenry County Historical Museum** is on Main Street (6422 Main Street), in the middle of town. The log cabin in the front yard makes it even more difficult to miss. The 1847 structure was built by Luke Gannon on a site 5 miles northeast of Huntley, in the southern part of the county, and donated to the museum in 1964 by the family. Pioneer exhibitions are held here during the season. The museum also houses a collection of nineteenth-century musical instruments, ladies' fashions and handiwork, a quilt collection, farm equipment, and Civil War memorabilia. An 1895 school building is part of the museum complex. Open May through October Tuesday through Friday from 1:00 to 4:00 P.M. and Sunday from 1:00 to 4:00 P.M. Admission, adults $5.00; seniors and children, $3.00. Family rate (two adults and two or more children): $12.00. Call for information on specially scheduled events; (815) 923–2267.

Just around the corner and a bit east of town on Olson Road in the middle of cornfields is one of our most recommended museums in northern Illinois, the **Illinois Railway Museum.** Here you can touch the solid, worn seats as you sit back and enjoy a short train ride. Feel the tingle of excitement as the train bell

"You Call This Prairie?"

Miles of lakeshore, sand dunes, marsh meadows, scores of lakes, and even soggy bogs make up some of the landscape of northeastern Illinois. It's not what lots of people expect from the Prairie State.

In the east, the magnificent shoreline of Lake Michigan dominates all geography. Up north, near the Wisconsin border, you can find the last great sand dunes of the Chicagoland area that haven't been destroyed by progress. There are also wooded ravines and narrow, winding roads through tree-filled towns that are some of the toniest in the country.

Move farther west and you'll find yourself in the winding hills of the Fox River Valley. It's a place to explore graceful historic towns that took advantage of the riverways. But as you travel southward, you'll start to discover lands more open—patches of prairie here, grassland there—really a kind of gateway to the great Midwest prairie everyone really expects to find in the Land of Lincoln.

rings and the whistle blows. And watch with loving affection as the old steam engine comes puffing into the station. The Railway Museum is a nonprofit organization run by volunteers, train buffs who love the thrill of classic locomotives as much as we do. And most important, the exhibit is a place the whole family can find fun. It's open-air, with plenty of places to go—fifty-six acres worth—cars to ride, noises to hear, and even a spot for picnics.

When is a train more than a train? Well, when it's one of the museum's 200 cars and locomotives, which include electric interurbans, streetcars, trolleys, diesels, Chicago elevated cars, and even a complete silver Burlington Zephyr streamliner. It's one of only two places in the state you can ride a steam engine. (The other's in Monticello.) One of the most exotic stars of the show is the Russian Decapod from the Frisco Railroad, built in 1917 by Baldwin for the czarist Russian government, but, due to a revolution, never delivered.

Dating from 1851, the depot originally served as the station in Marengo. Behind it are the gift shop and bookstore with a mountain of railroad lore. Throughout the summer special events are held, such as the July 4 Trolley Pageant, Railroad Day, and Diesel Day. Kids will especially love the Day Out with Thomas event held each year in late August. Trains operate daily June through August, but only on weekends in April, May, September, and October.

northeastern illinoistrivia

Lake Michigan is the world's sixth-largest freshwater lake.

The Baha'i House of Worship in Wilmette, which is open for tours, is a lakefront architectural jewel that took forty years to build.

On weekends the grounds are open from 9:00 A.M. till 6:00 P.M., yet park operations don't begin until 10:30 A.M. and end at 5:00 P.M. On weekdays the grounds open at 10:00 A.M. and close at 5:00 P.M., park operations begin at 10:00 A.M. and end at 4:00 P.M. Admission varies but includes unlimited rides; call (815) 923–4000.

South of town, at 8512 South Union, is *Donley's Wild West Town.* It's like someone's attic—someone who collected almost everything. One of the country's largest antique phonograph collections can be found along with records, cylinders, and needles.

A nickelodeon shows movies throughout the day right around the corner from the "Street of Yesteryear," a collection of old-time shops. Outside, the town has its own saloon, blacksmith shop, and pioneer cabin. Desperadoes shoot it out daily during the summer months in a flashy Wild West gunfight show. And conveniently nearby is the gallows, a real Chicago version, from the old Cook County jail on Hubbard Street, still waiting for "Terrible Tommy" O'Connor, who escaped on December 11, 1921, four days before his scheduled execution, the last one by hanging in the state. To record your day in the past, make a date with the photography studio, where you can get dressed up in Victorian garb or Wild West attire and have a sepia-toned souvenir in a matter of minutes. But certainly the favorite activity for kids is panning for gold (pyrite, that is). Try it—strike it rich! And afterward celebrate with a scoop at the ice-cream parlor. Open daily Memorial Day through Labor Day and weekends only in September and October. Call (815) 923–9000 for hours. Admission is $14.00 for everyone over three.

In the center of the county is Woodstock, the quaint Victorian county seat, named after the Vermont town from which many of its early citizens came. In the center of the town is the square, not with a courthouse (which is off to one side), but with a handsome park complete with bandstand, spring house, and classic Civil War statue.

Movie fans might recognize this location from the 1993 film *Groundhog Day,* starring Bill Murray. The novelty of posing as Punxsutawney, Pennsylvania, continues today with Woodstock's own **Groundhog Days** celebration beginning a few days before the annual national February 2 event. The festivities include a parade of decorated groundhog statues, a free screening of the movie, and the weather prognostication of local groundhog celebrity Woodstock Willie. Call (815) 338–4300.

Don't miss the official "lighting of the groundhog," which is stationed on top of the ornate **Woodstock Opera House** at 121 East Van Buren Street. Listed in the National Register of Historic Places, this is the year-round home of the Woodstock Musical Theatre Company; (815) 338–4212.

In mid-June, cartoon crime fighters prevail during Woodstock's **Dick Tracy Days.** And visit the **Chester Gould–Dick Tracy Museum** on the second floor of the Old Court House, open Thursday through Saturday 11:00 A.M. to 5:00 P.M. and Sunday 1:00 to 5:00 P.M.; $2.00 adult admission, $1.00 for seniors, children free. Register the kids for cartooning classes while you peruse the exhibits; (815) 338–8281.

Next, take Route 173 to Richmond, which is located blocks south of the Wisconsin state line. The legendary antique village is chockablock with antiques shops of every description. Most shops in town are closed on Monday. Whatever your weakness, chances are it will find you here—from oak furniture to primitives, from china dolls to heavenly homemade chocolates.

Since 1919 **Anderson's Candy Shop,** 10301 Main Street, has been bringing them in for hand-dipped English toffees, meltaway fudge, and old-fashioned "candy bars" that are really chocolate-covered apricot, orange peel, pudding, or "krispy" rice. This is a must visit for any candy lover—these homemade sweets might be the best in the state! Open Tuesday through Saturday 9:00 A.M. to 5:00 P.M., Sunday noon to 5:00 P.M.; (815) 678–6000.

Holy Cow!

No, this doesn't have anything to do with Harry Caray, the late legendary baseball announcer, who may have found his greatest fame with the Chicago Cubs. This is all about Harmilda.

Harmilda is a life-size fiberglass cow that sits in the middle of Main Street in Harvard. The village prides itself on its former reputation as one of the Midwest's top milk-producing regions. Now it recalls this heritage during its Milk Days festival, celebrated in early June. Of course, milking contests (with real cows) are part of the fun.

By the way, if you wondered about her name, Harmilda, think HARvard MILk DAys; (815) 943–4614.

Richmond holds special exhibits, such as a quilt show and an art glass exhibit, throughout the summer months. The last weekend in August is "Richmond Round-Up Days," where local service clubs, aided by the village, put on a "do" over at the Community Church. Fill up on a bratwurst, roasted ears of corn fresh from the field, and slabs of roast beef. Call (815) 678–4040 for more information.

A *moraine,* according to Webster, is "a mass of rocks, gravel, sand . . . carried or deposited by a glacier." And that's exactly what you'll find at **Moraine Hills State Park,** 3 miles south of McHenry. **Lake Defiance,** in the park, was created by a chunk of glacier left to melt there. Unusual natural features include a leatherleaf bog—120 acres of floating sphagnum moss and leatherleaf surrounded by a moat of open water. The pike marsh contains the largest known colony of pitcher plants in Illinois, along with cattails and bullrushes. It's a protected nature preserve and, as such, attracts a rich variety of wildlife as well. Visitors will want to stop at the interpretive center, which explains the park's natural resources. The **Pike Marsh Nature Trail** features a floating boardwalk perfect for exploration of park plant life. All state parks are open year-round except Christmas and New Year's Day. Contact the Site Superintendent, 1510 South River Road, McHenry; (815) 385–1624.

West Suburban Chicagoland

Of what are locally known as the collar counties—those surrounding Cook—DuPage County is surely the white collar enclosing the beefy neck of Chicago—buttoned down, starched, of oxford cloth. It's conservative, Republican, a place of manicured lawns and solid brick homes. As someone who grew up in

Wheaton—the county seat (where Prohibition didn't end until 1992)—I can personally vouch for this.

On its northeast corner DuPage County slices through O'Hare International Airport; on the south it encloses the Argonne National Laboratory; and on the west it bisects the grounds of the Fermi National Accelerator Laboratory, one of the world's largest particle accelerators, where scientists from around the world come to study quirks and quarks. There's a lot going on in the county.

The **Morton Arboretum** (630–968–0074) offers a spectacular year-round escape to nature for harried city dwellers. One mile north of Lisle, at the Route 53 exit of the East-West Tollway (I–88), the garden encompasses 1,700 acres of lush plants and trees and shrubs. Drive or stroll interpretive trails. Hours are 7:00 A.M. to 7:00 P.M. during daylight saving time, 7:00 A.M. to dusk or 5:00 P.M. after October 29. There is a $7.00 charge for adults; $5.00 for seniors; $3.00 for children three to twelve years. On Wednesdays: $4.00 for adults; $3.00 for seniors; $2.00 for children.

For history buffs (and kids), visiting the **Naper Settlement,** at 523 South Webster, Naperville (630–420–6010), makes an ideal afternoon. Here, seventeen historic buildings on a thirteen-acre site re-create a nineteenth-century village. Costumed interpreters lead tours. Visit the tiny gothic **Century Memorial Chapel** and the 1883 **Caroline Martin-Mitchell Mansion,** which is listed on the National Register of Historic Places. Open April through October 10:00 A.M. to 4:00 P.M. Tuesday through Saturday; 10:00 A.M. to 4:00 P.M. Sunday. Adult admission is $7.00, seniors $6.00, children $4.50.

Naperville hosts two award-winning festivals. Over the Fourth of July, thousands treat their taste buds to four days of world-class barbeque during

Naperville

Charm abounds along the 5-mile brick trails of Naperville's *Riverwalk,* which skirts the meandering banks of the DuPage River. Covered bridges, an amphitheater, and sculptures dot the path. Visit the *9/11 Memorial Wall* outside of City Hall, pause for a concert at the *Millennium Carillon Bell Tower,* view artwork along the *Century Walk,* or get your legs into shape peddling a boat on *Paddleboat Quarry.* There's even a public swimming quarry called *Centennial Beach.* Call the Naperville Park District; (630) 848–5000.

Don't forget the prime shopping along Chicago Avenue, Jackson, and Jefferson Streets. Feeling tired? Take the one-hour *Naperville Trolley* tour, which boards at the *Dandelion Fountain* on the corner of Jackson and Webster. Reservations recommended; dates flexible. Call (630) 420–2223. Adults, $8.00; ages four–seventeen, $5.00; one cent for three and under.

Ribfest, held noon to 10:00 P.M. at Knoch Park, West Street at Hillside Avenue. After several days of concerts, a carnival, and games, a dramatic fireworks display caps the event. Parking is limited; take the free shuttle; (630) 848–5000; adults $8.00; children eleven and under free. And as summer fades, the *Last Fling* celebration, held over Labor Day weekend, features a two-hour parade, a street full of carnival rides, and concerts in two locations. The Sled Hill stage features concerts by nationally known artists. Concert fees range from $5.00 to $10.00; (630) 961–4143.

The *Old Graue Mill* at York and Spring Roads in Oak Brook is grist for a nostalgic afternoon. It's the only operating waterwheel grist mill in the state, and a white-aproned miller turns out stone-ground cornmeal for sale in the country store. Upstairs are a Victorian drawing room, kitchen, and children's room with antique dolls and toys, plus exhibits of spinning and weaving. Visit the new exhibit commemorating this stop on the historic Underground Railroad. Open 10:00 A.M. to 4:30 P.M. daily (closed Monday except holiday weekends) mid-April through mid-November; (630) 655–2090. Admission, $3.50 adults, $1.50 children, and $3.00 seniors.

Wheaton, the DuPage county seat, is home to *Wheaton College,* founded in 1853, and the headquarters of a number of religious publishing houses and organizations. Wheaton College is Billy Graham's alma mater and the site of the *Billy Graham Center Museum* with its Walk Through the Gospel and scenes from American evangelism since 1702. Temporary exhibits change quarterly. I always enjoyed coming here as a kid. A couple of the rooms are almost Disneyesque in their special effects, so it's kind of like the *Pirates of the Caribbean*—only pious. I'm not sure if that was the effect Billy Graham was going for, but it did manage to bring me in time and again, and actually made me familiar with the name of Jonathan Edwards, one of the most important evangelists in early American history. Open Monday through Saturday 9:30 A.M. to 5:30 P.M., Sunday 1:00 to 5:00 P.M.; (630) 752–5909.

Not every county has its own mastodon, but at Armerding Hall on campus, a skeleton of the giant *Perry Mastodon,* which was found locally, is on exhibit; (630) 752–5010.

One of Wheaton's most famous sons is football hero Red Grange. At the *Red Grange Museum/DuPage Heritage Gallery,* 421 North County Farm Road, displays and films tell the story of his life. Open Monday through Friday 8:00 A.M. to 5:00 P.M.

If you love politics, there's nothing like Wheaton's *Fourth of July parade,* long a magnet for national and state politicians stumping for votes. Call (630) 367–1534.

The *DuPage County Fair* runs the fourth week of July and features traditional farm and home arts exhibits. Concerts by big-name artists are eclipsed by the perennial favorite Demolition Derby. Located off of County Farm Road; (630) 668–6681. Free parking; adults $6.00, seniors $3.00, children (three to eight) $1.00, under three free.

Also in Wheaton is *Cantigny Park,* the former estate of the late Colonel Robert R. McCormick, celebrated publisher of the *Chicago Tribune.* Tours of the restored mansion are free, but group sizes are limited, so make your reservation as soon as you arrive. Twenty-seven of the thirty-five rooms are open for viewing. Artifacts and antiques from ancient Chinese and European artists are displayed alongside the McCormick family's personal memorabilia. Colonel McCormick's private office features exotic wood paneling and a wet bar that raises from the floor behind a secret door, a requirement for entertaining during Prohibition. It's a real treat to stand on the veranda and view the unimpaired, impeccably manicured garden vista. Parking is $8.00. The entrance is at 1 South 151 Winfield Road; (630) 668–5161. Closed during January; open Friday through Sunday only during February, 9:00 A.M. to 4:00 P.M.; March to December hours are Tuesday through Sunday, 9:00 A.M. to sunset.

Also on the grounds is the *First Division Museum at Cantigny.* The brainchild of Colonel McCormick, the museum honors the "Big Red One," the First Infantry Division of the United States Army in which he served during World War I. The 38,000-square-foot homage features impressive, life-size dioramas and interactive experiences such as the illusion of riding a transport onto the shores of France during the heat of battle. The $8.00 parking fee applies at the entrance gate. A separate admission is charged for this venue. Adults $3.00; children, students, and seniors $2.00; under four free. Entrance at 1 South 151 Winfield Road; (630) 668–5185. Hours and days mirror those of the mansion tour, except the doors here open at 10:00 A.M.

Another worthwhile Wheaton attraction is the *DuPage County Historical Museum,* located in an 1891 Romanesque-style, limestone building. Visit the special interactive gallery (popular with families), the Victorian period room, and the permanent collection of DuPage history. Here, too, is almost a half mile of model railroad track. Watch trains chug along on select Saturdays and Sundays from 1:30 to 3:30 P.M. The museum is located at 102 East Wesley Street; (630) 682–7343. Its hours are 10:00 A.M. to 4:00 P.M. on Monday, Wednesday, Friday, and Saturday and 1:00 to 4:00 P.M. on Sunday. DuPage County, in fact, has no shortage of museums—over a dozen in all.

Equally numerous are golf courses, if history's not your game. DuPage boasts nearly fifty public courses, plus a handful of private courses, making it

Prohibition Suppositions

In 1933, Prohibition ended in the United States but not in Wheaton, Illinois. The entire time I lived in Wheaton—up into my late teens—the town was dry. You couldn't purchase beer, wine, or liquor anywhere. That's not to say beer, wine, and liquor weren't around. My parents and the parents of practically every childhood friend I ever had all had built-in bars in their basement rec-rooms, fully stocked from the liquor stores of neighboring towns like Glen Ellyn. Wheatonian prohibition, then, was simply a quaint holdover from a (supposedly) more innocent time and not something anyone took very seriously. Yet once I was living in Chicago, I was always surprised to hear the snorts of disbelief, and maybe derision, from fellow college kids when I told them I had grown up in Wheaton.

As my college years came to a close, I thought less and less about Wheaton, returning only to visit my parents. Yet there I was one day in 1992 right smack in downtown Wheaton, which I hadn't seen in quite a few years. A friend and I had just returned from a stint in New Orleans, and we had to drop off our rental truck. As we headed toward a restaurant I had frequented in my teen years to get dinner, I told him about the Prohibition deal and explained that beer would not be on the menu. His reaction was one of flat disbelief.

"That's ridiculous," he waved my comment away, "there's no Prohibition anymore."

Because my friend was not originally from Illinois, he knew nothing about Wheaton. His statement was based solely on his inability to believe there could be any such thing as a dry town only thirty miles from Chicago. Of course the two of us had just been living in New Orleans, where alcohol is available twenty-four hours a day. After the battering our livers and nervous systems had taken in that city, it was hard to imagine a place where you couldn't drink a beer while walking down the street or doing your laundry. He would realize soon enough, I figured.

We sat down at a booth in the restaurant, and—wonder of wonders—there were beer lights on the walls. And yes, we were able to order beer with our meal. "See, I told you," my friend indulgently smiled, as if I had been suffering from some delusions. It had finally happened—my hometown had finally emerged from the 1930s. You can now order a beer or a glass of wine or a mixed drink in a public place in Wheaton, just like you can in towns all across America.

This is progress, though in hindsight I would say Wheaton has definitely lost something. There was a certain charm in people's reactions when they learned you were from Wheaton. All that's gone now. In fact, Wheaton has softened up to the point that I recently heard the 1980s goth band Sisters of Mercy playing over the loudspeakers of a Whole Foods supermarket while people like my parents shopped without so much as a *"What is this?"* Ah well, it's all for the best, I suppose. But let's just hope they don't go the way of New Orleans and start opening bars where you can do your laundry as strippers gyrate on the dryers. That would send this native son straight to the Billy Graham Center.

DuPage County Historical Museum, Wheaton

one of the most golf-accessible counties in the state. This mania is no recent phenomenon. The Chicago Golf Club, a private club in Wheaton, claims to have been the first eighteen-hole course in the United States, having opened in 1892.

Plenty of other outdoor activities are available in DuPage County, as well. For example, if your interests are somewhat patrician, there are polo matches each Sunday afternoon at 1:00 from mid-June to mid-September at the *Oak Brook Polo Club,* 700 Oak Brook Road in Oak Brook; (630) 990–2394.

During mid-May Lombard is abloom for the annual *Lilac Festival,* making it one of the best-smelling towns in the county. Parades are scheduled and a Lilac Queen is named. Call (630) 620–7322 for more information.

Especially pleasant is the *Illinois Prairie Path,* beginning in Elmhurst at York Road south of North Avenue. This 62-mile-long biking and hiking trail follows an old railroad right-of-way, where wildflowers, prairie grasses, tiny parks, and rest stops are plentiful. For a color map, send $6.00 to Illinois Prairie Path, P.O. Box 1086, Wheaton, IL 60189. Yet I would be remiss if I didn't use this opportunity to caution you against drinking from one of the creeks that occasionally flow along the Prairie Path. Yes, I'm aware that all sensible adults and children know better than to do such a thing, but my cousins and I did it in our childhood, and we, too, knew better. I guess we had just gotten wrapped up in make-believe, pretending our bikes were not bikes at all but horses and the Prairie Path untrammeled wilderness. I forget who first cupped his hands into that little creek we had lunched beside, but soon we were all gulping

Movie Mania

Yorktown Cinema in Lombard is a movie lover's dream: eighteen screens! All of the theaters here feature stadium seating, but several include out of the ordinary perks such as leather seats, small tables, restaurant foods, and wine service. If you're running late and don't have time to search for a parking space, use the valet service.

If eighteen theaters are heaven, Warrenville's Cantera 30 is a movie lover's nirvana. Yes, it really has thirty screens, so if making a simple decision causes you anxiety, beware! All seats are great with stadium seating, plus a large video game arcade makes this place a veritable movie/amusement park.

down handfuls of the cool water, smacking our lips and pronouncing it good. I won't go into the consequences in detail, but as you can probably imagine, it involved several unpleasant trips to the bathroom later that day. So please remember, your bike is not a horse and the Prairie Path is not untrammeled wilderness. Don't drink the water.

At Glen Ellyn, the ***Willowbrook Wildlife Haven,*** 525 South Park Boulevard, is always popular with children. Here wounded, lost, and captured native wildlife are cared for. Take a self-guided tour and visit the ***Touch & Feel Museum.*** The haven's hours are from 9:00 A.M. to 5:00 P.M. daily; (630) 942–6200. Admission is free.

The county's forest preserves are among the finest in the area, with sixty-eight preserves encompassing 24,000 acres. At various locations you'll find dog training fields, model airplane runs, bird-watching facilities, cross-country skiing, ice skating, hiking, and equestrian fields.

Oak Brook Center, Twenty-second Street and Route 83, is the nation's largest upscale open-air shopping center with Macy's, Lord and Taylor, Nordstrom, and Neiman-Marcus as major tenants. More than 160 shops and restaurants are laid out around a landscaped courtyard.

The settlement of the Fox River Valley can be credited in great part to the Black Hawk War of 1832. As soldiers and militiamen from southern Illinois and neighboring states flooded into the region to chase down Black Hawk and his unfortunate band of Sauk and Fox, they became enchanted with the fertility of the land along the river. Thus communities sprang up beside the waterway, notably Geneva in 1833, as supply centers for area farms and pioneers traveling farther west.

For the weekend traveler on nothing more than a sightseeing excursion, a trip through the Kane County towns of the Fox River is richly rewarding. Follow Route 31 along the eastern edge of the county as it meanders along next to the Fox River. In the south begin with Aurora, one of the first major cities in the nation to light its streets with electricity (1881).

Here the best show in town is the *Paramount Theatre,* 23 East Galena Boulevard. Commanding a peninsula along the Fox River, the opulently stylish and historic art deco movie and vaudeville showcase was built in 1931 by noted theater architects Rapp and Rapp as a romanticized version of a Venetian palace. A 70-foot cascade light marquee adorns the redbrick and terra-cotta exterior. The Paramount was restored in 1978 and protected in the National Register of Historic Places two years later. In the theater's early days, Charlie Chaplin and the Marx Brothers were headliners. Today there's a varied schedule of visiting entertainers. Call (630) 896–6666 for program information.

West of town on Galena Boulevard (and about 2½ miles west of Randall Road) is *Blackberry Farm's Pioneer Village,* a dairy farm that has been converted by the Fox Valley Park District into a unique park with a collection of rides and historic exhibits.

Pony rides and an antique carousel vie for junior riders. A miniature steam train, Old Engine #9, takes visitors around the fifty-four-acre park and Lake Gregory to an 1840 *Pioneer Farm* where craftspeople demonstrate frontier skills are among the attractions.

Museums on the property exhibit early carriages, a one-room schoolhouse, and Victorian women's furnishings. Throughout the season special events are scheduled. Open May 1 to Labor Day; Monday through Friday, 9:30 A.M. to 3:30 P.M. and Saturday and Sunday 11:00 A.M. to 5:00 P.M. After Labor Day the park

Holy Cow! . . . er, Cougars

If you're a fan of baseball, then you must take in a game at Elfstom Stadium—home to the Kane County Cougars. The Cougars are the Class A affiliate of the Oakland Athletics. Fans view games at the Cougars' quaint Geneva stadium from April through September.

But it's not just the love of the game that brings fans to this picturesque ballpark. The stadium boasts great up-close looks at up-and-coming ballplayers.

Why not rent out the hot tub just over the left field wall? It's a great way to watch baseball, seated in your jet-streamed water pod, while sipping on a cool drink and witnessing some great all-out hustle from these young ballplayers. Let's face it: Some major leaguers could learn a thing or two about the love of the game from these guys. Box seats $12.00, reserved $10.00, lawn $8.00; free general admission parking; reserved parking is $5.00. Call (630) 232–8811.

is only open on Friday, Saturday, and Sunday. Call for times of special fall events. Admission, which includes all rides, is $6.00 for adults, $3.75 for seniors and children, free for children ages two and under. Call (630) 892–1550.

Between North Aurora and Batavia on Route 31 lies one of the most unusual communities in the entire state. *Mooseheart* is a wonderful, warm place you're certain to want to visit. Here children, whose families are unable to care for them, thrive in a nurturing homestead run entirely by the Loyal Order of Moose. On 1,200 acres are a dairy farm and garden, a post office and bank, a school, field house, and even a furniture shop for supplying the needs of the residents. Tours are Monday through Friday 9:00 A.M. to 4:00 P.M. and Sunday noon to 4:00 P.M.; (630) 906–3605.

North of Aurora in Batavia is *Fermilab,* the Department of Energy's laboratory for physics research, and home to the *Tevatron,* the world's most powerful particle accelerator. Visitors must stop their vehicle at an entrance checkpoint, provide identification, and use the map provided to navigate the grounds. Heed the posted signs. Ask for directions to see the herd of sixty buffalo that roam within a securely fenced area. The premises are open seven days a week, 8:00 A.M. to 6:00 P.M. from mid-October to mid-April, and 8:00 A.M. to 8:00 P.M. during spring and summer. Currently, *Wilson Hall* and the *Lederman Science Center* are open for self-tours. Hours are Monday through Friday, 8:30 A.M. to 4:30 P.M.; (630) 840–3000.

Next, take Route 38 West and catch Route 25 North toward Geneva, but keep your eyes open for the entrance to the *Fabyan Forest Preserve.* Suddenly you might think you've made a wrong turn and ended up in Denmark because a classic five-story windmill stands majestically in the middle of the grassy park. The *Fabyan Windmill* is recognized as a national and state landmark, and in 1980 it graced a commemorative U.S. postal stamp. Tours run from May 15 to October 15, Saturday and Sunday, 1:00 to 4:00 P.M.; (630) 232–5980.

This forest preserve was formerly part of the 600-acre estate of Colonel and Mrs. George Fabyan. Today their circa 1900s home, which was redesigned by Frank Lloyd Wright, contains family heirlooms and collections. The restored Japanese Gardens and Tea House attract picture takers, and fishing is prime along the banks of the Fox River.

Continuing north, the town of *Geneva* is the next stop. Its historic district is a bonanza of period architecture with more than 200 structures listed in the National Register of Historic Places. Geneva is the county seat, and the 1892 *Kane County Courthouse* is historically significant, with unique wrought-iron balconies gracing the first to the fourth interior floors. Also be sure to see the WPA mural in the post office at 26 South Third Street. Founded as a trading center, Geneva is still that, with dozens of charming shops.

One of the oldest annual festivals in the state, Geneva's *Midsommar Festival Swedish Days* is held each June to commemorate the area's Swedish heritage. Quilts, crafts, *rosemaling* (Swedish painted flower decoration on furniture), and an unforgettable Swedish buffet are part of the fun. Free admission; (630) 232–6060.

Although it might not be fair to the other towns along the way, it's not much of a stretch to proclaim *St. Charles* the jewel of the Fox River. Here pretty, wooded slopes fall away to the slow-running river where the *Fox River Trail* (a premier bicycle and walking path from St. Charles to Aurora and north to Elgin) hugs the water. It's the perfect walking town, bisected by a

strangebuttrue

The first medical school in Illinois—the Franklin Medical School in St. Charles founded in 1842—sparked a riot in 1849, when townspeople discovered two students robbing graves. In the ensuing scuffle, one of the offending students was killed.

river, with plenty of quaint shops, boutiques, and side streets to explore. It's nice to see a small town where things are going well, business is thriving, the economy healthy. You come away with an almost Disney-like impression of a town where clean streets and smiling faces are part of the package.

Make sure to schedule a visit to St. Charles during September for the "Grave Reminders" Cemetery Walk, sponsored by the *St. Charles Heritage Center.* Here you'll meet the likes of Caroline Howard, a psychic consulted by Mary Todd Lincoln, and S.S. Jones, Kane County's first practicing lawyer. You won't simply be visiting their gravestones, mind you, but mixing with actors portraying them in period dress. During the rest of the year, stop by the center at 215 East Main Street. Open Tuesday through Saturday, 10:00 A.M. to 4:00 P.M.; noon to 4:00 P.M. Sunday; (630) 584–6967.

St. Charles's claim to fame is antiquing. *Giant Antique Markets I, II, and III* are dealer cooperatives with a remarkable collection of stuff under each roof.

On the first Sunday of each month and the Saturday afternoon preceding it, the massive *Kane County Flea Market* takes over the County Fairgrounds with 1,000 dealers on twenty-five acres, attracting fifteen to twenty thousand or so shoppers. It has been called the largest flea market in the world, perhaps rightly so. The market ignores the weather and never cancels. Its success is the work of Helen Robinson, a grandmother whose nickname, Queen Flea, says it all. The monthly operation includes three kitchens and eight food trailers to feed the bargain hunters. Located on Randall Road just south of Route 64; (630) 377–2252. Open noon to 5:00 P.M. on Saturday and 7:00 A.M. to 4:00 P.M. on Sunday. Admission is $5.00; children under twelve are free. Free parking.

Shoppers, too, will enjoy the three restored areas in town—*Historic Downtown St. Charles, Century Corners,* and *Fox Island Square.* Lunch is

honeymoonhotel

When Hotel Baker, St. Charles' riverside retreat, was built in 1928 by local moneybags Edward J. Baker, it was the toast of the town, hosting the vaudeville stars who came to play the local theater. The hotel was in vogue and famous for its Rainbow Ballroom, which had a glass-block dance floor lighted from beneath in red, blue, amber, and green.

After a $10 million renovation in 1997, the hotel has recaptured its former elegance and refashioned itself into a "Honeymoon Hotel," a moniker it first received in the 1930s. The original Moorish-style architecture inspires romance—and you can still glide across the ballroom floor with your special someone.

a welcome respite, and the choices of restaurants are numerous.

In the handsome old 1928 *Hotel Baker,* a National Register building, the oval Rainbow Room has a backlit colored glass floor and a view of the river. The Moorish stucco interiors lead out onto a terrace with a gazebo that's perfect for photographing the waterfalls behind the hotel. Dine beside the river at the Baker's Waterfront Restaurant. At 100 West Main Street; (630) 584–2100.

But to *really* get the feel of the river, you have to get out on it. And the best way to do that is a ride on the *St. Charles Belle* or the *Fox River Queen,* 100-passenger paddle-wheelers. Adults $6.00; children, $4.50. June through August, the excursion boats leave from Potawatomie Park at 3:30 P.M. on weekdays and at 2:00, 3:00, and 4:00 P.M. on Saturdays and Sundays; also at 5:00 P.M. on Sunday. In May, September, and October, the boats operate on weekends only. Call (630) 584–2334. Also in this hilly, tidy park north of downtown are a swimming pool, a miniature golf course, and tennis courts. Note that there is a parking and use fee for nonresidents.

Professional entertainment in St. Charles is offered at the *Dellora A. Norris Cultural Arts Center,* 1040 Dunham Road (630–584–7200), and at the *Pheasant Run Resort and Spa* east of town on Route 64; (630) 584–6300. Both feature name entertainers and shows.

Just west of St. Charles in LaFox is the *Garfield Farm Museum,* at 3N016 Garfield Road, a living history farm of the 1840s. Roosters wander in and out of the weathered barns. Herbs and flowers grow in the curator's garden. In 1841 Timothy and Harriet Frost Garfield brought their eight children from Vermont to the prairie lands of Illinois. In 1977 the third-generation owner, Elva Ruth Garfield, donated the farm as a museum; one of the most intact historical sites in the country, it is used for ongoing archaeological studies. It's the largest Illinois farm in the National Register of Historic Places, and it gives the visitor an excellent idea of just how a farm family of the 1840s must have lived. Walk through the grounds and the interior of the brick (made locally) home and teamster tavern (inn). In August come to the farm's Heirloom Garden Show, where you'll see pioneer veggies like purple tomatoes, blue potatoes, and an 1800s carrot more than a foot and a half long. In early October join in the **Sunday Harvest Days,** which feature historical music, a storyteller, blacksmithing, craft demonstrations, and hearty farm cooking appropriate to the period. Open on Wednesday and Sunday 1:00 to 4:00 P.M., June through September or by appointment. Adults $3.00; children $2.00. Call (630) 584–8485 for a schedule of seasonal events.

Farther north on Route 31, in South Elgin, is the **Fox River Trolley Museum,** where you can take a 4-mile, thirty-minute ride along the Fox River on this electric railway. Vintage railway cars are on display. Open Sunday 11:00 A.M. to 5:00 P.M. May through early November; Saturday 11:00 A.M. to 5:00 P.M. late June through August and on select October Saturdays; (847) 697–4676. The museum is on Route 31 in South Elgin, 3 blocks south of State Street. Adults $3.50, children (ages three to eleven) and seniors $2.00. All day ticket $7.00.

In Elgin don't go looking for the Elgin Watch Factory, from 1866 the manufacturer of America's best-known timepieces. It closed in 1965. What you can explore, however, is the **Elgin Historic District.** The National Register district includes 667 structures, many of noteworthy architecture—Greek Revival, Queen Anne, Shingle style, and brick row houses. Walking tour or bicycle tour maps are available from the Elgin Visitors Bureau; (847) 695–7540.

The **Dundee area,** just north of Elgin, was once home to Allan Pinkerton, a cooper turned secret agent and spy who contracted his services during the Civil War. His motto, "We Never Sleep," featured the logo of a penetrating eyeball, and hence, the term "private eye" was born. A state historical marker along Third Street in West Dundee designates the site of his homestead.

In Dundee tour the family-owned **Haeger Potteries** at 7 Maiden Lane. From the banks of the Fox River, the company founder took clay to use in his Dundee Brickyards in 1871 to make bricks that were used to rebuild Chicago after the Great Chicago Fire. Haeger was bestowed a *Guinness Book of World Records* award in 1976 for its successful creation of "the world's largest hand-thrown vase," and it's quite a stunning specimen that you don't want to miss! The 8-foot-tall, 650-pound showpiece can be ogled at the free on-site museum. Factory outlet and museum on Van Buren Street 2 blocks south of Route 72. Open Monday, Thursday, and Friday 10:00 A.M. to 6:00 P.M., Saturday and Sunday 11:00 A.M. to 5:00 P.M., (847) 783–5420.

Next, backtrack south to the heart of Kane County's oldest city, **Batavia.** During the 1850s, Batavia emerged as the world's windmill manufacturing leader, earning the nickname "The Windmill City." Visitors to the **Batavia Riverwalk Park** can view seven faithfully restored examples of Batavia's windmills as produced from 1880–1942. The city celebrates its heritage each year in mid-July with a carnival, live music, plenty of arts and crafts booths, and lots of food during the *Windmill City Festival.* For a schedule of events, call (630) 897–5235.

At 155 Houston Street find the *Depot Museum,* a formerly abandoned depot from the Chicago, Burlington and Quincy Railroad which is now home of the Batavia Historical Society. The quaint, refurbished terminal offers an exhibit that gives a glimpse into one of Mary Todd Lincoln's most desperate times. A replica of her room during her incarceration at Batavia's Bellevue Place Sanitarium stands, eerily, exactly as when she lived there. Both the dresser and the bed are the same that Mrs. Lincoln used during her stay. Antiques of that era complete the display. Mrs. Lincoln was eventually freed from the hospital and sent to live with her sister in Springfield, Illinois.

Kids of all ages might like to try their dot and dash skills at the museum's antique telegraph station or tour the refurbished (circa 1907) train caboose. For a photo op, pose beside the life-size American Indian sculpture, the Newton Wagon (these were used to transport "salesman's samples" of windmills!), or the charming Victorian-era gazebo. The museum is open from March to Thanksgiving on Monday, Wednesday, Friday, and Saturday from 2:00 to 4:00 P.M.; (630) 406–5274.

South Environs of Chicagoland

Will County's seat, Joliet, may call to mind only *The Blues Brothers* (part of the movie was set here) and an infamous state prison. But this community of 78,000, 40 miles southwest of Chicago, has other, more pleasant features. For example, it's known as the City of Spires, for the 158 houses of worship that dot the area.

The temple of art, however, that attracts the cultural faithful from miles around is the historic *Rialto Square Theatre,* "The Jewel of Joliet." Opened in 1926 by the renowned theater designers Rapp and Rapp, this masterpiece is a remarkable example of theater baroque. Restored in 1981, it is in the National Register of Historic Places. Here where Fanny Brice and Al Jolson once performed, a list of modern-day luminaries headlines the bill at the new performing arts center: Broadway shows, orchestras, singers, and comedians.

But in this palace for the people, the real show's before the show. You enter a block-long lobby lined with mirrors, its splendor compared with that of the Hall of Mirrors at Versailles. This lobby leads into the domed rotunda with bas-relief sculptures by Eugene Romeo. From the dome hangs one of the largest hand-cut chandeliers in the United States, "The Duchess," over 20 feet long with eight arms of copper and bronze and more than 250 lights. Beyond the rotunda is the auditorium, no less impressive. The twenty-one-rank Barton Grande Theatre Pipe Organ is a prized instrument that is used in occasional recitals at the Rialto. Tours are scheduled each Tuesday at 1:30 P.M.; (815) 726–7171. Admission is $5.00. For performance information and tickets, call (815) 726–6600.

The city's historic districts are also worth inspection. The **South East Neighborhood Historic District,** south and east of downtown, is a Registered National Landmark District. The feature home is the opulent **Jacob H. Henry Mansion,** a three-story, forty-room Italian Renaissance mansion at 20 South Eastern Avenue. Just west of the Des Plaines River, on North Broadway and Hickory Streets, are splendid Second Empire–style homes and authentic examples of original Joliet limestone residences. Up the hill from downtown Joliet, west along Western Avenue, are turn-of-the-century Victorian mansions in all of their ornate glory.

northeastern illinoistrivia

Oak Park, one of Chicagoland's most historic nearby suburbs, is said to have been called a place with "neat lawns and narrow minds" by hometown boy Ernest Hemingway.

In 1990 the Illinois legislature approved gambling but with a twist: gaming was not permitted on land. The stipulation provided for the birth of riverboat gambling. Cities blessed with a river became candidates for the new income generator. Joliet won two of the nine statewide enterprises. Floating southwest of downtown along the Des Planes River is **Argosy's Empress Casino Joliet** at 2300 Empress Drive and **Harrah's Joliet Casino** at 151 North Joliet Street. Between the pair, patrons can test their luck on over 2,000 slot machines.

strangebuttrue

The town of Romeo (now Romeoville) was named as a sister city to Juliet (now Joliet).

Completed for the nation's bicentennial year, the **Billie Limacher Bicentennial Park** complex at Jefferson and Bluff Streets is home to an outdoor concert season and a beautiful 300-seat formal theater. Free weekly lawn concerts are offered each Thursday in June, July, and August at 6:30 P.M. Call (815) 724–3760 for more information.

The nation's first junior college was founded in 1901 by William Rainey Harper and J. Stanley Brown. Six students became the inaugural class of the Joliet Junior College. They matriculated in the stone building designed by Daniel Burnham and F. S. Allen at 201 East Jefferson Street, which now houses **Joliet Central High School.**

northeastern illinoistrivia

In 1900 the Chicago River became the first river in the world to have its course altered, engineered to flow westward into a canal system rather than eastward into Lake Michigan.

In the city's Highland Park is the *Bird Haven Greenhouse and Conservatory,* a repository for an exceptional collection of exotic flora. Featured are cacti more than a hundred years old and seasonal flower shows; (815) 741–7278.

An essential part of Joliet, as well as Will County as a whole (and Cook, La Salle, and Grundy Counties), is the Illinois and Michigan Canal. In 1984 it became the newest member of the National Park System, the *Illinois and Michigan Canal National Heritage Corridor,* running from Chicago to Peru, Illinois. It contains historic sites, residential neighborhoods, forest preserves for picnicking, fishing, hiking, canoeing, and camping, plus thirty-nine rare natural areas, remnants of the ancient Illinois landscape. Among them is the *Lockport Prairie Nature Preserve* at Route 53 and Division Street, south of Route 7, across from Stateville Correctional Center. Some of the best examples of native prairie grasses and wildflowers still may be found there; (815) 727–8700.

The canal was once the principal transportation link providing a continuous waterway from the Great Lakes and the Mississippi to the Gulf of Mexico. The I&M Canal, dug over 96 miles by hand between 1836 and 1848, made possible the settling of the northern part of the state and the growth of the city of Chicago. Settlement and industry followed the opening of the waterway, and with that, the growth of canal towns characterized by distinctive architecture.

A remarkable example of local limestone architecture is the *Gaylord Building Historic Site* at 200 West Eighth Street. Owned by the National Trust for Historic Preservation and superintended by the Canal Corridor Association, the 150-year-old structure is outstanding. Exhibits are always changing. The *Public Landing Restaurant* sets a relaxed tone. Open Tuesday through Saturday 10:00 A.M. to 6:00 P.M.; Sunday noon to 6:00 P.M.; (815) 588–1100.

The *Will County Historical Society* maintains the artifact-packed museum at 803 South State Street, in the former *I&M Canal Commissioner's Headquarters,* circa 1837. Well-informed docents provide tours Tuesday through Sunday noon to 4:00 P.M.; donations appreciated. *The Settlement* is a nearby open-air complex of twelve remarkable buildings open for exploration; (815) 838–4547.

At 201 West Tenth Street is the *Illinois State Museum Lockport Gallery,* which showcases Illinois art, from paintings to quilts. Hours are Tuesday through Saturday 10:00 A.M. to 5:00 P.M.; Sunday noon to 5:00 P.M.; (815) 838–7400.

The **Gladys Fox Museum,** at 231 East Ninth Street, features area memorabilia displayed in the restored 1839 Old Congregational Church building, which in itself is worth a look. Open Monday through Friday 1:00 to 4:00 P.M.; (815) 838–1183.

A 2½-mile trail follows the east bank of the canal through **Lockport.** Accessible year-round by hikers, joggers, bicyclists, and cross-country skiers, the trail is marked with interpretive signs explaining the history of the waterway. It crosses over old **Lock Number One,** where locally quarried stone walls remain. The trail terminates in **Dellwood Park,** originally built in the early 1900s by the Chicago and Joliet Electric Railway Company as an amusement park. Today it boasts tennis courts, picnic areas, playgrounds, hiking trails, and ball fields.

A side note: Some of the county's earliest steel plows were first fashioned in Lockport by inventor John Lane in 1835. Like those designed by competitor John Deere, Lane's plows shaped the destiny of Illinois agriculture.

After an afternoon of history, a delightful counterpoint is **Tallgrass,** a decidedly gourmet restaurant, 1006 South State Street, a place that's even been acclaimed by tough Chicago restaurant reviewers. Housed in what was once a barn used for I&M canal workers, the mood is elegant, the food epicurean, the prices steep.

Frankfort, forty-five minutes south of Chicago at US 30 and US 45, is known as the "town with 1890 charm." Listed on the Illinois Historic Landmark survey, the **Frankfort Historic District** contains many restored shops and homes typical of a nineteenth-century crossroads village. Today antiques hunters come from miles around for the village's growing collection of antiques stores. Most shops are closed on Monday. The Chamber of Commerce has further information, including walking maps; (815) 469–3356. An annual fall festival is scheduled over Labor Day weekend. Visit, too, the **Frankfort Area Historical Society Museum** at 132 Kansas and Hickory Streets, open Sunday 1:00 to 4:00 P.M.; closed January and February; (815) 469–6541.

In the southern part of the county, **Wilmington** is one of northern Illinois's most unusual towns. On the Kankakee River it's known as the "Island City" because the river runs through downtown, forming an island home to two city parks, **North and South Island Parks.**

Architecturally significant is the **Schutten-Aldrick House,** 600 South Water Street, a landmark octagonal residence built in 1856. The 1836 **Peter Stewart House,** at Kankakee and the Outer Drive, was an important stop on the Underground Railroad during the Civil War.

During most of the year, visitors come to Wilmington for the dozens of antiques shops in the area.

The Schutten-Aldrick House

The little village of New Lenox is home to a historically important building—the *Gougar Residence* at Gougar Road and US 30, home of the first county postmaster. On the last Saturday in June, the village holds its *Old Campground Festival.*

Perhaps nothing demonstrates quite as eloquently the changes in our society as the juxtaposition of the historic and the futuristic. In Morris, the seat of Grundy County, the towering shapes of the Dresden Nuclear Power Station form a striking contrast to the waters of the old Illinois and Michigan (I&M) Canal, which flow past town and through *Gebhard Woods State Park.*

The thirty-acre park, named after its donor, Fred Gebhard, is situated off Route 47 at the southwest edge of Morris on the north bank of the I&M Canal. The park has four ponds for children's fishing plus adult fishing in the canal and in *Nettle Creek,* which form the north and east boundaries of the park. Largemouth bass, bluegill, sunfish, and catfish are plentiful. With an impressive collection of shade trees—walnut, oak, cottonwood, ash, and maple—picnicking is a popular activity here. Gebhard Woods is part of the *I&M Canal State Trail* and the *I&M Canal National Heritage Corridor.* For further information contact: Site Superintendent, Gebhard Woods State Park, P.O. Box 272, Morris 60450; (815) 942–0796.

East of Morris in *Evergreen Cemetery,* lies the grave of *Shabbona* (1775–1859), a Potawatomi chief who was much beloved by the early settlers of the region. Though he had fought with Tecumseh on the side of the British during the War of 1812, he afterwards proved a steadfast friend of Americans. During the Winnebago War of 1827, he reconnoitered a hostile Winnebago encampment, sending word of their violent intentions back to Chicago. During the Black Hawk War, he had his son ride throughout the white settlements of the area to warn of the approach of Black Hawk's warriors. For this a murder attempt was made on his life a year later, but he escaped unscathed. He didn't, however, survive the encroachments of the settlers—he and his band were forced to emigrate west of the Mississippi with the rest of the Potawatomi after the signing of the Chicago Treaty of 1833. He later returned to Illinois, where he died peacefully at the ripe old age of eighty-four. The city of Morris honors him with one of the last working steam pump fire engines in the country. *Old Shab-a-nee,* in use from 1868 to 1922, still appears today in parades.

The last weekend in September, Morris hosts the *Grundy County Corn Festival,* one of the largest county agricultural festivals in the state. Parades, exhibits, musical concerts, and boat excursions on the Illinois River make it a perfect family outing. Call (815) 942–2676 for information.

About 8 miles southeast of Morris and south of the Illinois River is one of my favorite Illinois natural preserves, *Goose Lake Prairie State Park,* one of the last remnants of prairie left in this, the Prairie State, and one of the largest preserves in the tall grass region of North America. As such it has national significance. Of its 2,537 acres, 1,537 are dedicated as an Illinois Nature Preserve.

There is, however, no lake at Goose Lake, having been drained at the end of the last century for farming and for the clay deposits under it. Instead, the grasses and flowers are much like what the state's earliest settlers would have encountered. The palette of wildflowers changes in hue throughout the seasons: in spring the violet shooting star and blue-eyed grass; in summer false indigo and blazing star; and in fall aster and goldenrod.

The park's *Tallgrass Nature Trail* offers a fascinating walk through 1½ miles of prairie and across potholes, marshes, and a unique floating bridge.

The two-story reconstructed 1834–35 *John Cragg Cabin,* nicknamed the Palace, stands in the park as a tribute to Illinois' pioneers.

An interpretive program is offered at the visitor center open Monday and Thursday 10:00 A.M. to 4:00 P.M., Friday 10:00 A.M. to noon and Saturday and Sunday 10:00 A.M. to 4:00 P.M. except winter weekends from December to February. The park's address, on Jugtown Road, comes from an early settlement here. For information on the park, contact: Site Superintendent, 5010 North Jugtown Road, Morris 60450; (815) 942–2899.

The Kankakee River, the namesake of the county and city, offers more than just scenic beauty. Six miles northwest of Kankakee on Route 102, along the river's banks, is the *Kankakee River State Park,* 4,000 wooded acres spread out along 11 miles of the river. The first European to travel down that river was

An Empty Jug (Town)

"Jugtown" was the name of an informal settlement of potters who lived along Goose Lake's clay-rich banks and worked in what is thought to be Illinois' first pottery manufacturing enterprise. In October 1855, a potter named William White joined with financier Charles Walker to form White and Company. At the peak of business, Walker had invested over $12,000 in the firm, a whopping sum in 1860. Unfortunately, money couldn't solve the challenges that beset them. Although Chicago provided an eager marketplace for drainage tiles, moving the heavy tiles across rutted roads to the canal for transport into the city proved impossible. The Panic of 1857, which bankrupted many businesses, didn't help either. Faced with creditor's lawsuits, the partners ended their ten-year alliance, leaving a skilled worker population without a means of income and sealing the demise of the hamlet.

Rene Robert Cavalier, Sieur de la Salle, who, with a party of fourteen men, traveled from the headwaters of the Kankakee down to the Illinois River in 1679.

Modern explorers make the trip downstream daily throughout the summer on one of the cleanest waterways in the state. **Reed's Canoe Trips,** 907 North Indiana Avenue, Kankakee 60901, books canoe trips from two hours to six hours. Canoes, paddles, life jackets, and return transportation are provided. The service operates daily 8:00 A.M. to 5:00 P.M., May 1 to September 30; (815) 932–2663.

The state park's **Rock Creek Canyon** is especially pretty with its picturesque waterfall and gnarled cedars growing from its steep, limestone walls. Hiking, equestrian, and snowmobile trails are laced throughout the park's forested acres. Picnic facilities and camping (with electric hookup) are available. In the summer the park rangers present an informative interpretive program. For information contact the Park Ranger, P.O. Box 37, Bourbonnais 60914; (815) 933–1383.

Each July, anglers from around the Midwest gather to try their luck in the annual **Kankakee River Valley Fishing Derby.** More than $300,000 is awarded in prizes to those who land the tagged fish. For more information call (800) 747–4837.

Golf, too, has its proponents, and Kankakee County has the courses to satisfy even the most avid. There are eight courses, including the **Bon Vivant Country Club** (815–935–0403), ranked second in the district only after Butler National by the Chicago District Golf Association.

During Labor Day weekend, the **Kankakee River Valley Regatta** brings powerboats to the river from miles around for fast and wonderful racing championships; (800) 747–4837.

In the southwest part of Kankakee, at Eighth Avenue and Water Street, is the boyhood home of Len Small, twenty-eighth governor of Illinois. Situated on a twenty-five-acre park, the home is part of the **Kankakee County Histori- cal Society Museum.** The 1855 Italianate limestone building has been restored and rooms furnished in period style. On the grounds visitors can tour a historic one-room schoolhouse. Admission is free. Open year-round 10:00 A.M. to 4:00 P.M. Tuesday through Friday and 1:00 to 4:00 P.M. on Sunday. Call (815) 932–5279.

Kankakee's **Bradley House,** at Harrison and the river, was designed by Frank Lloyd Wright as a private residence, the first in his famous "Prairie style." The 1901 structure is true to form with long, low lines and overhanging eaves. Set in a grove of trees on the Kankakee River, the effect is a natural, harmonious one. Wright also designed the original furnishings, china, and rugs for the home. Although the home is privately owned, a business that sells museum gifts, called the Stable Shop and Museum Store, is open at the 701 South Har- rison Avenue address. For hours call (815) 935–5056.

Bourbonnais, just north of Kankakee, was one of the earliest settlements on the Kankakee, dating from the founding of a French trading post here in 1832. An influx of French Canadians followed, giving the region its French fla- vor. In Bourbonnais is the **Olivet Nazarene University** (formerly the Catholic St. Viator College), with its renowned **Strickler Planetarium.** More than 4,800 stars are projected onto a 30-foot dome. A separate laser show is also offered. Program dates and times vary based on the academic year so contact the plan- etarium by using the hotline at (815) 939–5308 or the general number at (815) 939–5395. Admission is $1.00 for adults and children; laser shows are $2.00.

Momence, too, is a historic community, once known as the Old Border Town (between wilderness and civilization), and situated on the Hubbard Trail linking Fort Dearborn (Chicago) to Vincennes, Indi- ana. The road, also known as the Vincennes Trail, later became state road Illinois 1 of the Dixie Highway.

Momence today boasts a number of historic homes. The

The Bradley House

Momence Historic House, 117 North Dixie Highway, is a furnished home that lets the visitor see what life was like in the period 1870–1900. The kitchen, with its dry sink and pump, pie safe, and butter churn, speaks of a time without modern appliances. Open in June only, Saturday and Sunday, 2:00 to 4:00 P.M. Free; (815) 472–2670.

A major industry in the area is the growing of gladioli—more than 150,000 are harvested annually. In mid-August the ***Momence Gladiolus Festival*** draws thousands from across the country. In addition to lovely flowers, there are parades, antique car shows, a flea market, a garden show, and a family fun run. Call (815) 472–6353 for more information.

Places to Stay in Northeastern Illinois

ELMHURST

Holiday Inn,
624 North York Road,
(630) 279–1100

FRANKFORT

Abe Lincoln Motel,
10841 West Lincoln
Highway,
(815) 469–5114

GENEVA

The Herrington,
15 South River Lane,
(630) 208–7433

GURNEE

Sweet Basil Hill Farm,
15937 West Washington
Street,
(847) 244–3333

LAKE FOREST

Deer Path Inn,
255 East Illinois,
(847) 234–2280

LIBERTYVILLE

Best Western Hitch-Inn
Post Motel,
1765 North Milwaukee
Avenue,
(847) 362–8700

LINCOLNSHIRE

Marriott Lincolnshire
Resort,
10 Marriott Drive,
(847) 634–0100

LISLE

Hyatt,
1400 Corporetum Drive,
(630) 852–1234

LOMBARD

Embassy Suites,
707 East Butterfield Road,
(630) 969–7500

NAPERVILLE

Fairfield Inn Marriott,
1820 Abriter Court,
(630) 577–1820

Hampton Inn,
1087 East Diehl Road,
(630) 505–1400

Holiday Inn Select,
1801 Naper Boulevard,
(630) 505–4900

OAK PARK

Under the Ginko Tree B&B,
300 North Kenilworth
Avenue,
(708) 524–2327

ST. CHARLES

Hotel Baker,
100 West Main Street,
(630) 584–2100

WAUKEGAN

Illinois Beach Resort and
Conference Center,
1 Lake Front Drive,
(847) 625–7300

Ramada Inn,
200 North Green Bay Road,
(847) 244–2400

WINNETKA

Chateau des Fleurs,
552 Ridge Road,
(847) 256–7272

Places to Eat in Northeastern Illinois

EVANSTON

Blind Faith Cafe,
525 Dempster Street,
(847) 328–6875

Oceanique,
505 Main Street,
(847) 864–3435

Pete Miller's Steakhouse,
1557 Sherman Avenue,
(847) 328–0399

GENEVA

Mill Race Inn,
4 East State Street,
(630) 232–2030

LAKE FOREST

Deer Path Inn,
255 East Illinois,
(847) 234–2280

Egg Harbor Cafe,
512 North Western Avenue,
(847) 295–3449

South Gate Cafe,
665 Forest Avenue
at Market Square,
(847) 234–8800

LEMONT

White Fence Farm,
11700 Joliet Road,
(630) 739–1720

LIBERTYVILLE

**The Country Inn
Restaurant of Lambs Farm,**
I–94 and Highway 176,
(847) 362–5050

MCHENRY

Le Vichyssois,
220 Rand Road (Lakemoor),
(815) 385–8221

NAPERVILLE

BD's Mongolian Barbeque,
221 South Washington
Street,
(630) 428–0300

SELECTED VISITORS BUREAUS AND CHAMBERS OF COMMERCE

**Illinois Bureau of Tourism—
Travel Information,**
(800) 2–CONNECT
(226–6328)

**DuPage Area Convention and
Visitors Bureau,**
915 Harger Road, Suite 240,
Oak Brook, 60523
(630) 575–8070

**Elgin Area Convention and
Visitors Bureau,**
77 Riverside Drive,
Elgin, 60120
(847) 695–7540

**Heritage Corridor Convention and
Visitors Bureau,**
81 North Chicago Street,
Joliet, 60432
(800) 926–2262

**Lake County Convention and
Visitors Bureau,**
5455 West Grand Avenue, Suite 302,
Gurnee, 60031
(847) 662–2700

Oak Park Visitors Bureau,
1118 Westgate,
Oak Park, 60301
(708) 524–7800

**St. Charles Convention and Visitors
Bureau,**
311 North Second Street, Suite 101,
St. Charles, 60174
(630) 377–6161

WEB SITES

Illinois Bureau of Tourism,
www.enjoyillinois.com

Meson Sabika Tapas,
1025 Aurora Avenue,
(630) 983–3000

Sullivan's Steakhouse,
244 South Main Street,
(630) 305–0230

Traverso's Restaurant,
2523 Naperville-Plainfield
Road,
(630) 305–7747

ST. CHARLES
Francesca's by the River,
200 South Second Street,
(630) 587–8221

WHEATON
Suzette's Creperie,
211 West Front Street,
(630) 462–0898

WHEELING
Bob Chinn's Crab House,
393 South Milwaukee
Avenue,
(847) 520–3633

Don Roth's Blackhawk,
61 North Milwaukee Avenue,
(847) 537–5800

Le Francais,
269 South Milwaukee
Avenue,
(847) 541–7470

Weber Grill Restaurant,
920 North Milwaukee
Avenue,
(847) 215–0996

WILMETTE
Walker Bros. Original
Pancake House,
153 Green Bay Road,
(847) 251–6000

OTHER ATTRACTIONS WORTH SEEING IN NORTHEASTERN ILLINOIS

Argonne National Laboratory,
Argonne

Walter Payton's Roundhouse
Complex,
Aurora

Sci Tech Hands-On Museum,
Aurora

Villa Olivia Ski Area,
Bartlett

McDonald's Museum,
Des Plaines

Wandschneider Park and Museum,
Downers Grove

Lizzadro Museum of Lapidary Art,
Elmhurst

Northwestern University Sculpture
Garden and Galleries,
Evanston

Chicago Botanic Garden,
Glencoe

Medieval Times Dinner Theater and
Tournament,
Schaumburg

River Trail Nature Center,
Northbrook

Ernest Hemingway Museum and
Birthplace,
Oak Park

Westfield Old Orchard Center,
Skokie

Kohl Children's Museum,
Wilmette

Kline Creek Farm,
Winfield

Health World Museum
Barrington

Brookfield Zoo,
Brookfield

Gross Point Light House and
Lakefront,
Evanston

The Grove,
Glenview

Marytown/St. Maximilian
Kolbe Shrine,
Libertyville

Frank Lloyd Wright Home and Studio,
Oak Park

Woodfield Shopping Center,
Schaumburg

Hawthorne Race Course,
Stickney

Nathan Manilow Sculpture Park,
University Park

Cuneo Museum and Gardens,
Vernon Hills

Cosley Zoo,
Wheaton

Baha'i House of Worship,
Wilmette

Seven Bridges Ice Arena,
Woodridge

Northwestern Illinois

Mississippi River Banks

The scenery along the Mississippi River, down into the Mississippi River Palisades State Park, is one of the prettiest and hilliest terrains in the state. Beginning at the northwestern corner of the state is the historic lead-mining town of *Galena,* the third-largest tourist attraction in Illinois (after Chicago and Springfield). Although it wouldn't quite be considered "off the beaten path," so many small-town charms are here that it would be a mistake to overlook it.

Galena's life as a tourist attraction began about thirty years ago as a spot to spend the day, browse through quaint shops, hunt for antiques, and visit the home of General Ulysses S. Grant.

As an introduction to the town, the *Galena/Jo Daviess County History Museum,* 211 South Bench Street, is an excellent place to visit. Here you can see a slide-tape presentation and tour the museum, which is chock-full of nineteenth-century artifacts—from Civil War items to clothing and toys. Most interesting of all is an actual mine shaft from the 1830s. Afterwards you can mosey into Galena's historic downtown district. The museum is open daily 9:00 A.M. to 4:30 P.M. Admission, $4.50

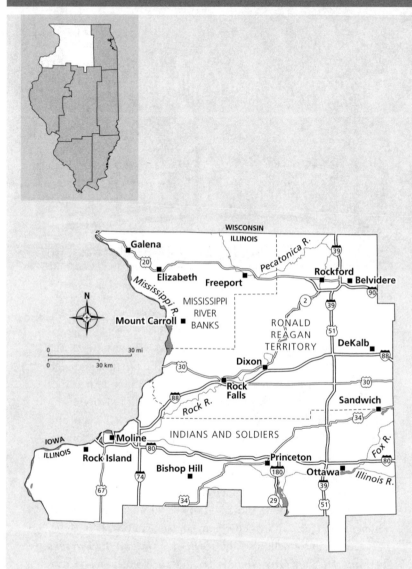

adults; $3.50 children, ten to eighteen years of age. The museum also offers a one-hour walking tour of Galena's Main Street every Saturday, May through October, or by appointment. The tour begins at 10:00 A.M. in the lobby of the DeSoto House Hotel, 230 South Main Street; $5.00 per person. For more information, call the museum at (815) 777–9129.

Galena's main attraction is the *Ulysses S. Grant Home.* Presented as a gift to Grant in 1865, this Italianate home is filled with period furnishings and Grant family effects. The house is open seasonally, April to October, Wednesday through Sunday, 9:00 A.M. to 5:00 P.M.; winter months, November to March, Wednesday through Sunday, 9:00 A.M. to 4:00 P.M. A $3.00 donation is suggested; 500 Bouthillier Street; (815) 777–0248.

The *Belvedere Home,* at 1008 Park Avenue, is just one of the notable Galena properties that have been lovingly restored. Visitors are transported to a bygone era as soon as the door opens. Tours daily, 11:00 A.M. to 5:00 P.M. from late May to November 1. Admission $10.00; (815) 777–0747. Another remarkable example is the *John Dowling Stone House* at Main and Diagonal Street. Daily tours 10:00 A.M. to 5:00 P.M., Memorial Day to December 31; (815) 777–1250.

The *Old Market House,* located at 1123 North Commerce Street, is open during hours similar to the Grant Home; calling ahead for firm times is recommended. Admission is free, though a $2.00 donation is suggested for adults and

AUTHOR'S TOP TEN PICKS

Galena,
Illinois,
(877) 464–2536

White Pines Forest State Park,
Mt. Morris,
(815) 946–3717

Starved Rock State Park,
Utica,
(815) 667–4726

Tinker Swiss Cottage Museum,
Rockford,
(815) 964–2424

Bishop Hill State Historic Site,
Bishop Hill,
(309) 927–3345

Sandwich Antiques Market,
Sandwich,
(815) 786–3337

John Deere Historic Site,
Grand Detour,
(815) 652–4551

Magic Waters,
Cherry Valley,
(815) 332–3260

Oregon,
Illinois,
(815) 732–2100

Apple River Fort State Historic Site,
Elizabeth,
(815) 858–2028

Galena Nuggets

The recorded history of Illinois began just north of present-day Galena. On June 20, 1673, explorers Père Jacques Marquette and Louis Joliet paddled their canoe along the Mississippi River and put ashore on its sandy banks, thereby becoming the first Europeans to have ever set foot in what would become known as Illinois.

To explorers, Illinois was a wilderness to be tamed. The missionary priest and his companion were followed by French fur traders and trappers, who plied the state's inland waterways and carved out a crude but vast river transportation system. These men also struck up trading relationships with native Illinois peoples, like the Illiwek, Sauk, and Fox. Eventually, trading posts were established, many of which turned into towns.

However, the French influence in Illinois came to an end largely because of the results of the French and Indian War (1754–1763), which pitted France against England for control of the vast resources of North America's interior regions. England won, the French were forced out (though you can still see some remnants of their occupation, especially in southwestern Illinois), and English and Irish pioneers poured in.

$1.00 for children. Inside its Main Hall are wall panel photos, diagrams, and a short, narrated slide show about architecture. The South Wing has a commerce and mining exhibit, and the basement has a collection of photos and documents.

Galena Cellars Winery, 515 South Main Street, 61036, (815) 777–3330, is just inside the Flood Gates on Galena's Main Street in a restored 1840s granary building. You'll enjoy watching the working of this operating winery. The family-owned business produces 20,000 cases a year, most sold at the winery. The forty-five-minute tour includes wine tasting. Admission is $4.00, and the winery is open daily except major holidays. Call for tour times.

Golden Dudes

Dude, if you can go from a backside melon to a stalefish, then to a cab 1080 melon, you're gold. At least gold's what our American snowboarders earned at the Winter Olympics at Salt Lake City, Utah. What if the team was, as one newspaper account put it, "stoked by nutballs"? Our wacky snowboarders helped the United States to its first medals sweep in the Winter Olympics in forty-six years.

At Chestnut Mountain Resort, just outside downtown Galena, you can try a mute grab, switch McTwist, or a Kasserole spin on the resort's snowboard runs. It's extreme sport, but it's real cool. Wait, scratch that. It's radical, dude.

Boom . . . and Bust

Galena's lead-mining history would make a good television miniseries. How did it happen?

Since the last great glacier bypassed what we call northwestern Illinois, most of the landscape remained as it had developed naturally—with mineral deposits lying just beneath the surface of the ground.

Fox and Sauk Indians had mined the abundant lead and used it for trade with other tribes. In fact, they operated small lead mines and smelters even before the French came here in the 1720s, the first Europeans to mine this area, who used 200 of their own men and slaves from San Domingo to get the lead out.

When this region became part of the United States, it was incorporated into a huge Federal Mining District. In 1822 the first mining lease was granted to a Col. James Johnson, who brought twenty of his hardened Kentucky miners (and a number of slaves) to work the mines. (Even though laws prohibited the use of slaves in the old Northwest Territory, they were used in the mining industry here until the 1840s.)

The real lead boom began in the late 1820s with the arrival of the steamboats at Galena. Before the decade was over, more than 4,000 mining permits had been granted. By 1828 the tiny hamlet of Galena had grown to an important city of more than 5,000 people.

In 1845, 54 million pounds of lead (more than 80 percent of the nation's total) was mined here. But surface deposits quickly played out, and the discovery of gold in California in 1848 drew miners west. By the 1870s Galena was reduced to a tiny hamlet again, filled with abandoned mines and abandoned houses.

Galena boasts plenty of places to stay, and that includes resorts, hotels, and more than thirty-five bed-and-breakfasts. The Chamber of Commerce and the Visitors and Convention Bureau have listings. Many of the guest houses and bed-and-breakfasts are in restored historic homes and are a delightful way to spend time here in this "town that time forgot."

For additional information you can contact the Convention and Visitors Bureau, 101 Bouthillier Street, Galena 61036; (877) 464–2536.

The *Galena Public Library & Historical Collection,* 601 South Bench Street; (815) 777–0200, includes a mosaic fireplace in a wisteria pattern, done in the style of Frank Lloyd Wright. Among its historic collections are Galena newspapers from 1834 to the present. Historical Collection hours are Monday, Tuesday, Thursday, and Friday from 3:00 to 5:00 P.M.; Wednesday 3:00 to 8:00 P.M.; Saturday noon to 4:00 P.M. Library hours are 11:00 A.M. to 8:00 P.M. Monday through Thursday; 11:00 A.M. to 5:00 P.M. Friday and Saturday.

The ***Old Stockade Refuge,*** 208 Perry Street; (815) 777–1222, has American Indian and pioneer history displays—and includes a spot where settlers hid from Indian braves during the 1832 Black Hawk War. Watch your head on the low timbers here! Open Sunday 1:00 to 4:00 P.M. or by appointment.

Galena also offers river cruises. The **Twilight,** (815) 777–1660, is a three-deck steamboat-style ship. A two-day cruise on the Mississippi departs from LeClaire, Iowa, docks overnight near Galena, and returns to LeClaire. Reservations are required.

In nearby Elizabeth, the ***Apple River Fort State Historic Site,*** 311 East Myrtle, is a must-visit. The Apple River Fort is an exact reconstruction of the fort built on this site in 1832 in response to the Black Hawk War. Unlike many hastily erected stockades throughout northern Illinois in 1832, this one actually repelled an attack by Black Hawk and two hundred of his warriors. Within the fort itself you can see period furnishings and can climb up into the sleeping

The Winnebago War

The Black Hawk War figures prominently in Galena history, but Galena was the actual flashpoint for a lesser-known conflict, the so-called Winnebago War of 1827. As hordes of whites flocked to the region during the lead-mining boom of the mid-1820s, they increasingly angered the local Winnebagos on whose lands they were illegally establishing their mines. Those government agents who were sincere about keeping whites out of Indian territory simply didn't have the backing or man power to stanch the flood. On June 26, 1827, a small group of Winnebagos attacked a farmstead just outside Prairie du Chien across the modern-day Wisconsin border. Later that day, a keelboat crew traveling down the Mississippi above Prairie du Chien came under attack by about thirty Winnebagos.

Though only five people were killed by the Winnebagos, the attacks set off a panic throughout the frontier. As for Galena itself, one eyewitness claimed it descended into chaos. Thousands of refugees poured into the city, and the roads were clogged with hysterical men, women, and children convinced they were about to be overtaken and scalped at any moment.

The episode came to a conclusion two months later with no other bloodshed than what took place on June 26, but contemporaries were in agreement that it had been the unbridled influx of miners into Galena and its hinterlands that had sparked the conflict. To relieve the situation, the federal government obtained a massive land cession of the entire lead-mining region in 1829. Rather than solve the problem, however, this brought thousands of new whites to the area, many of whom headed south of Galena in search of available farmland. Unfortunately, the best farmland in the region was in the vicinity of Saukenuk near modern-day Rock Island, which was home to Black Hawk and his band of Sauk and Fox. Hence, the Black Hawk War.

lofts and firing stands. The nearby interpretive center offers exhibits and arti- facts from the site, in addition to a short but very informative video describing the Black Hawk War and the Apple River Fort incident All in all, this is a first- rate site. Open daily, mid-April to September, 9:00 A.M. to 5:00 P.M.; call for win- ter hours; (815) 858–2028.

The new *Elizabeth History Museum* was unveiled at 231 North Main Street in 2006. Exhibits cover village history, lead mining, and local people. Open weekends, May through October, 11:00 A.M. to 3:00 P.M.; (815) 858–2343.

North of Elizabeth, *Apple River Canyon State Park* has 297 acres for pic- nicking, camping, fishing, cross-country skiing, and five great hiking trails. Entrance at 8763 East Canyon Road; (815) 745–3302.

The town of Hanover, called the "Mallard Capital of the World," sits about 30 miles from Apple River Canyon. Here thrives the *Whistling Wings Duck Hatchery,* which raises more than 200,000 mallards every year. This is the world center of mallard duck production, most of which are sold for release. The hatchery is on Route 84, in the middle of town. View a video, newly hatched ducklings, or select something for your dinner table from the gift shop. Just don't tell the kids that they're eating Daffy Duck for dinner! (815) 591–3512.

In mid-September the community celebrates *Mallardfest,* a party that includes a parade, live music, and fire- works. The height of the event is the duck call contest, so start practicing! Held at White Park; contact Village Hall at 207 Jefferson Street; (815) 591–3800.

roomwithaview

To be rewarded with some of the best vistas in Galena, book a room at the Hellman Guest House, built on Quality Hill, with views of Horseshoe Mound. Especially noteworthy is the view from the 1895 merchant home's main tower, overlooking the "town that time forgot" and its many church spires and steeples, gingerbread houses, surrounding bluffs, and more.

Of course, the bed-and-breakfast guest rooms at this historic home are top quality, too. Victorian elegance sprinkled with authentic antiques, brass beds, and claw-foot tubs are part of the ambience that makes the Hellman House one of the premiere overnights in the Galena area.

Mount Carroll is pure nineteenth-century Midwest America with its cob- blestone courthouse square in the center of town, Victorian architecture, and 1870s-style storefronts lining Main Street. In fact, Mount Carroll was chosen from among seventy-six other Illinois towns as a "Main Street, Illinois" town based on the concept of "building on yesterday for tomorrow."

Mount Carroll, located in the northwest corner of the state, about 10 min- utes east of the Mississippi River, was named after Charles Carroll, a Maryland signer of the Declaration of Independence. The town was created by an Act of Legislature in 1839.

Appreciative of its architectural treasures, Mount Carroll has preserved many of its original buildings, and a major portion of them are listed in the National Register of Historic Places. A self-guided walking tour through the historical sites is available from the Chamber of Commerce, Mount Carroll 61053; (815) 244–2255.

Highlights of the tour include the **Hotel Glenview,** 116 East Market Street, built in 1886 at a cost of $20,000. The hotel remained open until 1976.

The **Owen P. Miles Museum,** 107 West Broadway, houses the Carroll County Historical Society, which is a good place to brush up on local history. Tours of the 1873 Italianate mansion are also offered. Open Monday, Tuesday Thursday, Friday, 10:00 A.M. to 2:00 P.M.; and every other weekend, Saturday, 10:00 A.M. to 2:00 P.M., Sunday noon to 3:00 P.M.; $2.00 donation suggested; (815) 244–3474.

The Main and Market Streets **Commercial Core** architecturally dates back to the 1850s, and a number of buildings were faced with galvanized steel and cast iron. These decorative **Mesker Brother** facades are said to make up one of the finest collections of metal-faced buildings in the United States.

Mount Carroll War Memorial and Annex

Inside City Hall, 302 North Main, the United States Hissem brass bell, on loan from the Washington, D.C., Naval Historic Center, is on display.

In the center of the town square is the **War Memorial and Annex,** which is listed in *Ripley's Believe It or Not* as the only memorial with an annex. The annex was built to accommodate the 1,284 names listed on the monument. The monument is crowned with a cavalryman designed and sculpted by Lorado Taft, a renowned Midwestern sculptor, lecturer, and author.

Mount Carroll's annual **Mayfest** celebration is held on Memorial Day weekend. Visitors are treated to live music, art, food, and sports activities at the Campbell Center, 600 South College Street. Request information at

TOP ANNUAL EVENTS

Bald Eagle Days,
Rock Island, mid-January,
(309) 788-5912

Fulton Dutch Days Festival,
Fulton, early May,
(815) 589-2626

Annual Wildflower Pilgrimage,
Starved Rock State Park, Utica,
early May,
(815) 667-4906

Suak Valley Fly-In Airshow,
Dixon, late July,
(815) 284-3361

Annual Steam Threshing and Antique Show,
Freeport, late July,
(800) 369-2955

Ottawa's Riverfest,
Ottawa, late July–early August,
(815) 434-2737

DeKalb Corn Festival,
DeKalb, late August,
(815) 748-CORN

Autumn Pioneer Festival,
Belvidere, late September,
(815) 547-7935

Sycamore Pumpkin Festival,
Sycamore, late October,
(815) 895-5161

Julmarknad,
Bishop Hill, late November–early December,
(309) 927-3345

Mayfest, P.O. Box 191, Mount Carroll 61053; (815) 244-2411, or visit www .mount-carroll.il.us.

The *Raven's Grin Inn,* at 411 North Carroll Street; (815) 244-4746, is an out-of-body experience for those interested in local artist Jim Warfield's fun house. Every room is packed with sensory and intellectual experiences. Warfield personally conducts the tours and no two of them are quite the same. Hours 7:00 P.M. to midnight; reservations recommended; admission $10.00.

The Campbell Center is a complex of Georgian Revival buildings previously occupied by Frances Shimer College. The college was established at Mount Carroll in 1853 and closed in 1978. The center was purchased by local investors after Shimer College closed, and the campus now houses the *Campbell Center for Historic Preservation Studies.* The center offers workshops in architectural and fine arts preservation, archaeology, and the educational, policy, and planning aspects of preservation. To contact the Campbell Center, call (815) 244-1173; www.campbellcenter.org.

The *Oakville County School Museum Complex,* 4 miles southeast of Mount Carroll, is also nostalgic of the nineteenth-century Midwest. A one-room country schoolhouse, a blacksmith shop, and two log cabins are on exhibition.

The Carroll County Historical Society operates the complex, which is open by appointment only; (815) 244–3474.

Four miles east of Mount Carroll is the *Timber Lake Playhouse,* a live, semiprofessional summer stock theater. The season runs from June 1 to late August, and there are evening and matinee performances. New productions are offered every two weeks along with special children's shows. The 375-seat theater is air-conditioned. For information and tickets call (815) 244–2035. Tickets should be purchased in advance.

Farther south along the banks of the Mississippi River is *Thomson,* home of *Melon Days,* a yearly festival held over Labor Day weekend in which watermelon is the star attraction. Thomson has restored its *Burlington Railroad Depot* and turned it into the *Thomson Depot Museum,* which is open to the public from Memorial Day to October, Friday to Sunday 1:00 to 4:00 P.M. Free. For information contact the Thomson Chamber of Commerce at (815) 259–7378.

northwestern illinoistrivia

East Dubuque is the "northwesternmost" town in Illinois.

Abraham Lincoln served here as a company officer in the Black Hawk War of 1832.

Mississippi Palisades State Park heads up the natural beauty in Carroll County. The 2,500-acre preserve is located 4 miles north of Savanna and is registered as a National Historic Landmark by the Department of the Interior. Its location near the confluence of the Apple and the Mississippi Rivers gives a breathtaking resemblance to tree-lined bluffs along the Hudson River in New York, thus the name palisades. Unusual rock formations have been sculpted by water and wind along the cliffs; among them are Indian Head and the Twin Sisters. There are 15 miles of heavily wooded trails for hiking (the back trails giving the best view of the Mississippi), 5 miles of snowmobile trails, and one hundred acres of open snow area. There are also facilities for picnicking, boating, and camping; a playground; and nature and equestrian trails. For information contact Mississippi Palisades State Park, 16327A Route 84, Savanna 61074; (815) 273–2731. Hours are from sunup to sundown for the park and 7:30 A.M. to 10:00 P.M. for admittance to the campground.

In Lanark, the *Standish House,* built in 1882, has been renovated into a bed-and-breakfast. The rooms are furnished with eighteenth- and nineteenth-century English antiques and reproductions. And yes, Puritan Miles Standish is part of the historic family tree. Contact the Standish House at (815) 493–2307 or 540 West Carroll Street, Lanark 61046.

William "Tutty" Baker, one of the early settlers in Freeport, is responsible for naming the town. Actually it was his wife who teased him about running a "free port" for everyone coming along the trail. Legend has it that one night a group of settlers were discussing a name for the town and Mrs. Baker suggested Freeport because of her husband's generosity.

At *Lincoln-Douglas Debate Square,* located at the corner of Douglas and State Streets, two of America's greatest patriots met in the second Lincoln-Douglas debate. Today a life-size statue of the two famous orators, created by artist Lily Tolpo, depicts Lincoln sitting and Douglas standing, and commemorates the August 27, 1858, meeting that put forth the Freeport Doctrine on slavery.

The *Stephenson County Courthouse,* at the junction of U.S. Highway 20 and Route 75, has a *Civil War Monument,* which was dedicated in 1871. On the four corners are life-size figures of a Civil War sailor, militiaman, cavalryman, and artilleryman. Engraved on the sides are the names of battles in which Stephenson County volunteers fought. Near the entrance of the courthouse is a plaque commemorating Col. Benjamin Stephenson, Illinois militiaman of 1812.

A bronze statue of Lincoln titled **Lincoln the Debator,** stands near the entrance to *Taylor's Park,* a mile east of the courthouse on Route 75.

The *Stephenson County Historical Museum* features memorabilia of early social worker Jane Addams, nineteenth-century furnishings, and an 1840s log cabin. Part of the museum is a farm exhibit, which displays a typical farm kitchen, a blacksmith shop, and many farm machines and tools. A furnished one-room schoolhouse dates from approximately 1910.

The museum is located at 1440 South Carroll Avenue, 4 blocks south of US 20 on Carroll Avenue between Jefferson and Pershing Streets. Admission is $3.00 for adults and $1.00 for children; hours are Wednesday through Sunday noon to 4:00 P.M. May through October; Friday through Sunday noon to 4:00 P.M. November through April. Open in January by appointment only; (815) 232–8419. Closed on holidays.

The *Freeport Arts Center,* at 121 North Harlem Avenue, has a collection of primitive, Asian, and American Indian art; European paintings and sculpture; old and new world antiques; and a contemporary exhibit. It is open Tuesday 10:00 A.M. to 6:00 P.M.; Wednesday, Thursday, and Friday 10:00 A.M. to 5:00 P.M.; Saturday and Sunday noon to 5:00 P.M. Closed on Sunday during winter. Donations appreciated. For exhibit information call (815) 235–9755.

Krape Park on Park Boulevard in Freeport is open year-round and has a merry-go-round, flower garden, duck pond, band shell, boat rentals, tennis courts, miniature golf, and concessions. One dollar buys four carousel rides! Call (815) 235–6114.

Lake Le-Aqua-Na State Park, 6 miles south of the Illinois-Wisconsin state line and 3 miles north of Lena off Route 73, got its name for the nearby town of Lena and *aqua,* the Latin word for water. Road cuts near the park entrance and to the north contain excellent examples of glacial till with varieties of igneous rock foreign to Illinois. Hours are 6:00 A.M. to 10:00 P.M. from March 16 to November 14, and 8:00 A.M. to 10:00 P.M. from November 15 to March 15. Camping, picnicking, fishing, boating, hiking, and winter sports are available.

The Second Battle of Black Hawk was fought near *Kent,* and a monument in Kent commemorates the event. The *Black Hawk War Monument* is listed in the National Register of Historic Places, and every year the town remembers the battle with a memorial. For information contact the Stephenson County Clerk's Office, 15 North Galena Avenue, Freeport 61032; (815) 235–8266.

Ronald Reagan Territory

Dixon has gained new stature on the Illinois map as the *Ronald Reagan Boyhood Home.* Reagan lived at 816 South Hennepin Avenue, from 1920 to 1923, from his ninth to twelfth year. Dixonites consider these his formative years. This house is the only family home in Dixon mentioned in Reagan's autobiography.

After the Republican National Convention in the summer of 1980, a local mailman noticed that the house was for sale. To preserve the house for future generations, he put down a $250 deposit and raised the remainder of the down payment through donations. A group of local businesspeople signed a note to guarantee the mortgage. The house was purchased for $31,500. Fundraising activities and donations paid off the balance of the mortgage by the winter of 1981.

The house and adjacent barn are restored to their 1920 condition; although the furnishings are not those of the Reagan family, they are typical of the time period. The refurbishing was completed in time for Reagan's birthday visit on February 6, 1984.

Listed in the National Register of Historic Places, the home is open to the public, and volunteers serve as tour guides. Hours are Monday through Saturday 10:00 A.M. to 4:00 P.M., Sunday 1:00 to 4:00 P.M. April through October; Saturday 10:00 A.M. to 4:00 P.M. and Sunday 1:00 to 4:00 P.M. in March. Closed November through February. Admission $3.00 for adults, twelve and under free; (815) 288–5176. Call (815) 288–5176.

Dixon is the petunia capital of the world, and to celebrate the city holds a *Petunia Festival* every Fourth of July weekend. The city boasts that more than 7½ miles of city streets are lined with petunias. The festival also includes a carnival, games, races, an arts and crafts show, parade, and fireworks over the Rock River. For more information, contact the Chamber of Commerce, 101 West Second Street, Suite 210, Dixon 61021; (815) 284–3361.

Dixon is rich in history as its many monuments to nineteenth-century pioneers testify. On the west bank of the Rock River is the site of **Fort Dixon,** built during the Black Hawk War. On May 13, 1832, a twenty-three-year-old volunteer marched here from Sangamon County. That volunteer was Abraham Lincoln. The **Lincoln Statue,** a statue of Captain Abraham Lincoln when he served in the Black Hawk War of 1832, and the **Old Settler's Memorial Log Cabin** are located on Lincoln Statue Drive on the north bank of the Rock River between Abraham Lincoln Bridge and Ronald Reagan Bridge. The cabin is open on summer weekends, or by appointment; (815) 284–1134.

A nearby granite boulder summarizes Lincoln's military service in the summer of 1832 on a bronze tablet in bas-relief. Another bas-relief shows founding father John Dixon with a picture of Fort Dixon and Dixon's ferry and tavern.

The **Nachusa Hotel,** 215 South Galena Avenue, is the hotel of the presidents. Five U.S. presidents have stayed there: Abraham Lincoln, Ulysses S. Grant, Theodore Roosevelt, William Howard Taft, and Ronald Reagan. The hotel was built in 1837 and is the oldest hotel in Illinois. It also claims to have had the first bathtub in Illinois. It is refurbished, and the Abraham Lincoln Room is decorated in authentic 1840 decor. The hotel is no longer operating and is not open to the public, but it's worth driving by.

Nachusa Grasslands on Lowden Road just east of Grand Detour is a privately held nature preserve comprised of sandstone buttes, rolling hills, oak savannahs, wetlands, and a sea of little bluestem grass. For information call (815) 456–2340.

Loveland Community House Museum, 513 West Second Street; (815) 284–2741, exhibits local history. Pictures and personal items of John Dixon furnishings from pioneer homes, Indian artifacts, and a library with county books and records are part of the exhibit. There is also a Reagan memorabilia section. The curator, a classmate of the former president, has yearbooks and other souvenirs on display and some personal memories to share. Museum hours are Wednesday, Thursday, and Friday 9:00 A.M. to noon, and the first Saturday of the month 9:00 A.M. to 3:00 P.M.

Lowell Park, 3 miles north of Dixon, is a 240-acre park on the Rock River. Ronald Reagan served as a lifeguard here for seven years from 1926 to 1932; (815) 284–3306. On display at Loveland Community House Museum is a plaque, which at the time was affixed to a log on the beach. Reagan notched the log every time he saved a life; (815) 284–2741.

The ***Amboy Depot Museum*** in Amboy was once the Illinois Central Railroad depot. The 131-year-old building is now a nineteen-room museum telling the history of Amboy. Museum hours are year-round; Wednesday, Thursday, and Sunday 1:00 to 4:00 P.M.; Friday and Saturday 10:00 A.M. to 4:00 P.M., May through September. Admission is free. Amboy is a small community and the museum is easy to find at 50 South East Avenue; (815) 857–4700.

Near the depot are two plaques: one marks the site of the first Carson, Pirie, Scott and Company store while the other stands as tribute to the early believers of the Reorganized Church of Latter-Day Saints who settled here (now the Community of Christ).

Grand Detour is a modest township in Ogle County with about 750 inhabitants, but thousands of tourists visit each year because of a blacksmith named John Deere who opened a shop there in 1836. The shop was the beginning of Deere and Company, one of the largest manufacturers of plows in the world.

Grand Detour was named by the Indians because of the oxbow bend in the Rock River at this point. In 1834 pioneer Leonard Andrus came to the Rock River Valley and made a claim to the land. He laid out the village of Grand Detour, but, unfortunately, the town was passed over by the railroad and never grew to its early promise of prosperity.

When Deere started farming here, he found that plowing the heavy prairie soil was a difficult job and that most settlers gave up in despair. He experimented with different shapes and materials for plows, and in 1837 he developed a steel plow that worked. Deere and Company is now the oldest major manufacturing business in Illinois and the largest producer of farm implements in the world.

The John Deere Foundation maintains a brand-new museum and exhibit center, original buildings, and other features of the original property in Grand Detour. An archaeological exhibition building covers the site of the original blacksmith shop and displays various machines and how they work. The ***John Deere Historic Site*** also includes Deere's house, authentically furnished from the 1830s; a visitor center; and a blacksmith shop reconstructed on the basis of archaeological findings. The shop has a working forge and equipment used by nineteenth-century iron craftsmen.

The John Deere Historic Site is open daily 9:00 A.M. to 5:00 P.M. April 1 through November 30. Admission is $3.00 for ages twelve and older. For further information contact the John Deere Historic Site, 8393 South Main Street, Grand Detour, Dixon 61021; (815) 652–4551.

Another attraction in Ogle County is the ***Ogle County Courthouse*** in the center of Oregon. The building is listed in the National Register of Historic Places, and the Soldiers' Monument designed by Lorado Taft adorns the lawn.

John Deere Historic Site

Lowden State Park, across the river from Oregon, is on a bluff overlooking the Rock River. *Black Hawk,* Lorado Taft's most famous statue, stands 50 feet high overlooking the area. Taft and a few artists retreated to this area every summer beginning in 1898 and created an artists' enclave known as Eagle's Nest Art Colony. The public library in Oregon has a collection of works by Taft on display in the second-floor gallery. Lowden State Park; (815) 732–6828.

White Pines State Park, 8 miles west of Oregon, has 385 acres of recreation and forest area. The lodge has a restaurant, gift shop, and lounge. Best bet here is to reserve one of sixteen cabins that the park offers to overnight visitors, though the rustically inclined can choose from 103 campsites. The park is open from 8:00 A.M. to sundown year-round. For information concerning the lodge and restaurant, call (815) 946–3817.

Mount Morris, northwest of Oregon, has the ***Official Illinois Freedom Bell*** dedicated by Ronald Reagan in 1963. The bell was hung in the Illinois Pavilion in the 1964 World's Fair and again at a 1965 Cubs game in Wrigley Field. It is a replica of the Liberty Bell in Philadelphia and is the focal point of the ***Let Freedom Ring Festival*** every Fourth of July in Mount Morris.

Fulton celebrates its Dutch heritage on the first weekend in May every year. ***Dutch Days*** are highlighted by *klompen* (wooden shoe) dancing in the streets of the town. A parade is preceded by the *burgemeester* (mayor) and the town crier inspecting the streets to see if they are clean. When the mayor announces that "We must scrub the streets," costumed street cleaners come out with brooms and pails and scrub until the streets are declared clean.

One part of the parade is the "Parade of Provinces," where townspeople wear native costumes from each province of the Netherlands. Sinterclas, the Dutch version of Santa Claus, brings up the rear of the parade.

Delft jewelry and dishes, wooden shoes, and authentic costumes are on sale. Local stores offer tastes of Dutch cheese and pastry. Traditional Dutch meals, which include corned beef, potatoes and cabbage, pea soup, and currant buns, are served.

The townspeople plant more than 10,000 tulip bulbs every year, and windmills and tulips are in great profusion in Fulton. Even the information booth is housed in a windmill.

During Dutch Days the town crier walks the street announcing special events, and the library displays Dutch books and shows films of the Netherlands (no admission charged).

The festival ends Sunday afternoon with a traditional Dutch worship at a Fulton church. Men and women sit on opposite sides of the church, and part of the service is conducted in Dutch.

For information contact Fulton Chamber of Commerce, 415 Eleventh Avenue, Fulton 61252; (815) 589–4545.

Prophetstown State Park, in ***Prophetstown,*** was once the site of a Winnebago village, though it also contained large numbers of outcasts from other regional tribes. The park derives its name from the American Indian prophet Wa-bo-kie-shiek (White Cloud), who held sway over the village somewhat in the manner of a modern-day cult leader. The village was destroyed in the Black Hawk War. The park borders the Rock River on the northeast side of Prophetstown. Picnicking, fishing, and camping are available, but with no lifeguards here, plan on swimming at the city park, just 4 blocks away. Call (815) 537–2926 for more information about Prophetstown State Park.

Artists' Aerie

It's no coincidence that the magnificent **statue of Chief Black Hawk** (actually named *Eternal Indian*) stands on a high bluff overlooking the Rock River just across from the town of Oregon.

Legend has it that renowned sculptor Lorado Taft got the idea for the statue when observing some of his fellow artists standing on that very same bluff with their hands folded across their chests. By the way, it's a hollow statue of poured concrete fashioned with iron reinforcing rods and weighs about one hundred tons. It is thought to be the second largest concrete monolith in the world.

Sterling is the location of the **P. W. Dillon Home Museum.** The Italian Renaissance-style brick home at 1005 East Third Street, was built on the five-and-one-half-acre lot in 1857. Paul W. Dillon, owner of Northwestern Steel and Wire Company, lived there for ninety-six years from his birth in 1883 until his death in 1980. The home has antiques and artifacts on display, plus an Engine #73 steam locomotive and caboose. Hours are Tuesday, Thursday, and Saturday 10:00 A.M. to noon and 1:00 to 4:00 P.M., and Sunday 1:00 to 5:00 P.M.; (815) 622–6202.

The two **Lincoln historical markers** in Sterling are at 607 East Third Street, and at Sixth Avenue and Sixth Street. The Sterling **Municipal Symphony Band** performs ten concerts at the **Grandon Civic Center,** on Wednesdays, June through August, at 7:30 P.M. The band once performed for a Republican rally during Abraham Lincoln's presidential bid.

strangebuttrue

The towns of Sterling, Nebraska, and Sterling, Colorado, were both founded by former residents of Sterling, Illinois. Now for the strange part. On a road trip to Denver some years back, my van broke down in Sterling, Illinois. On the trip back, it broke down in Sterling, Colorado. Coincidence?

Morrison-Rockwood State Park on Route 78 is located 2½ miles north of Morrison. Lake Carlton, at the center of the park, has a 38-foot-high, 1,800-foot-long dam with a road across it. Fishing, boating, camping, picnicking, and hiking are available. Call (815) 772–4708.

For country fun, visit the **Whiteside County Fair** in mid-August. There's a draft horse show and tractor pull, too. At 201 West Winfield Street, Morrison; (815) 772–7329.

Union Grove Cemetery, also on US 30 just outside Morrison, dates back to the early 1800s and is open to the public.

Route 84, running along the west edge of Whiteside County, is part of the **Great River Road** that parallels the Mississippi River and is one of the most scenic drives in Illinois.

Rockford has many museums for those who love browsing. The **Midway Village and Museum Center,** 6799 Guilford Road, has buildings featuring local history and industry, the Old Dolls' House Museum, and Midway Village, a turn-of-the-century village of twenty-four buildings complete with stagecoaches. It also features an annual Civil War reenactment, complete with authentically dressed Blue and Gray troopers as well as soldiers' encampments that visitors can walk through to soak up some "living history." Admission fees are $5.00 for adults, $3.00 children three to seventeen. The center is open year-round, but hours vary depending on exhibit, so call (815) 397–9112.

The *Burpee Museum of Natural History,* 737 North Main Street; (815) 965–3433, is housed in a Victorian mansion and is open Monday through Saturday 10:00 A.M. to 5:00 P.M., Sunday noon to 5:00 P.M. Admission is $5.00, Wednesdays free. The *Rockford Art Museum,* 711 Main Street; (815) 968–2787, is open Monday, Tuesday, Wednesday, and Saturday 10:00 A.M. to 5:00 P.M., Thursday 10:00 A.M. to 7:00 P.M., Sunday noon to 5:00 P.M. Adults $5.00, seniors $3.00, children free.

The *Discovery Center Museum,* 711 North Main Street; (815) 963–6769, is a hands-on participatory museum where you can explore scientific and perceptual principles. The center is open Monday through Saturday 10:00 A.M. to 5:00 P.M., Sunday noon to 5:00 P.M., Thursday to 7:00 P.M. in summer. Adults $5.00, children $4.00, under two free.

For ethnic flavor the *Erlander Home Museum,* operated by the Swedish Historical Society, has mementoes of Rockford's rich Swedish history. It is located at 404 South Third Street; (815) 963–5559. Hours are Tuesday through Friday 1:00 to 4:00 P.M., and Sunday 2:00 to 4:00 P.M. Admission $5.00 for adults, children three to seventeen $2.00, seniors $3.00, family rate $15.00.

The *Graham-Ginestra House,* 1115 South Main Street; (815) 968–6044, is an example of classic Greek Revival and Italianate architecture. It has elaborately painted ceilings and authentic furnishings. It is open Sunday 2:00 to 4:00 P.M. May through October, and is listed in the National Register of Historic Places.

Another interesting architectural gem is the *Tinker Swiss Cottage,* built in the Swiss-chalet style after its owner, Robert Hall Tinker, visited Switzerland in 1862. The cottage's antique treasures include a 300-year-old painting, diamond-dust mirrors, Lincoln memorabilia, and dozens of family heirlooms. The cottage is open Tuesday through Sunday, with tours at 1:00 P.M., 2:00 P.M., and 3:00 P.M. Call (815) 964–2424 or write 411 Kent Street, Rockford 61102. Admission is $5.00 for adults, seniors $4.00, children five to seventeen $2.00.

northwestern illinois trivia

Legend says the town of Aledo got its name by chance, with town founders picking letters out of a hat; the first pronounceable name spelled A-L-E-D-O.

Today Aledo is most proud of its *Rhubarb Festival,* which grew from a backyard gathering of neighbors and friends into an annual event that has attracted an estimated 10,000 visitors. Held in early June, the townsfolk hold a tremendous bake sale, which in recent years has resulted in the sale of over 1,000 homemade rhubarb pies! Live music is featured at the new band shell at Central Park. Vendors and businesses offer rhubarb samples or provide recipes. Free admission, but bring your appetite! Contact (309) 582–2751.

Cool off at **Magic Waters,** a wave pool that offers a playground beach, 40-inch-wide roller slide, a tunnel slide with a heart-stopping 30-foot drop, a lazy river, organized games, and competitions. Magic Waters is located just off I–90 at the US 20/US 51 interchange near Rockford. Call (815) 332–3260 or write Magic Waters, 7820 North Cherryvale Boulevard, Cherry Valley 61016. Open late May to Labor Day.

Rock Cut State Park, off Route 173 about 6 miles northeast of Rockford, boasts picnicking, camping, trails, fishing, boating, ice skating, ice fishing, cross-country skiing, and snowmobiling. From Rockford take US 51 to Route 173. For information contact the Site Superintendent, 7318 Harlem Road, Lores Park 61111; (815) 885–3311.

prairiesurprises

If you're driving through northwestern Illinois, you'll note that the landscape is actually quite remarkable in some spots.

Far northwestern Illinois claims the state's most exciting topography up this way, especially if you head far west, from Stephenson County near Freeport into Jo Daviess County and on to the Mississippi River. Here the great glacier never leveled out the topography, and you'll note steep valleys and sharply sloping wooded hills. Of course, once you reach the river, you'll see magnificent bluffs lining both sides of it.

Much of the region south of here is undulating prairie, but it's still intriguing, especially when running through the Illinois and Rock River Valleys, where soaring cliffs and wooded bluffs jump out of the prairie flatness, only to disappear too quickly.

One of the best ways to see this area is to follow the carefully mapped Boone County Historical Trail. Originally compiled by the Boone County Bicentennial Commission and the Boone County Conservation District in 1976, the guide to the trail is available by calling (815) 547–7935.

The trail follows four different routes: the South Pacific Route, running through a region once covered by more than 50 miles of native prairie grasslands; Belvidere/Caledonia Route, covering the county seat, Belvidere, and the Scottish settlements at Caledonia and Argyle; Piscasaw Route, which follows the Kishwaukee River and Piscasaw Creek to the Norwegian village of Capron; and the Blaine/State Line Route, beginning in the Kinnikinnick Creek Conservation Acre and traveling through historic Blaine village and across the rolling hills of the Illinois-Wisconsin border. Each route is about 30 miles long, approximating the length of one day's wagon trip in the early settlement days of the 1830s. The trail is designed to be covered by car, on foot by hikers, or on bicycles.

The first three routes begin in Belvidere's **Spencer Park,** on the western edge of the city on South Appleton Road. Before the arrival of white settlers, this was the permanent gathering place for the local Potawatomi Indians. At nearby Belvidere Park, the old **Baltic Mill** dates from 1845 and was in use up until 1918. The fall of water through the Kishwaukee River provided the energy to turn the heavy grinding wheel.

At 534 East Hurlbut Avenue, is the former home of one of its early Civil War heroes, Gen. Stephen A. Hurlbut. Hurlbut's forces at the Battle of Shiloh won an important victory for the Union, earning him national recognition. He served as a member of the Illinois Constitutional Convention, a state representative in the Illinois Legislature, a U.S. congressman, and a minister to Colombia and Peru. Hurlbut is buried in Belvidere Cemetery along with dozens of the city's pioneers.

Usually cemeteries are repositories of an area's history, and **Belvidere Cemetery,** at 1121 North Main and Harrison Streets, is no exception. Stop at the cemetery office for a copy of their historic walking tour. Established in 1847, the burial ground holds the graves of two Revolutionary War soldiers, Thomas Hart and Timothy Lewis; the first white woman in the county, Sara Loop; an African American soldier in the Civil War and former slave, John Lawson; and blacksmith Samuel Longcor. Longcor was an early Illinois manufacturer of scouring plows, known as the S. Longcor's Iron Beam, a significant development in the cultivation of the state's prairie lands.

The **Pettit Memorial Chapel,** listed in the National Register of Historic Places, was designed by Frank Lloyd Wright in 1907 as a monument to a local physician, Dr. William H. Pettit. The chapel was restored by the Belvidere Junior Women's Club in 1977. It is a fine example of Wright's Prairie School style, with long, low lines. The stucco exterior is painted pale green with dark green wood trim and has a rough-sawn cedar shingle roof. Tours by appointment; (815) 547–7642.

Another historic home, the **Colonel Joel Walker Home,** stands at the corner of Lincoln Avenue and Main Street. The 1840 structure was the residence of a noted hero of the War of 1812.

Big Thunder Park honors the Potawatomi Indian Chief Big Thunder, who died in the 1830s. Local lore says his method of burial became the town's very first tourist attraction. Following Indian custom, he was buried seated in his best attire, along with food, tobacco, and implements necessary in the afterlife, then surrounded by a 6-foot-tall log stockade and left to the elements. Early visitors, including travelers on the Chicago-Galena stagecoach who stopped here, were very curious and—like tourists today—took souvenirs. Soon, very little was left of Big Thunder. It's rumored that the local citizenry substituted bones of hogs and sheep as relics for the eager and gullible tourists. A boulder with a bronze plaque on the grounds of the Boone County courthouse serves as a memorial.

A greater exploration of local history can be undertaken at the **Boone County Historical Museum,** 311 Whitney Boulevard; (815) 544–8391. Featured are farm implements as well as a log cabin, civil war artifacts, and a 1906 Eldredge Runabout car. Hours are Monday through Friday 9:00 A.M. to 4:00 P.M., and Saturday 10:00 A.M. to 4:00 P.M.

The fall in Belvidere is the time for festivals. The fourth weekend in September each year, the Boone County Conservation District sponsors the **Autumn Pioneer Festival,** with pioneer ethnic gardens, produce, samples and crafts, volunteers in authentic period dress, and an Indian village. Call (815) 547–7935.

Northwest of Belvidere are remnants of the county's immigrant past when Scottish and Scandinavian settlers arrived to take up farming. **Caledonia** and **Argyle** (on the Winnebago County line) were, of course, Scottish settlements. In 1834 two Armour brothers and their cousin came to Ottawa, Illinois, from Kintyre, Scotland. Shortly thereafter they moved to this part of Boone County, which came to be known as Scotch Grove.

Capron, on Route 173 in the northeast part of the county, was home to Norwegian settlers. The first two Norwegian pioneers came to the area in 1842 and called their settlement Helgesaw, later known as Long Prairie.

The town of DeKalb was once known as the "World's Barbed Wire Capital." It was here in 1874 that inventor Joseph F. Glidden patented an improved method of producing barbed wire. An industry grew up around his invention, with other DeKalb pioneers involved in its manufacture—Jacob Haish and Isaac Ellwood. The **J. F. Glidden Homestead and Historical Center,** at 921 West Lincoln Highway, is undergoing extensive renovation. Exhibits open May to November, the first and third Sunday each month noon to 4:00 P.M.; (815) 756–7904.

The **Ellwood House and Museum,** 509 North First Street, is an imposing Victorian mansion appointed with the finest furnishings of the period. Call (815) 756–4609. Guided tours take place Tuesday through Friday at 1:00 and 3:00 P.M.; Saturday and Sunday at 1:00, 2:00, and 3:00 P.M. Closed the second week of December until March 1. Also in Ellwood Park is the **Little House,** a 10-foot

Apple Pickin'

Not far from DeKalb, you can spend a wonderful autumn family afternoon at the **Kuiper Family Farm,** 01N145 Watson Road, Maple Park; (815) 827–5200. Take a hayride, pick some apples or pumpkins, or find your Christmas tree here. At the Old Barn Store or the Orchard Shop and Bakery, select from homemade goodies. Open September and October, Tuesday through Friday 9:00 A.M. to 6:00 P.M., Saturday and Sunday 10:00 A.M. to 6:00 P.M.; November and December, Tuesday through Sunday 10:00 A.M. to 5:00 P.M.

miniature mansion with carefully crafted interiors. The carriage house on the property has a fine collection of buggies and sleighs and samples of—what else?—barbed wire. Admission is $8.00 adults, children ages six through seventeen $3.00.

Northern Illinois University, founded in 1895, is located in DeKalb. The school, with over 25,000 students enrolled, is the second largest state university in Illinois. The architecture of some of the older buildings is worth exploring. Check with the Office of Admissions in Williston Hall for guided campus tours; (815) 753–0446. NIU's O'Connell and Players' theaters offer performances throughout the year; (815) 753–1337. Admission is free to the anthropology museum in the Stevens Building. Open Monday through Friday 9:00 A.M. to 5:00 P.M.; (815) 753–0230.

The *Egyptian Theater,* on North Second Street near Lincoln Highway, is a National Register of Historic Places building with a unique terra-cotta exterior and excellent acoustics. Built in the Egyptian Revival style, the theater is used for productions by traveling companies and local performing arts groups, as well as for movies; (815) 758–1215. Tours are scheduled by appointment.

The 1931 *Haish Memorial Library,* at Oak and North Third Streets, was a gift from barbed-wire baron Jacob Haish. Its art deco Indiana limestone structure, designed by White and Weber of Chicago, is also on the National Register.

And the *Gurler House,* 205 Pine Street, is home to a series of special events, such as the Summer's Eve Festival. The Greek Revival farmhouse, set in a parklike environment, is listed in the National Register. DeKalb may have chartered the nation's first county farm bureau in 1912.

Festivals of all kinds are important in the county. Among the most popular is the annual *DeKalb Corn Fest* held each August, when thousands of pounds of fresh-roasted, hot, buttered sweet corn are given free to all "corny" visitors; (815) 748–2676.

sandwich sampler

Sandwich Antiques Market might be the best place in Illinois to find a real deal on antiques and collectibles. The massive show, whose organizer holds to strict standards so that only authentic merchandise is sold, features more than 550 dealers, offering more than 330,000 items in a parklike setting of 160 acres.

The popular antiques market prides itself on fine nineteenth- and twentieth-century American and English furniture. Of course, primitives are still hot as collectibles, too.

But whatever kind of antique you're looking for, just figure that you'll find it here. Call (815) 786–3337. Admission is $5.00 per person, kids twelve and under free. Dates vary but usually fall on the third or fourth Sunday from April to October.

Sycamore, the county seat, hosts a yearly **Pumpkin Festival** the last weekend in October with a variety of old-time activities, including a parade and decorated pumpkins, some in fantastic shapes and others lampooning the politicians of the day, on the courthouse lawn; (815) 895–5161.

Shabbona Lake State Park, in the southwest part of DeKalb County, encompasses 1,550 acres and a 318-acre lake. Fishing is the thing here, and boats can be rented ($50/day for motorboats, $30/day for rowboats; 815–824–2581) at the marina. One hundred fifty campsites are available (all with electrical hookups), and hiking trails, horseshoe pits, and a baseball diamond are in place. In the winter, cross-country skiing, ice fishing, and snowmobiling are enjoyed here. Write the Site Superintendent, 4201 Shabbona Grove Road, Shabbona 60550; (815) 824–2106.

In the southeast corner of the county, Sandwich is home of the immensely popular **Sandwich Fair.** Catch the western horse show, sheep dog demonstration, harness racing, and even a fiddle contest that you can enter with your ticket stub as your entry fee! Events begin on Labor Day and continue all week; (815) 786–2159.

Indians and Soldiers

Ottawa is a town that remembers its soldiers well. **Washington Park,** in the center of town between Lafayette and La Salle Streets, has two war memorials, one dedicated to veterans of World Wars I and II, Vietnam, and Korea, and the other to the county soldiers in the Civil War. The Civil War monument was designed and erected by Edward McInhill.

The park also has a boulder for commemorating the first Lincoln-Douglas debate here on August 21, 1858, erected by the Illinois Chapter of the Daughters of the American Revolution.

In 1856 Sheriff William Reddick built what is known as the **Reddick Mansion.** The building is at 100 West Lafayette Street, across the street from Washington Park and is listed as a National Historic Landmark. For tours, contact the Ottawa Visitor Center at (815) 434–2737.

The **Third District Appellate Court of Illinois,** just east of the Reddick Mansion, was built in 1857 and served as the state's supreme court building for a decade. The building is open to visitors during business hours.

Ottawa's favorite son, William Dickson (W. D.) Boyce, founded the Boy Scouts of America in 1910, after encountering a helpful British scout in London. Boyce died in 1929 and is buried in the **Ottawa Avenue Cemetery,** just feet from a life-size statue of a young scout. Many call the figure the **Unknown Scout,** referring to the British boy who inspired Boyce to become the Father of American Scouting. The *Ottawa Scouting Museum,* at 1100 Canal Street, provides the history of scouting through displays and memorabilia. Open Thursday through Monday 10:00 A.M. to 4:00 P.M.; (815) 431–9353.

You must visit *Christ Episcopal Church,* the first Episcopal church to hold services in Ottawa in 1838. It is an example of English High Victorian Gothic architecture. The Wallace Window, patterned after a cathedral in Glasgow, Scotland, is a depiction of the Resurrection. It was designed by Professor Julius Herber of Dresden, Germany, one of Germany's finest artists. The church is located at 113 East Lafayette Street.

The *Ottawa Avenue Memorial Columns* are classic Roman architecture. The columns were built in 1918 as a memorial to Ottawa in honor of the centennial celebration of Illinois statehood. The columns are located next to the Ottawa Avenue Cemetery. Allen Park, along the Illinois River where it joins the Fox River, is a scenic park with tennis courts, public boat launches, picnic areas, and a beautiful view of the two rivers.

The Ottawa Chamber of Commerce publishes an auto tour of historic sites in the city. Contact the chamber for a copy of the tour at Ottawa Visitor Center, 100 West Lafayette Street, Ottawa 61350; (815) 434–2737.

Two miles west of Ottawa in the Illinois Michigan Canal National Heritage Corridor is the *Effigy Tumuli.* These five massive earth sculptures, inspired by the Native American burial grounds, have been shaped into a 1½-mile-long work as a tribute to Native Americans. This is one of the largest outdoor sculptures in the country. Call (815) 433–2220.

The *Starved Rock Land Tour* begins just outside the Ottawa Avenue Cemetery in the village of Naplate. The village was named for the former National Plate Glass Company and is now the home of Pilkington Glass.

The tour continues west through *Buffalo Rock State Park* to the Half-Way House, once the Sulphur Springs Hotel. The house is privately owned and not open to the public.

The *Grand Village of the Kaskaskia Indians* (1678 to 1687) is the site of three archaeological excavations near the Illinois River. The digs are not open to the public, but artifacts are on exhibit at the LaSalle County Historical Museum in Utica.

The *Starved Rock Lock and Dam* and *Illinois Waterway Visitor Center* offer the chance to see an operating lock, although weather dictates viewing; (815) 667–4054.

The *LaSalle County Historical Museum* in Utica, just outside Starved Rock State Park, was built during the term of President Zachary Taylor in 1848; 101 East Canal Street, Utica; (815) 667–4861.

The tour ends at the visitor center in **Starved Rock State Park,** one of the finest state preserves in the Midwest. Starved Rock State Park is located 10 miles west of Ottawa on Route 71 or south of I–80 on Route 178.

The park's name was derived from an Indian legend, which originated during the 1760s when Pontiac, an Ottawa chief (who lived upriver from this area), was murdered by an Illinois Indian while attending a tribal council in southern Illinois. Many battles to avenge the death of Pontiac were fought, and a Potawatomi band, allies of the Ottawa, fought the Illinois Indians in the area now called Starved Rock. The Illinois Indians took refuge on top of a butte and were surrounded by the Ottawas and Potawatomis. They eventually starved atop the rock.

There is evidence the Archaic Indians as well as the Hopewellian, Woodland, and Mississippian tribes lived in the area. Village sites and burial mounds have been mapped by archaeologists within the park boundaries.

The largest group of Indians to inhabit the area was the Illinois. They are believed to have lived here from the 1500s to the 1700s. The tribe's population was between 5,000 and 10,000 and was divided into subtribes. The Kaskaskias were a subtribe whose village extended along the north bank of the Illinois River, directly across from the park.

northwestern
illinoistrivia

Legendary Old West gunfighter and lawman Wild Bill Hickok, killed in a Deadwood, South Dakota, saloon holding the "dead man's hand" (aces and eights), was born in Troy Grove.

French explorers Louis Joliet and Father Jacques Marquette were the first known Europeans to visit the area. They canoed up the Illinois River from the Mississippi and stopped at the Kaskaskia village. Two years later, Father Marquette founded the Mission of Immaculate Conception, Illinois' first Christian mission, on the site of the Kaskaskia village.

Rene Robert Cavalier, Sieur de La Salle, came to the area to build a chain of forts to confine the English colonies in the East. Fort St. Louis was built on top of Starved Rock in the winter of 1682–83. It was a strategic post, towering above the rapids of the Illinois River and thereby controlling passage from Canada south. Many Indians settled near the fort for protection from the Iroquois tribe and to be near French trade goods, though the Iroquois eventually drove the French to abandon the area and retreat to Peoria.

In the 1800s there was a movement to make Starved Rock the "Gibraltar of the West," but this plan was unsuccessful. The area was later developed into a vacation spot. In 1911 the State of Illinois purchased Starved Rock and the surrounding area. The park now consists of 2,630 acres and is bordered by a 582-acre nature preserve.

Many interesting rock formations are found in the park; they are primarily of St. Peter's sandstone, laid down by a huge, shallow inland sea more than 425 million years ago. It was brought to the surface by an enormous upfold known as the La Salle Anticline. Continual erosion has formed the existing flat surface.

Most of the flat land was glaciated during the past 700,000 years, resulting in a flat and gently rolling plain formed after the last glacier. Most of the prairie is now farmland, and the areas along the river are predominantly forest.

There are eighteen canyons in the park; they were formed by streams feeding into the Illinois River. The streams cut channels through the rock as they followed the cracks and crevices of the sedimentary layers. Waterfalls are found at the heads of fourteen of the canyons, especially after a hard summer rain. The most popular waterfalls are at the St. Louis, French, La Salle, and Ottawa Canyons.

The park has a wide variety of plant and animal life. Red oak, basswood, and sugar maple trees grow in the moist, sandy soil along the northern slopes. Woodchucks feed on the lush undergrowth, and moles live on insects found in the soil. Vireos and catbirds fly above the ferns and shrubs. Trillium, Dutchmen's-breeches, and the large white flowers of the mayapple tree can be seen in spring.

Along the floodplain cottonwood, black willow, and ash trees grow. Skunk cabbage, marsh marigold, and wild iris live in the marshy areas. Wood ducks nest in hollow trees and can be seen paddling along the river's edge. Beaver and muskrat sometimes appear along the river.

The park has 13 miles of marked hiking trails, and hiking information is available at the visitor center and park office. The trails are open year-round, but hikers should be cautious near bluffs and stay on official park trails. Metal trail maps are located at all trail access points, trail intersections, and points of interest. Colored dots along the trails and on trees assist the hiker; they correspond to letter symbols on trail maps.

Picnicking is permitted, and picnic tables, drinking water, toilets, litter cans, and metal grills are provided at no charge.

Fishing is permitted, but anglers must stay 600 feet from the dam. Channel catfish are caught between the lock and dam, bullheads from the seawall, white bass from both ends of Plum Island, sauger and walleye from below the dam in fast water, carp from both banks, and crappies from around the small Leopold Island.

Boats may be launched from the ramp at the west end of the park, and canoes and paddle wheels are available for rent.

Ice skating is permitted at parking lot C, and cross-country skiing and snowshoeing are allowed in the picnic area and at **Matthiessen State Park** (just southeast of Starved Rock State Park off Route 178). Equipment can be rented on weekends, and tobogganing, sledding, and ice skating are permitted east of the main parking lot. Heated washrooms are accessible from these areas. Snowmobiling is not allowed in the park.

The visitor center displays the park's cultural and natural history. A park interpreter posts a weekly schedule of activities. The center is usually open daily. If the center is closed, contact the park office, which is open daily from 9:00 A.M. to 4:00 P.M.

Contact the visitor center or park interpreter at Starved Rock State Park, Box 509, Utica 61373; (815) 667–4726.

Camping is permitted except in the winter and during the spring thaw. There are 133 sites, and permits are obtained at the campground or park office.

There are horseback riding trails and a horseback riders' campground along Route 178 in the far western side of the park. Horse rentals are available on Route 71, just west of Route 178; April and November weekends, May through October, Wednesday through Sunday.

The wonderful **Starved Rock Lodge,** inside the state park, is located on a high bluff overlooking the Illinois River. The Civilian Conservation Corps (CCC)–built lodge boasts seventy-two rooms and a rustic lounge with a large double fireplace. An indoor swimming pool, Jacuzzi, and sauna are also available. Twenty-two cabins adjacent to the lodge are also for rent. Lodging is available year-round. For reservations and information call (815) 667–4211 or write Starved Rock Lodge and Conference Center, P.O. Box 570, Utica 61373.

Norway, 12 miles northeast of Ottawa, is the site of the first permanent settlement of Norwegians in 1834. Inspired by their leader, Cleng Peerson, fourteen families purchased a tiny sailing vessel and set sail for America. They left Norway because of economic, political, and religious domination by the Swedes. Peerson became known as the Norwegian Daniel Boone because he helped settle the new land in America.

A historical marker on Route 71 commemorates the hundred-year anniversary of the settlement, and a plaque tells the Norsk story. The **Norsk Museum,** off Route 71 on County Road 2631, is open June through September, Saturday and Sunday from 1:00 to 5:00 P.M.

Great elm trees planted by the founding fathers line the streets of **Princeton,** a prosperous small town much as it was when it was part of the pioneer path to the west.

Princeton was the home of the abolitionist preacher Owen Lovejoy. Lovejoy, an acquaintance of Abraham Lincoln, was elected to the state legislature in

1854 and then to the U.S. House of Representatives in 1856 where he served five terms. Lovejoy became nationally known for his work on behalf of the abolition of slavery. His house was one of the most important stations on the Underground Railroad in Illinois. Runaway slaves were hidden here by the Lovejoy family until plans could be made for them to travel to the next station on their way to Canada.

The *Owen Lovejoy Homestead* is now a museum. Listed in the National Register of Historic Places, it has fifteen rooms and has been restored to reflect the typical furnishing of its era. The home is on US 6 in Princeton. Hours are 1:00 to 4:00 P.M. Friday through Sunday, May through September. Nominal admission; (815) 875–2616.

More recent history can be found on the shelves of *Hoffman's Patterns of the Past,* a china and crystal replacement service at 513 South Main Street, 61356. More than 100,000 hard-to-find patterns are stocked. Hours are 9:00 A.M. to 5:00 P.M. Monday through Saturday; (815) 875–1944.

Other buildings to look for in Princeton are the *Cyrus Bryant House,* 1110 South Main Street, and the *John Bryant House* at 1518 South Main Street. For other gems, pick up a *Historical Homes and Architecture of Princeton* driving guide for 50 cents at the Chamber of Commerce (815–875–2616) or at the *Bureau County Historical Society Museum,* 109 Park Avenue West. Open Wednesday through Monday 1:00 to 5:00 P.M.; (815) 875–2184. Just 2.5 miles north of Princeton on Route 26, stop by the *Bureau County Red Covered Bridge,* built in 1863 and one of only five specimens still open to traffic in Illinois.

The second weekend in September is the *Lovejoy Homestead Festival and Pork Day,* complete with an ice-cream social, art show, beer garden, street dance, flea market, antique car show, pioneer crafts, horse-drawn wagons, and horse show. For information contact the Princeton Chamber of Commerce, 435 South Main Street, Princeton 61356; (815) 875–2616.

The *Hennepin Canal Parkway State Park,* 1 mile south of I–80 at Route 88, is a 104-mile waterway with canoeing, boating, hiking, and snowmobiling (some restrictions on snowmobiles). Visi-

Covered Bridge in Princeton

tor center hours are Monday through Friday 8:00 A.M. to 4:00 P.M.; hours vary with weather. Call (815) 454–2328.

In 1846 a group of idealistic Swedish immigrants came to the Midwest looking for a place to build a communal society. Under the leadership of Erik Jansson, a religious zealot, the group founded a commune in **Bishop Hill.** The group, industrious and optimistic, suffered through a harsh winter and epidemics. That year took many of its inhabitants with it. The survivors did establish their version of utopia, but dissension spread among the ranks, and in 1861 the commune dissolved. With the dissolution Bishop Hill faded into history.

Efforts to preserve the physical remains of the utopian village began in 1896 when members formed the Old Settler's Association. Today, the settlement's buildings are protected by registration on the National Register of Historic Places, and with national Historic and Illinois Landmark status. Several entities own and maintain portions of the settlement, causing some independence in hours open to the public, so call ahead.

wheredoesthe timego?

Perhaps the most unusual (and character-driven) feature of the Bishop Hill utopian village is found at the Steeple Building, completed in 1854, and constructed of handmade bricks and plaster.

But look up at that two-story wooden steeple with the clock. There are four faces to the clock—but only one hand!

The mystery might be explained by local folklore, which notes that this speaks directly to the colony's work ethic: "If you take care of the hours, you don't have to worry about the minutes."

The Illinois Historic Preservation Agency manages the **Colony Church** where visitors can watch an orientation video and admire ninety-six paintings of renowned artist Olof Kranz. Open Wednesday through Sunday 9:00 A.M. to 4:00 P.M., November 1 to February 31; Wednesday through Sunday 9:00 A.M. to 5:00 P.M., March 1 to October 31; (309) 927–3345.

The **Colony Steeple Building** is maintained by the Bishop Hill Heritage Association. Register for an hour and a half walking or riding tour. Reservations advised. Adult admission is $3.50, students $2.00; (309) 927–3899.

Fifteen of the twenty-one buildings are open as antique, quilt, and furniture shops or restaurants, and about 125 residents, including skilled artisans, currently call Bishop Hill home.

Annual Swedish festivals include the May 31 **Midsommer Celebration** with the decoration of the *midsommerstang* (maypole), traditional dances, music, and food. During the last weekend of November and the first weekend of December is the **Julmarknad** (Christmas market), where a cookie and chocolate walk (bake sales) are big draws. Guests attending *Lucia Nights* on the second weekend of December are served sweets by girls wearing candle-and-greens head wreaths; (309) 927–3345.

The *Julotta,* a 6:00 A.M. Christmas service at the Colony Church (non-denominational) is conducted in both English and Swedish. For more information, call the *Bishop Hill State Historical Site,* 200 South Bishop Hill Street, 61419; (309) 927–3345.

While in Henry County, stop by *Kewanee,* where the "world's best bar-beque" is served for "ninety-six hours a year" during *Hog Days* over Labor Day weekend. Events include a Hog Day Stampede (5K run for people), mud volleyball, and a "hoggatta regatta." Contact the Kewanee Chamber of Commerce, 112 East Second Street, Kewanee 61443; (309) 852–2175.

The *Henry County Historical Museum* also maintains a building in Bishop Hill, at 202 South Park Street. Exhibits include examples of Illinois prairie life from home to farm. Special seasonal events include quilt displays or photograph histories. Open 10:00 A.M. to 4:00 P.M. Monday through Sunday, May 1 to October 31; tours by appointment November 1 to April 30; (309) 927–3528.

Soprano Jenny Lind was known as the "Swedish Nightingale" when she arrived to tour America as a headliner for P. T. Barnum. In 1850 she became the benefactor for the then Augustana Lutheran Synod of America, donating more than half of the funds required to build a church for the Illinois Swedish community. The church, at the southwest corner of Sixth and Oak Streets in Andover, was named the *Jenny Lind Chapel* in her honor. Hours vary. Call (309) 521–8501.

The *Henry County Courthouse,* built in 1878–80, is located in Cambridge, the county seat. The main courtroom is worth a look. It is decorated with murals depicting the principal communities in the county.

strangebuttrue

Back in 1830, Bureau County was thrown into a panic by a report of an attack by Native Americans. A resident of the county, Mike Leonard, had been ambushed while hunting and had barely managed to get away—two ball holes in his hat were testimony to his narrow escape. After he gave the alarm, hysteria and confusion ensued as every settler in the area immediately began fleeing toward the town of Hennepin. It wasn't until after they had all reached Hennepin that somebody decided to examine Mike Leonards hat more closely. That's when they discovered that had Leonard actually been wearing the hat at the time the balls had passed through it, there would be two holes in his head, as well. Whereupon Leonard admitted that it was all just a practical joke—he had shot the holes in the hat himself. Everyone returned to their homesteads the next day.

Henry County has a number of lakes and recreational parks. *Johnson Sauk Trail State Park,* off Route 78, 6 miles south of the Anna-wan exit of I–80, has 400 acres of recreation along the Old Sauk Trail. Near the entrance take note of *Ryan's Round Barn.* Built in 1910, it's a "true" round barn (not polygonal). Tours every other Saturday, May to October. Call for schedule; (309) 853–5589. *Izaak Walton League Park,* Route 82, 1½ miles north of Geneseo on Hennepin Canal Parkway, has eight acres of camping, fishing, hiking, and water sports. The *Timber Lake Resort and Campground,* 5 miles north of Bishop Hill, has cabins, campsites with lake swimming, fishing, a pavilion, and planned activities. It is located on Route 81, 3 miles east of Cambridge and 1 mile north; (815) 244–1600.

Rock Island, one of the Quad Cities, has the Mississippi River as its frontyard and the Rock River as its back. During the 1840s and 1850s, the height of the steamboat era, as many as 1,900 steamboats docked in Rock Island annually.

It was here in 1675 that explorers Marquette and Joliet came on their trip down the Mississippi River. Seven years later they were driven out by the Sauk and Fox tribes. In 1805 Zebulon Pike traveled up the Mississippi on a government inspection trip and found the land inhabited by more than 5,000 Indians.

In 1816 Rock Island was fortified by the government and Col. George Davenport became the first resident-settler. In 1828 other settlers started moving here in large numbers and began battling with the Indians. The Indians retaliated, and the settlers sent for help from the governor. They wrote that the Indians "threaten our lives if we attempt to plant corn, and say that we have stolen their land from them, and they are determined to exterminate us."

The result was the Black Hawk War in which the Sauk and Fox lost their fight, opening up all of northern Illinois for settlement.

The Rock Island Railroad, the first to come to the area, completed its railroad bridge in 1856, the first bridge to span the entire Mississippi River.

In 1863 the *Rock Island Arsenal* was established. It originally served as a prison for Confederate soldiers, and more than 12,000 prisoners were confined here. When the Civil War ended, the arsenal was converted to its present use as the U.S. Army Armament, Munition, and Chemical Command.

The Rock Island Arsenal was built on what is now known as Arsenal Island, in the middle of the Mississippi River. The arsenal is the largest in the Western world.

The *Clock Tower,* the first permanent building of the Rock Island Arsenal, has a giant clock, over a hundred years old and still running. Visitors can tour the Clock Tower (on weekends and by appointment only) and other sights on the island: a replica of the *Fort Armstrong blockhouse,* the

The Black Hawk War

The Black Hawk War of 1832 has gotten plenty of mention in this book so far, but now that we're in Rock Island—Black Hawk's hometown, so to speak—it's time to give it a closer look. The groundwork for the war was laid as early as 1804, when three Sauk and Fox from Black Hawk's band signed away a vast portion of their lands—the large, permanent village of Saukenuk included—under distinctly shady circumstances. Black Hawk had never considered the treaty valid, as he claimed the individuals had had no authority to make such a decision and had been pressured into it while drunk. Nevertheless, the U.S. government had still allowed the Sauk and Fox to live on the land, for heavy white settlement had not yet reached the area. After the Winnebago War and the cession of the lead-mining lands, however, whites flooded into the region.

In the winter of 1829, while Black Hawk's people were away at their winter hunting camps, white squatters moved into Saukenuk and fenced off the Indian fields as their own. Black Hawk, investigating the matter, found a white family living in his own lodge. Incredibly, this did not lead to bloodshed. Come spring, the Indians and whites lived amid each other uneasily, squabbling over cornfields and livestock. Eventually, Black Hawk ordered the whites to leave. By now, the U.S. government had begun selling the lands acquired in 1804 to private individuals, and much of the land being purchased was in Saukenuk. Many of the squatters were squatters no longer but legal landowners. Thus when they petitioned the governor of Illinois to come to their rescue, he responded by calling up hundreds of militiamen and federal troops.

Black Hawk and his people wisely retreated across the Mississippi into Iowa, and in subsequent treaty talks, promised to remain there. Yet after one harsh winter—in which the government failed to supply an adequate amount of corn as promised—they returned. Wa-bo-kie-shiek at Prophetstown had invited them to live with his people, and Black Hawk had convinced himself that they wouldn't be troubled as long as they settled down peacefully on the Rock River and planted their crops. Instead, their reappearance in Illinois threw the frontier into a panic. Militia companies were quickly mobilized and federal troops were rushed into the field, forcing Black Hawk and his people, unwilling to risk an armed encounter, to flee northward.

On May 14, 1832, over two hundred mounted militiamen were reported to be settling in for the night only 8 miles from Black Hawk's camp. He sent three messengers under a flag of truce to report that they had no hostile intentions and hoped now only

Court of Patriots Memorial Field, and a *Confederate Soldier cemetery.* For tour information contact the visitor center at (309) 782–0799.

The *Mississippi River Visitor Center* at Lock and Dam 15 stands above the Mississippi Waterway System, where you can get a great view of barges passing through the lock system. Admission is free. The center is open daily 9:00 A.M. to 5:00 P.M.; (309) 794–5338.

to be allowed to return to Iowa in peace. Five more men were sent to observe the proceedings from afar. The militia, lubricated by whiskey, rudely escorted the message bearers into camp, but upon sighting the observers, rode off in pursuit—shooting and killing two of them. Back in camp, they killed one of the messengers, but the other two managed to escape in the confusion, as the militiamen mounted up and rode off pell mell after the fleeing Indian observers.

When the Indians returned to Black Hawk's camp and informed him of what had happened, he became enraged. With barely any time to react before the whites bore down on them, he spread his men out and awaited their arrival in the growing dusk. After the first Indian volley, the whites panicked and fled in disarray. With Black Hawk's men in pursuit, most did not stop until the following morning—each man certain he was the sole survivor. The incident became known as Stillman's Run, after the commander in charge.

Blood having been shed, there was no turning back. Black Hawk's band continued to flee, splitting into smaller groups to avoid detection, their ultimate goal to cross the Mississippi as soon and as safely as possible. They were pursued into Wisconsin, as skirmishes and battles raged across the frontier. The climax came at the confluence of the Bad Axe and Mississippi rivers, when an army-commandeered steamboat arrived just as Black Hawk's haggard band was getting ready to cross into Iowa. The Indians raised a white flag, attempting to surrender. The steamboat opened fire, and mounted volunteers bore down on the Indians from behind. As Sauk and Fox warriors tried to hold off the volunteers and return fire on the steamboat, scores of old men, women, and children tried to swim across the river, most of whom were killed or drowned in the attempt. Those who made it across were killed by Sioux warriors working for the U.S. government. Black Hawk himself escaped, only to be captured soon after. Overall, some six hundred Indians died in the war, along with seventy-two whites.

The war cleared the way for the final cession of Indian lands in the state, which were in northeastern Illinois under Potawatomi control. Seeing what had happened to the Winnebago, Sauk, and Fox, the Potawatomi had had no choice but to sign the Chicago Treaty of 1833—the most expensive Indian treaty of its time—and remove west across the Mississippi. Thus was Illinois finally spared, as one high-ranking government official phrased it, "the embarrassment of Indian relations."

The restored *Colonel Davenport Home* is open for viewing Thursday through Sunday from noon to 4:00 P.M., from May through October. It is located on Davenport Drive on Arsenal Island (which was called Rock Island when he settled here). Adult admission $5.00, students/seniors $3.00; (309) 786–7336.

For bikers a 7-mile bike trail around Arsenal Island begins at Terrace Drive at the corner of Gillespie Street.

To reach Arsenal Island take I–74 in Rock Island, exit at Seventh Avenue, and go west to Fourteenth Street. Take Fourteenth Street north to the bridge to the island.

Rock Island is on the site of *Black Hawk State Historic Site,* 1510 Forty-sixth Avenue; (309) 788–0177. This is the site of the westernmost battle of the Revolutionary War. On the grounds are three places to explore: the *Hauberg Indian Museum,* the *Watch Tower Lodge,* and the *Singing Bird Nature Center.* The museum contains a collection of Indian artifacts, paintings, and relics. There are three rooms, one devoted to Black Hawk items including portraits of the chief, another devoted to the daily lives of the Sauk and Fox, and the third is a gallery of Indian chiefs and the soldiers who opposed them during the Black Hawk War.

The bird center maintains a research area for bird enthusiasts and features windows that overlook bird feeder stations so visitors may view birds feasting away in their natural surroundings. Call for information on scheduled nature programs.

The park is open daily from sunrise to 10:00 P.M. Museum, lodge, and bird center hours: March through October, 9:00 A.M. to noon, and 1:00 to 5:00 P.M., Wednesday through Saturday; call for winter hours, (309) 788–9536.

The *Fryxell Geology Museum,* 639 Thirty-eighth Street, on the Augustana College campus, has a collection of fossils, which includes sauropod dinosaur eggs. Admission is free, and hours are Monday through Friday 8:00 A.M. to 4:30 P.M., Saturday and Sunday 1:00 to 4:00 P.M. during the academic school year; (309) 794–7318.

The *Denkmann Library,* also on campus, has the Augustana Historical Society collection of almost all the Swedish-American newspapers of North America.

Moline has a heritage of Belgian immigrants, and the *Center for Belgian Culture,* 712 Eighteenth Avenue, offers demonstrations of Belgian lace being made. Occasionally you can purchase samples. Call (309) 762–0167 for information. Open Wednesday and Saturday.

A landmark in Moline is *Lagomarcino's Confectionery* at 1422 Fifth Avenue, 61265. The shop's specialty is golden sponge candy—dark chocolate coating around a crisp blond center. Everything is handmade and hand-dipped. Try the homemade ice cream and sinfully rich hot fudge sauce; (309) 764–1814.

Coal Valley is the home of the *Niabi Zoo.* Translated from an Indian language, *niabi* means "spared of the hunter's arrow." The zoo is located on U.S. Route 6, 10 miles southeast of Moline. Besides a variety of animals, the zoo has a miniature railroad and a petting zoo designed for children. It is open daily 9:30 A.M. to 5:00 P.M. mid-April through early September; hours modified in fall and winter, so call ahead; (309) 799–5107. Admission is $5.00 for adults, $4.00

for seniors, and $3.50 for children three to seventeen; children under three are free. There are various free days through the year. Rides on the miniature railroad and the Endangered Species Carousel are $1.50.

Trackside Quad City Downs offers telecasts of thoroughbred and harnessraces, from all over the United States. Located in East Moline at Morton Drive and Route 5, it is open daily from 8:30 A.M. to 12:00 A.M.; call (309) 792–0202 for specific times.

Places to Stay in Northwestern Illinois

DEKALB

Baymont Inn and Suites DeKalb,
1314 West Lincoln Highway,
(815) 748–4800

Best Western DeKalb Inn and Suites,
1212 West Lincoln Way Highway,
(815) 758–8661

DIXON

Comfort Inn,
136 Plaza Drive,
(815) 284–0500

Quality Inn and Suites,
154 Plaza Drive,
(815) 288–2005

EAST DUBUQUE

Timmerman's Hotel and Resort,
7787 Timmerman Drive,
(815) 747–3181

ELIZABETH

Elizabeth Guest House,
101 West Main,
(815) 858–2533

FREEPORT

AmeriHost Inn and Suites,
1060 Riverside Drive,
(815) 599–8510

Country Inn & Suites-Carlson,
1710 South Dirck Drive,
(815) 233–3300

GALENA

Aldrich Guest House,
900 Third Street,
(815) 777–3323

Chestnut Mountain Resort,
8700 West Chestnut Road,
(815) 777–1320

DeSoto House Hotel,
230 South Main Street,
(815) 777–0090

Eagle Ridge Inn and Resort,
444 Eagle Ridge Drive,
(815) 777–5000

Galena Log Cabin Getaway,
9401 West Hart John Road,
(815) 777–4200

Hellman Guest House,
318 Hill Street,
(815) 777–3638

Pine Hollow Inn,
4700 North Council Hill Road,
(815) 777–1071

Queen Anne Guest House,
200 Park Avenue,
(815) 777–3849

Stoney Creek Inn,
940 Galena Square Drive,
(815) 777–2223

LANARK

Standish House,
540 West Carroll Street,
(815) 493–2307

MOLINE

Hampton Inn,
6920 Twenty-seventh Street,
(309) 762–1711

Holiday Inn Express,
6910 Twenty-seventh Street,
(309) 762–8300

La Quinta Inn,
5450 Twenty-seventh Street,
(309) 762–9008

Radisson on John Deere Common,
1415 River Drive,
(309) 764–1000

MORRIS

Comfort Inn,
70 West Gore Road,
(815) 942–1433

Holiday Inn,
200 Gore Road,
(815) 942–6600

MORRISON

Hillendale Bed and
Breakfast,
600 West Lincolnway,
(815) 772–3454

MOUNT CARROLL

Prairie Path Guest House,
1002 North Lowden Road,
(815) 244–3462

MOUNT MORRIS

Kable House Country Inn,
1 Sunset Lane,
(815) 734–7297

OREGON

Pinehill Inn,
400 Mix Street,
(815) 732–2067

PRINCETON

Days Inn,
2238 South Main Street,
(815) 875–3371

Econo Lodge,
2200 North Main,
(815) 872–3300

ROCKFORD

Clock Tower Resort and
Conference Center,
7801 East State Street,
(815) 398–6000

Fairfield Inn by Marriott,
7712 Potowatomi Trail,
(815) 397–8000

Hampton Inn,
615 Clark Road,
(815) 229–0404

Sweden House Lodge,
4605 East State Street,
(815) 398–4130

ROCK ISLAND

Four Points Sheraton,
226 Seventeenth Street,
(309) 794–1212

Top O' the Morning
Bed & Breakfast,
1505 Nineteenth Avenue,
(309) 786–3513

SYCAMORE

Stratford Inn,
355 West State Street,
(815) 895–6789

UTICA

Starved Rock State
Park Lodge,
Route 178 and Highway 71,
(815) 667–4211

SELECTED VISITORS BUREAUS AND CHAMBERS OF COMMERCE

Illinois Bureau of Tourism/Travel
Information,
(800) 2–CONNECT

Blackhawk Waterways Convention
and Visitors Bureau,
201 North Franklin,
Polo 61064
(815) 946–2108

Galena/Jo Daviess County
Convention and Visitors Bureau,
101 Bouthillier Street,
Galena 61036
(877) 464–2536

Rockford Area Convention and
Visitors Bureau,
102 North Main Street,
Rockford 61101
(815) 963–8111

Quad Cities Convention and
Visitors Bureau,
2021 River Drive,
Moline 61265
(800) 747–7800

Stephenson County Convention
and Visitors Bureau,
2047 Ayp Road,
Freeport 61032
(800) 369–2955

Places to Eat in Northwestern Illinois

FREEPORT

Beltline Cafe,
325 West South Street,
(815) 232–5512

GALENA

Bubba's,
300 North Main,
(815) 777–8030

Cafe Italia,
301 North Main,
(815) 777–0033

Fried Green Tomatoes,
213 North Main Street,
(815) 777–3938

Market House Tavern,
204 Perry Street,
(815) 777–0690

Log Cabin,
201 North Main,
(815) 777–0393

MOLINE

C'est Michele,
1405 Fifth Avenue,
(309) 762–0585

ROCKFORD

Great Wall Chinese Restaurant,
4228 East State,
(815) 226–0982

OTHER ATTRACTIONS WORTH SEEING IN NORTHWESTERN ILLINOIS

Fiorello's Pumpkin Patch,
Caledonia

Pecatonica Prairie Path,
Freeport

Silver Creek and Stephenson Railroad,
Freeport

Chana School Museum,
Oregon

Hauberg Indian Museum and Chief Black Hawk State Historic Site,
Quad Cities

Klehm Arboretum and Botanic Gardens,
Rockford

Channel Cat Water Taxi,
Rock Island

Stockton, Illinois' "highest" town

Warren Cheese Plant,
Warren

Eastern Illinois

The Heartland

Illinoisians tend to whiz through Vermilion County and its county seat, Danville, along Interstate 74 en route to Indianapolis and other points east. Why, I haven't really figured out. Besides being the easternmost big city in Illinois (apart from the really big one, Chicago), Danville has its charms. Among those are the area's many parks—15,000 acres of parks, in fact, for only 33,000 residents, making this one of the most heavily "parked" cities in the state.

The largest is the 3,000-acre **Kennekuk Cove County Park,** where you will find the 170-acre **Lake Mingo,** which sounds like something from Flash Gordon. There's fishing in the lake, for channel catfish, bass, and sunfish, but due to high insurance costs and low attendance, Stephens Beach is closed to swimming.

Follow **Lookout Point Trail** along a lush ravine system, through meadows and natural prairies. Stop to examine some of the 400 species of wildflowers, plants, and trees that grow in the park. Watch for the population of white-tailed deer and dozens of species of birds that are occasional visitors. The

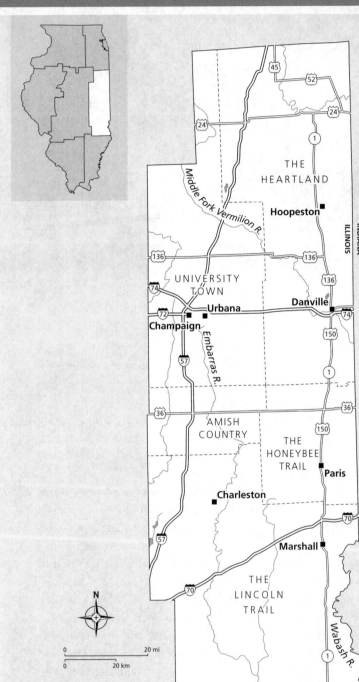

park's solar-heated visitor center houses an interpretive display of area Indian history. Kennekuk Cove County Park is 5 miles northwest of Danville at Henning Road off U.S. Highway 150. Park hours are 6:00 A.M. to 11:00 P.M. during the summer; (217) 442–1691.

What once was an ugly strip mine is today **Kickapoo State Park,** 2,842 acres of woods and ponds popular for picnicking and camping. The Middle Fork of the Vermilion River flows through the park, offering the opportunity for fishing and boating. It's a nationally designated scenic river—the only one in Illinois. Half-, one-, and two-day canoe trips begin here, with overnight accommodations either at a park campsite or—for the less adventuresome—at a hotel in Danville. Canoes, paddles, and life vests are provided. Scuba diving is also allowed; this is one of the few state parks where you can do so.

State park employees conduct interpretive programs year-round. In the summer there is hiking and horseback riding. The park's winter activities include ice fishing, ice skating, cross-country skiing, and sledding. Kickapoo State Park is at exit 210 off I–74. Park hours are 8:00 A.M. to 10:00 P.M. summer, 8:00 A.M. to 5:00 P.M. winter; (217) 442–4915.

In the southern part of the county, near Georgetown, **Forest Glen Preserve** is unique because of its **Grove Handicapped Trail,** paved for access by wheelchairs and said to be the only nature trail for the handicapped in the Midwest. It boasts an unusual restored tall grass prairie. Among the park flora, surprisingly, are several varieties of orchids. Also, in mid-September each year, a one-day Pioneer Craft Day is held here, complete with a pioneer homestead. On I–74, take the Main Street exit right onto Route 150. At the intersection of Main and Gilbert, turn right onto Route 1. Drive into the town of Westville, turn left (east) at the stoplight. The preserve's hours are 8:00 A.M. to 11:00 P.M. in the summer; (217) 662–2142.

AUTHOR'S TOP FIVE PICKS

Amish Country Inn,
Arthur,
(800) 72–AMISH

The Heartland Spa,
Gilman,
(800) 545–4853

Lincoln Log Cabin State Historic Site,
Lerna,
(217) 345–1845

Kickapoo State Park,
Oakwood,
(217) 442–4915

University of Illinois,
Urbana-Champaign,
(217) 333–1000

But as a major city, Danville has much more to offer than its parks. Its Civic Center, called the **David S. Palmer Arena,** built in 1980, is home to entertainment year-round, ranging from concerts to exhibitions to hockey games played by the local team. The Civic Center is at 100 West Main Street; call (217) 431–2424 for information.

The **Vermilion County Museum** (116 North Gilbert, open Tuesday through Saturday 10:00 A.M. to 5:00 P.M.) includes an 1850-era house, once the home of Dr. William Fithian, a friend of Abraham Lincoln. Lincoln, in fact, spoke from the balcony while running for the U.S. Senate. The bed he spent the night in is still here. The local visitors bureau acknowledges the Lincoln connection with the slogan, "We knew Abe *before* they called him Mr. President." Of special note are the doll collection in the Child's Room and the summer herb garden on the southwest corner of the grounds. The house is listed on the National Register of Historic Places. The museum has recently added a new building to house the collection. Admission for adults is $2.50. For children ages thirteen to seventeen admission is $1.00. Children twelve and under are admitted free. Call (217) 442–2922 for information.

strangebuttrue

During the early frontier days near Danville, settlers had a unique custom. Various days throughout the year were set aside as "fight" days, which took place in a special field designated solely for these events. On such days, whoever wished to fight—for whatever reason—could brawl to their hearts content. These were festive occasions, with sometimes a dozen or more fights taking place at one time. Spectators would wander from scuffle to scuffle, egging on the participants. Afterwards, the fighters would shake hands, knock back some whiskey, and watch a horse race or two.

The restored **Lamon House,** at 1031 North Logan in Lincoln Park, is open from 1:30 to 4:30 P.M. on Sundays, May through October, or by appointment through the museum; (217) 442–2922. Built in 1850, it is possibly the oldest frame house extant in Danville. It is furnished with furniture of the period.

With a list of such celebrated native sons as Gene Hackman, Bobby Short, Donald O'Connor, and Dick Van Dyke, it's not surprising that the arts scene in Danville is an active one. Community theater, the Danville Light Opera, the Red Mask, and the Danville Symphony Orchestra—named Illinois Orchestra of the Year in 1982—provide cultural sustenance. Call the Danville Convention and Visitors Bureau at (217) 442–2096.

For an evening of entertainment, visit **The Heron** in Danville at 34 North Vermillion Street. Start with a gourmet meal downstairs, and then take your nightcap upstairs at *The Up Club,* where classic jazz reigns. Dinner served Wednesday through Saturday 5:30 to 9:30 P.M.; (217) 446–8330.

In the northern part of the county, Hoopeston and Rossville are good places to look for antiques. Hoopeston hosts the *National Sweetcorn Festival* each September. A beauty pageant, tractor pulls, and—of course—plenty of hot corn and butter are hallmarks of this event; (217) 283–5833.

Rossville, on the other hand, calls itself "the village of unusual shops," a very apt description. Along Main Street shops selling antique furniture, glass, china, primitives, and country crafts provide ample fodder for the most ambitious shopping spree. Canine lovers will get a lick out of Rossville's *Dog Days of Summer* annual dog show and parade held the first Saturday of August. Admission: adults $5.00 per dog, children twelve and under $3.00; (217) 748–6914.

Serendipity is opening an oyster and discovering a pearl. Serendipity, too, is driving through miles of central Illinois farmland and coming upon *The Heartland Health Spa.* Here in Gilman this comfortable spa is remarkably unexpected, a Thoreauvian vision of a peaceful retreat some 28 miles from Kankakee down country back roads.

The facility was once the bucolic country estate of Dr. Karl A. Meyer, former medical director of Cook County Hospital. Meyer transformed the farmland, planting thirty-one acres of woods and creating Kam Lake. When Chicagoans Gerald S. Kaufman and Charlotte Newberger bought the property in 1983, they decided to preserve much of Dr. Meyer's healthful environment and to expand upon it.

What's Canoe with You?

Do you have your canoe handy? The Little Vermilion River State Natural Area and the Middle Fork River near Oakwood boast some of the state's top paddling possibilities.

About 2.2 miles of the Little Vermilion is listed as a statewide significant stream because its shoreline supports twelve state-endangered or threatened species and offers habitat for almost twenty-five additional forest interior species. The Middle Fork, the first Illinois stream included as part of the National Wild and Scenic River System, is contained in a narrow river valley, with 90-foot bluffs and few water ripples.

What all this means is some of the best scenery the state has to offer canoe lovers. Tulip trees 50 to 80 feet tall blossom here in springtime. Five natural prairies along the river are filled with 243 species of birds. You'll see Illinois' largest concentration of wild orchids. There are Indian mounds and burial sites with archaeological digs everywhere. There's even an active 50-foot beaver dam.

Yes, these rivers are something special. For more information, call (217) 442–4915.

TOP ANNUAL EVENTS

From Sheep to Clothing, Lincoln Log Cabin State Historic Site,
Lerna, early May,
(217) 345–1845

Sweetcorn Festival/ National Sweetheart Pageant,
Hoopeston, early September,
(217) 283–7873

Raggedy Ann and Andy Festival,
Arcola, early June,
(800) 336–5456

Broom Corn Festival,
Arcola, mid-September,
(800) 336–5456

Taste of Urbana-Champaign,
Champaign, late June,
(800) 544–7270

University of Illinois Football Games,
Champaign, September–November,
(217) 333–3470

World Free-Fall Convention,
Rantoul, late July
(217) 222–5867

Prairie Christmas, Lincoln Log Cabin State Historic Site,
Lerna, early December,
(217) 345–1845

At the edge of the spring-fed lake sits the main house—Meyer's mansion—with accommodations for only thirty-two guests and a pretty little dining room overlooking the lawn and lake. Here, too, are the Wood Room, where Heartland Institute lectures are held, and the cozy White Room for reading and conversation. An underground passageway leads to the old barn, magically transformed into a three-story fitness center with an aerobics loft, a state-of-the-art gym, sauna, whirlpool, and massage and facial rooms. Behind it is an enclosed swimming pool.

Guests begin their stay on Friday or Sunday for either a two-day weekend or a five- or seven-day program. The all-inclusive holiday begins with a tour of the facilities and an orientation, where one of the friendly staff members explains The Heartland fitness and nutrition philosophy. Guests exchange tired big-city clothes for loose-fitting workout togs, the uniform for all occasions throughout the stay. It's all part of the comfortable, casual attitude here.

After an optional body-fat evaluation, guests move on to dinner; like all meals, it's a fish or vegetarian affair, beautifully presented and served. Meals are kosher supervised, as well. Calories are limited to 1,500 for women and 1,800 for men. Cholesterol, sodium, and fats are also limited. But no one goes hungry here. Seconds are okay, if you're not trying to lose weight. In addition to breakfast, lunch, and dinner, snacks are available at midmorning and in the afternoon. A fruit basket is always standing ready on the sideboard for those who just can't make it through. One of Chef Barb Peters's menus might look like this: minestrone soup, eggplant Parmesan, steamed zucchini, fruit garnish, and carob coconut cookie. Or for lunch: Waldorf salad, frittata, green beans, and almonds.

A day's activities begin early. Wake-up comes at 7:00 A.M. (optional), followed by a morning stretch and a walk before breakfast. After the morning meal is a ninety-minute aerobics class in the fitness center where inhibitions are shed along with pounds and friendships are formed as guests struggle together through exercise class. By the end of a visit, the spirit of camaraderie is strong, along with the commitment to take home this awareness of healthy living.

Activities, it should be noted—like dance classes or horseback riding (extra fee)—are optional. So at any time you can wander away for a swim or a hike around the lake, or just take a lazy siesta in the sun with a good book. If it sounds like work, it isn't. As members of the staff explain, rest and relaxation are among the important benefits of The Heartland, as are the challenging daily issues of dieting and stress management.

The Heartland advocates a three-part approach to stress management. The first phase, exercise, focuses on increasing body awareness. Guests explore a variety of exercise techniques. Yoga, guided relaxation, and stretching classes increase the participants' awareness of their bodies, using progressive muscle relaxation and controlled breathing.

Education is the second component of the program. Instruction here will help guests become more aware of how tensions accumulate and will introduce various attitudinal approaches, from positive thinking and calming mental imagery to improved communication strategies for defusing harmful stress.

eastern illinoistrivia

Mammoths and mastodons once lived in east-central Illinois, and were driven out of the state during the Ice Age.

Step three is nutrition, and the spa's balanced vegetarian menus serve that role.

For reservations call (800) 545–4853. To reach the spa from Chicago, take the Dan Ryan Expressway south to I-57. Go 52 miles to Kankakee exit 308. Turn right at the top of the cloverleaf onto U.S. Highway 52/45 (which becomes Route 49) to U.S. Highway 24 (at the flashing red light). Turn right onto U.S. Route 24 for 2 miles to The Heartland sign and Camp Wahanaha sign (County Road 1220E). Turn left and continue for 2 miles to The Heartland sign. Turn left. The driveway to The Heartland is on the immediate right. The Heartland is 80 miles south of Chicago.

University Town

The 62,000-student *University of Illinois* campus, the state's largest, shapes the landscape of the twin cities of Urbana-Champaign like nothing else. Lying at the dividing point of the two towns, the university, founded in 1867, is internationally known for its physics and engineering departments. It houses the National Center of Supercomputing Applications facility, one of the nation's first academically owned supercomputers. It's a mecca for computer buffs with Marc Andreessen, of Web designer fame, as an alumni.

Historic . . . Haunted Hotel?

Nestled in downtown Urbana is the sprawling *Historic Lincoln Hotel,* 209 South Broadway Avenue. Built in 1924 to resemble some sort of gigantic Bavarian chalet, you'll find the Historic Lincoln Hotel to be both imposing and a bit . . . well, creepy. In the main lobby and dining areas, you'll find a high, beamed and buttressed ceiling, elegant chandeliers, a grand piano, and more grandfather clocks, fireplaces, paintings, and books than you can shake a copy of the Gettysburg Address at. The rooms feature four-poster beds and oak and cherry furniture and cabinets. And it's not overly expensive, either. You would think people are lining up to get rooms here, wouldn't you?

Such does not appear to be the case, though in all fairness the one Friday night my wife and I spent here was in late June, and there were not—to the best of my knowledge—any big events about town. Still, my wife expressed some reservation that we appeared to be among only a handful of guests in such a large hotel. She was also a bit creeped out by the darkened hallways and weathered furnishings of the rooms, which would have made Lincoln's ghost feel downright cozy. Afterward we learned from some friends in Urbana that many people find the place haunted and have even had lightbulbs shatter on them and lamps throw sparks. We, however, did not experience any problems. In fact, I appreciated the hotel's rather faded, battered air, for our teething, drooling son was just starting to crawl—not exactly the type of creature you feel comfortable letting loose in pristine, fancy-pants surroundings.

As for the staff itself, we had nothing but praise, and that's why I would recommend this unique, somewhat gloomy hotel. Though our son was in a particularly foul mood, we still attempted to have breakfast in the dining room before checking out. Despite our little darling's earsplitting caterwauls, one of the cooks actually hoisted him up into her arms and kept him entertained so that we could eat in peace. Granted, we were the only people in the dining room, but hey—that's service above and beyond the call of duty! You might also like to know that there's an indoor pool at the hotel, but, unfortunately, we were too afraid to wander the halls to find it. For reservations and directions to the pool, call (217) 384–8800.

Wander around campus and enjoy the architecture, or stop at the ***Krannert Art Museum,*** 500 East Peabody Drive, for its collection of sculpture, old masters, and the Ewing collection of Malayan art (open daily except Monday); call (217) 333–1860. Also on campus is the ***Spurlock Museum,*** 600 South Gregory Street, open Tuesday through Sunday; (217) 333–2360.

Another treasure house, the ***Museum of Natural History,*** 1301 West Green, is one of the finest in the Midwest, with thousands of specimens on display. It's the perfect place to take children. The Discover Room has hands-on exhibits—shells, teeth, and other artifacts—that kids can touch and examine closely. Open daily except Sunday. For the lively arts the ***Krannert Center for the Performing Arts,*** 500 South Goodwin Avenue, offers a full program of dance, theater, and music throughout the year. For schedule information call (217) 333–6280. Lively sports are represented each season when the "Fighting Illini" play in the Big Ten at ***Memorial Stadium,*** (217) 333–3630. For maps, walking tours, or directions, check in at the information desk at the Illini Union building at Wright and Green Streets; (217) 333–4666.

Other sites associated with the University of Illinois are worth a visit, too. The ***Morrow Plots,*** at Gregory near Mathews Street in Urbana, are the oldest permanent soil experiment fields in the country, in continuous use since 1876, in keeping with the original agricultural mission of the land grant school. Similarly, three round dairy barns built between 1902 and 1910 are part of the university's agricultural program (St. Mary's Road, Urbana). Renowned sculptor Lorado Taft studied here, graduating in 1879. ***Taft's boyhood residence,*** built in 1871, is located at the Illini Grove on South Maryland Avenue. One of his works, a ***Lincoln statue,*** sits opposite Urbana High School on Race Street.

A number of historic buildings are scattered throughout Champaign. The ***Cattle Bank Building,*** 102 East University Avenue, is the oldest remaining business building in the city, incorporated as a branch of the Grand Prairie Bank of Urbana in 1856. The building was bought by and is now occupied by the ***Champaign County Historical Museum.*** The purchase was part of the museum's twenty-fifth anniversary celebration in 1999. The museum has filled the former bank with exhibits, a library devoted to local history, meeting rooms, and a gift shop. The museum is open Wednesday through Friday 10:00 A.M. to 5:00 P.M.; Saturday and Sunday 1:00 to 4:00 P.M. Closed on holidays;

eastern illinoistrivia

Sullivan, originally known as Asa's Point and founded by a frontier hunter, is home to the Little Theater, the only professional Equity summer stock theater in east-central Illinois.

please call ahead. A donation is requested. For more information call (217) 356–1010 or visit www.champaignmuseum.org.

that'sflat!

If it's flat, open prairie you're aiming to see, you're in the right part of Illinois. The eastern portion of the state, and to an even greater extent, the central breadbasket of Illinois, is the heart of the heartland, where your car will roll past neat rows of croplands planted with everything from sweet corn to soybeans.

It's where Amish buggies clip-clop past black earth that has nurtured a nation for more than 200 years. And where for miles and miles you'll see nothing but miles and miles.

So you've made it to the prairie flatlands, where the spirit of the sodbuster lives proudly among the fields of harvest. Enjoy the heartland hospitality. Feel the sun on the back of your neck. Relax and look around.

One unique museum at the University of Illinois is the *Sousa Archives and Center for American Music,* located in the Harding Band Building, 1103 South Sixth Street. The collection includes the world's largest compilation of original John Philip Sousa music manuscripts, plus period uniforms and historical instruments. Free admission; open Monday through Friday 8:30 A.M. to 5:00 P.M. Call to schedule tour; (217) 244–9309.

A great place to bring kids is the *Prairie Farm* at Centennial Park, 2202 West Kirby Avenue. Here you'll find a replica of a turn-of-the-century farm with barns, a pond and pasture, and a flower garden. The usual menagerie of farm animals is present, with a separate petting area, and special events take place throughout the summer. Open daily 1:00 to 7:00 P.M., Memorial Day through Labor Day. The petting area is open daily 3:00 to 5:00 P.M., June 9 through September 1. Admission is free, though donations are certainly appreciated; (217) 398–2583.

In Mahomet, on Route 47, 10 miles west of Urbana-Champaign, *Lake of the Woods County Park* is a pleasant diversion in the Illinois farm country, though boating and swimming are no longer allowed on the twenty-six acre lake.

Visitors often come for the unique *Early American Museum and The Mabery Gelvin Botanical Garden,* located within the park. The museum, opened in 1968, began with the collection of local history buff William Redhead and has grown over the years. Volunteers present a fascinating series of pioneer-life programs year-round—from a colonial muster in September to an exhibition of farm life a century ago. You might encounter a costumed interpreter making soap or stitching a quilt, dipping candles, or spinning a tall folk tale. The demonstration of Christmas past is especially nice during the holidays. For children five to nine years of age, Wednesday mornings in June and

July mean a chance to put on a pioneer costume and spend time just as a youngster of the 1800s might have, learning antique crafts, games, and music; (217) 586–2612.

In the garden special plantings include the Heritage Garden, the Roses of Yesteryear, the Dye-Plant Garden, and a Prairie Sampler of native prairie plants. An eighteen-hole golf course, hiking trails, plus a covered bridge round out the park's attractions. Call (217) 586–3360 for information. The park is open daily year-round, 7:00 A.M. to sundown. Admission is free.

Two other parks in the Champaign County Forest District are worth mentioning. *Middlefork River Forest Preserve* near Penfield has year-round camping in addition to three fishing lakes, swimming, and an activity center. The preserve is on County Road 22, about 5 miles north of Penfield; (217) 595–5432. *Salt Fork River Forest Preserve* near Homer encompasses the eighty-acre Homer Lake, popular with area fishing enthusiasts. The Trailside Visitor Center features nature displays, live animals, and educational exhibits. In early June stop by for the *Salt Fork Summerfest,* with nature walks, fishing demonstrations, and canoe and kayak races; (217) 896–2733. From I–74, exit at Ogden and proceed south on Route 49 for 3 miles. Turn right at the sign for the preserve onto County Road 19. The entrance to the preserve will be in 1 mile.

Amish Country

Douglas and its neighboring county, Moultrie, are the center of Amish culture in Illinois. The first Amish in Illinois, however, came to the area around Peoria along the Illinois River in the 1830s. These early settlers immigrated from Europe: Alsace and Lorraine, Bavaria, and Hesse-Darmstadt. In the succeeding decades, though, Amish from Ohio and Pennsylvania joined those pioneers in Illinois, settling around Arcola and Arthur in the years immediately following the Civil War.

Today things haven't changed that much. You can still see a plainly dressed family riding to town in a black, horse-drawn buggy. One of the best ways to learn about the Amish way of life is by taking a tour arranged through the *Amish Interpretive Center,* 111 South Locust Street. You will see the Amish community that is hidden to the public. Visit a working Amish farm, admire the quiet countryside, stop by an Amish-run business and

eastern illinoistrivia

In Arcola's pharmacy, its Coffee Club displays more than 150 coffee cups, with customers' names affixed to them, behind the counter.

Amish Country

watch the craftsmen at work, or eat a meal at the home of a hosting Amish family. The center also provides an informative video and museum. Hours are Monday through Saturday 9:00 A.M. to 5:00 P.M. in March through November; by appointment only December through February; (217) 268-3599. As you drive down country back roads, you'll find horsepower of the original sort on display—Amish farmers hitched to teams of plow horses. Tractors are not used. Visiting this part of the state is a bit like stepping into a time machine, going back to an era when things were simpler.

You can begin a trip here with a stop at *Rockome Gardens,* a park 5 miles west of Arcola on Route 133. Here, on fifteen landscaped acres, nearly everything—from fences to arches to garden walls—is constructed of rocks inlaid in cement. Reopened in 2006 under new management, the focus here is decidedly 1940s family friendly. Rent a kayak (extra fee) or fish along the Kaskaskia River. If you've forgotten your gear, stop by the park's *Outdoor Store* and pick up whatever you need. The shop also rents bicycles and sells hearty picnic lunches.

strangebuttrue

The local Hardee's fast-food restaurant in Arcola, the largest of the twin towns that claim most of the state's Amish population, actually has a hitching post right out front of its building to accommodate those Amish families with horse and buggy who might want to stop in and grab a bite to eat.

There's horseback riding on Saturday and Sunday at 11:30 A.M. and 1:30 P.M. for $20 per person. Hiking tours focus on discovering native flowers and trees, or take the trails on your own. Next stroll through *Small Town USA.* There are cooking demonstrations and wine and cheese tastings daily at the *Harvest Time Store,* ice-cream treats at *Elvan's Soda Fountain,* and wares from books to lace at the *Rockome Five and Dime* general store. Buy some sweets at the *Candy Shack and Bakery,* and for a rib-sticking meal, try the family-style dinner at the *Days Gone By Restaurant,* open daily for lunch and evening dinner, often featuring live jazz or big band music. Throughout the season, special events include a model railroad show, a horse farming festival, quilt show, and the Old Fashioned Fiddlers competition. Call for schedule. Admission: adults $5.00, seniors $4.00, children $3.00. Open throughout the year with minimal schedule in winter. Park hours are 9:00 A.M. to 5:30 P.M., and extended for the restaurant; (217) 268–4106.

For shopping the *Arcola Emporium,* at 201 East Main Street in downtown *Arcola,* offers the conveniences of a mall with a collection of charming shops selling antiques, art, women's fashions, toys, cookware, gourmet foods, and handcrafted solid wood furniture. A number of antiques shops are also in the region.

The weekend after Labor Day, Arcola hosts the annual *Broom Corn Festival,* recalling the days when it was Broom Corn Capital of the world. A parade, a 10,000-meter road race, a flea market and street fair, plus demonstrations of broom making and other old-fashioned crafts, highlight

eastern illinoistrivia

In Arcola's Dutch Kitchen restaurant, Amish German sayings are translated on the walls; a couple of the more colorful ones are: "Don't eat yourself full. There's more back yet"; and "Eat your mouth empty before you say."

the celebrations. Arcola is the birthplace of Johnny Gruelle, the artist/creator of Raggedy Ann, and home to the *Raggedy Ann Museum,* at 110 Main Street. Free admission; open from March 15 to December 30, Tuesday through Saturday 10:00 A.M. to 5:00 P.M.; by appointment January 1 to mid-March; (217) 268–4908.

The town celebrates the *Annual Arcola Raggedy Ann and Andy Festival* the first week of June, with a parade and auction. Contact the Arcola Chamber of Commerce, 135 North Oak Street, Arcola 61910, for more information; (217) 268–4530.

The Lincoln Trail

The *Lincoln Log Cabin State Historic Site* near Charleston was the last home of Thomas and Sarah Bush Lincoln, Abraham Lincoln's parents. The cabin was built in 1837 and is now reconstructed on an eighty-six-acre lot that includes a pavilion, picnic area, and historical farm museum. The cabin is furnished with period pieces, and a kitchen building, log barn, and smokehouse from the 1840s have been added to the site. They are being restored to represent New England or "Yankee" culture in Illinois, in contrast to the Lincolns' southern upland culture.

The site is open 8:30 A.M. to sunset daily. The visitor center in Lerna is open May through October, Wednesday through Sunday 9:00 A.M. to 5:00 P.M.;

Lincoln Log Cabin State Historic Site

it closes at 4:00 P.M. November through March; (217) 345–6489. Costumed guides conduct tours during the summer, and admission is free. Special events at the cabin include draft-horse plowing demonstrations in May, the Bluegrass Festival in August, the Harvest Frolic and Trades Fair in October, and the 1840s Prairie Christmas in December. You'll see signs for the site on South Fourth Street Road, 8 miles south of Charleston.

Fox Ridge State Park is 8 miles south of Charleston on Route 130. A wooded tract with rolling hills running along the Embarras River, the park has fishing, boating, hiking, picnicking, and camping. For information contact the Park Manager, 18175 State Park Road, Charleston 61920; (217) 345–6416.

The **Thomas Lincoln Cemetary and Shiloh Church** is located about 1½ miles southwest of Campbell, along the Lincoln Heritage Trail. Previously called Gordon's Cemetery, it is the resting place of Thomas and Sarah Bush Lincoln. When historians discovered Thomas Lincoln's cabin and began to restore it, the citizens of Coles County dedicated themselves to perpetuating the gravesite. It is also a major cemetery for Civil War veterans.

One mile north of the Lincoln Cabin on the Lincoln Heritage Trail is the **Moore House** in Campbell. It was the home of Matilda Moore, the daughter of Sarah Bush Lincoln and Abraham Lincoln's stepsister. In January 1861 Lincoln paid his last visit to Coles County and his stepmother and stepsister at this home. The grounds of the home are open 9:00 A.M. to 5:00 P.M.

The **Stephen Sargent Farm** is located 10 miles south of the Lincoln Cabin. It is open to the public when staffing permits. It is a fine example of progressive farming of the 1840s. This is in contrast to the Lincoln Farm, which exemplifies subsistence farming. For more information contact the Lincoln Log Cabin State Historic Site, 400 South Lincoln Highway Road, P.O. Box 100, Lerna 62440 or call (217) 345–6489.

The **Indian Church** is 3½ miles west of the Lincoln Heritage Trail between County Roads 1150E and 250N. Built in 1832, this was the first church on the Little Indian Creek.

The **5-Miles House** at the corner of Route 130 and the Westfield Road (about 5 miles southeast of Coles County Courthouse in Charleston) was built in 1836. It was originally a wayside tavern and a place to water and care for horses. In 1849 it was an outfitting shop for travelers to the gold fields. The home is undergoing restoration and currently not open to the public.

Eastern Illinois University is the cultural center of Coles County. The battlements of Old Main, an example of German Gothic architecture, tower over the campus. The museum and greenhouses of the Life Science Building are open to the public. The **Tarble Arts Center,** housing the **Paul Sargent Art Gallery,** displays fine art and has changing exhibits. Open Tuesday through Friday, 10:00 A.M. to 5:00 P.M., Saturday 10:00 A.M. to 4:00 P.M., Sunday 1:00 to 4:00 P.M.; (217) 581–2787. Admission is free. The **Booth Library** is a stunning building to explore.

The university sponsors a **Celebration in Arts Festival** the last weekend in April. Call (217) 581–5326 for information.

A **replica of the Liberty Bell** became part of Charleston's heritage during the Bicentennial celebration of 1976. The bell hangs in Morton Park on Lincoln Street (Route 16).

The **Coles County Courthouse,** built in 1898, was remodeled in 1951. Located in Charleston's town square, it is where Lincoln practiced law, and it is the scene of the Charleston Riot, which involved 300 men in an armed conflict during the Civil War.

Riot!

Ever hear about the "Charleston Riot"? In March 1864 six Union soldiers and three civilians were killed here when a riot broke out right before a local Democratic congressman was about to give a speech about reuniting the country. It is said to be "the largest battle fought between soldiers and civilians in the North over an issue other than the draft."

Eventually fifteen people were arrested and imprisoned at Fort Delaware, Delaware. Eight months later, President Abraham Lincoln stepped in and ordered all fifteen to be returned to their homes in Coles County, Illinois.

The authorities here in Charleston released thirteen of the rioters on their arrival, while two stood trial and were eventually acquitted of inciting a riot. A marker on the Coles County Courthouse lawn (Monroe and Seventh Street), marks the site of the tragic incident.

The **Will Rogers Movie Theater,** 705 Monroe Street, named after the actor/comedian and philosopher, is an example of art deco architecture and is listed on the National Register of Historic Places.

The fourth Lincoln-Douglas debate was held in Charleston on September 8, 1858. The site of the debate is now the **Coles County Fairgrounds** on Route 316 on the west end of Charleston. Here you will find a museum devoted to the history of the debates, called the **Lincoln-Douglas Debate Museum.** Although each of the seven debates are memorialized by the hosting cities, this museum covers all of the 1858 Senatorial debates, including the Charleston match. The exhibit features hands-on displays and an interactive film and audio layout that invites participation from all age groups. Fairground hours are dawn to dusk; museum hours are 9:00 A.M. to 4:00 P.M. year-round. Call (217) 348–0430.

East of the debate site are the **Old Cemetery** and **Chambers Cemetery.** Here are the graves of Col. and Mrs. Augustus C. Chapman and Mr. and Mrs. Dennis Friend Hanks, relatives of Lincoln. Hanks supposedly taught Lincoln to read and write. There are also graves of many of the early settlers, including Charles Morton, founder of Charleston.

free-fallin'

Ever see more than 2,000 skydivers bail out of their planes and head earthbound at the same time? That's what happens every August at the World Free-Fall Convention at the Rantoul National Aviation Center. If you'd like to take the plunge, call (217) 222–5867 for more information.

For additional information on the Lincoln sites or other activities, contact the Charleston Tourism Office, 520 Jackson Avenue, Charleston 61920; (217) 348–0430.

Although primarily an agricultural county, Clark County has two literary associations worth noting. James Jones, author of *From Here to Eternity,* made his home in Marshall, the county seat. Indiana writer Booth Tarkington visited Marshall often as a boy and then recounted those experiences in his nostalgic novel *Penrod.*

Marshall has about 4,000 residents and a wealth of charm that could easily serve as writerly inspiration—quiet streets with leafy canopies of oak and maple, solid turn-of-the-century brick homes. One of the best examples is the 1907 **Lewis Home,** 503 Chestnut, with its dramatic two-story columned veranda (listed in the National Register of Historic Places, but not open to public inspection). The old-fashioned bandstand at the county courthouse is home to the oldest continuing city band in the state. The band, with a century-long history, performs every Friday night on the courthouse lawn from the end of May through August.

The original inhabitants of the county were the Kickapoo Indians, who ceded the land to the United States government in 1819. By 1832 they had been moved from the area. A year later the site on which Marshall was built was purchased by Col. William Archer and Joseph Duncan, later the sixth governor of Illinois. The town was named after the fourth chief justice of the United States, John Marshall.

Like the eastern states, which are dotted with spots that claim "George Washington slept (or ate or visited or whatever) here," we in Illinois have the Lincoln legend at every turn. The **Lincoln Heritage Trail,** created in 1963, marks the route the family traveled from their original home in Kentucky, through Indiana, to Macon County, Illinois. Here in Clark County, the **Lincoln Trail State Park** marks the area through which the Lincolns passed in 1830 on their way to a new home in Decatur. The 146-acre Lincoln Trail Lake is its focal point. The park offers camping (electricity, showers, and toilets available), fishing (bass, bluegill, crappie, channel catfish), picnicking, and hiking on trails up to 2 miles long. Boats are available for rental. In the winter enjoy ice fishing, ice skating, and cross-country skiing. For information contact the Site Superintendent's office at (217) 826–2222. The recreation area is 2 miles south of Marshall on Route 1, then drive 1 mile west.

Mill Creek Park, 7 miles northwest of Marshall, is operated by the Clark County Park District, the first county park district to be formed in Illinois (1967). The 2,600-acre park encloses Mill Creek Lake, an 811-acre flood control reservoir. The park opened in 1982. The campground has 139 sites (electric hookups available). For reservations call (217) 889–3901. Besides fishing for bass, walleye, catfish, crappie, and bluegill, sample the equestrian or RV trails and the

The Lewis Home

picnicking and swimming areas in the park. Mill Creek Park is on the Lincoln Heritage Trail 1 mile west of Clarksville.

In Marshall visit the **Clark County Museum,** 502 South Fourth Street, built in 1838 as the home of early postmaster Uri Manly. The museum is open free of charge on Sunday 1:00 to 4:00 P.M., and for tours by appointment; (217) 826–8570. At the First Methodist Church, the **Hinners Track Action Pipe Organ** dates from 1909. Find these sights on the walking tour sponsored by the Marshall Area Chamber of Commerce. Write for a brochure: 708 Archer Avenue, P.O. Box 263, Marshall 62441; phone (217) 826–2034.

Casey, on U.S. Highway 40 at Clark County's western border, is famous for **Richard's Farm Restaurant,** which is situated in an old barn. The specialty of the house is a "one-pound pork chop." Enjoy the decor and a seat in the hayloft and perhaps a chat with owners Diane and Gary Richards. Open daily for lunch and dinner; (217) 932–5300. Dinners range from $11 to $24. The restaurant is 1 block east of the intersection of Route 49 and US 40.

Plan a visit for Saturday night and take in Casey's famous **Saturday Night Auction,** held weekly at 5:30 P.M., with collectibles from area shops and individuals. It's held at the auction house in downtown Casey on Route 49; (217) 932–6186. Or stop by the auction house's salesroom any day from 8:00 A.M. to 4:00 P.M.

The Honeybee Trail

This may be Illinois' most international county, with a Paris, Scotland, and even a Palermo within its borders. The county seat, Paris, lies in the heart of a rich farming area. Both Paris and the county date from 1824 when pioneer Samuel Vance donated twenty-six acres. Today's wonderfully ornate **county courthouse** (listed in the National Register of Historic Places) sits at the center of that land. Vance laid out many of the county's earliest roads, some still traveled today. Forty years later those Southern settlers sympathized with the Confederacy during the Civil War and came to be known as Copperheads. When first established, Edgar County extended north all the way to Lake Michigan. Paris was incorporated as a village in 1849 and today approximately 9,000 citizens call Paris home. The downtown architecture harkens back to a simpler era.

A number of historic homes grace this lovely little town. The **Milton K. Alexander Home,** at 132 South Central Avenue, was the residence of a brigadier general in the Illinois Mounted Volunteers during the Black Hawk War of 1832. The house was built in 1826, with additions in 1840. It is now home to the **Bicentennial Art Center,** open Tuesday through Friday 10:00 A.M. to 4:00 P.M.; (217) 466–8130.

The **Daniel Arthur Home,** 414 North Main Street, was built in 1872 and now houses the **Edgar County Historical Society.** Open Wednesday through Friday 9:00 A.M. to 4:00 P.M., other times by appointment. For more information call (217) 463–5305.

Each year at the end of September, the town is abuzz with the excitement of the annual **Paris Homecoming and Honeybee Festival.** Known as the honeybee capital of the nation, the community features the best-known product as well as arts and crafts, an antique car show, and a parade. Concurrently, the museum sponsors **Prairie Settler Day,** with exhibits and demonstrations of pioneer life. Call the Paris Chamber of Commerce for further information, (217) 465–4179.

Twin Lakes Park, the largest of eleven in the city, offers camping (tent or RV, toilets, showers, electric hookups), boating, fishing, picnic areas, and cooking grills. The star attraction of West Lake is a small amusement park.

eastern illinoistrivia

By 1824 Illinois had begun to attract more and more settlers from New England and Europe. In response, those pro-slavery settlers who had originally come from the South felt it was their last chance to push for a convention to revise the Illinois Constitution, hoping to allow slavery in the state. Northern counties were heavily against the convention, while southern counties were heavily for it. Central counties were more ambivalent. Edgar County along the Indiana border near Terre Haute, however, was particularly adamant. Out of 277 votes cast, only three favored a convention, the lowest percentage in the state.

Palermo, in the northwest corner of the county, is the site of a historic meeting and peace council between Ottawa Indian Chief Pontiac and George Croghan, the British deputy superintendent of Indian Affairs. The 1765 parley settled the uprising known as Pontiac's Conspiracy, which occurred shortly after the French and Indian War.

Places to Stay in Eastern Illinois

ARCOLA

Budget Inn,
640 East Springfield Road,
(217) 268–3031

Comfort Inn,
610 East Springfield Road,
(217) 268–4000

ARTHUR

Arthur's Country Inn,
785 East Columbia Street,
(217) 543–3321

CHAMPAIGN

Comfort Inn,
305 West Marketview Drive,
(217) 352–4055

Courtyard by Marriott,
1811 Moreland Boulevard,
(217) 355–0411

Hampton Inn
1200 West University
Avenue,
(217) 337–1100

Hilton Garden Inn,
1501 South Neil Street,
(217) 352–9970

DANVILLE

Comfort Inn Danville,
383 Lynch Drive,
(217) 443–8004

Days Inn,
77 North Gilbert Street,
(217) 443–6600

Fairfield Inn by Marriott,
389 Lynch Drive,
(217) 443–3388

URBANA

Historic Lincoln Hotel,
209 South Broadway
Avenue,
(217) 384–8800

Holiday Inn,
1001 Killarney Street,
(217) 328–7900

Illini Union Guest Rooms,
1401 West Green Street,
(217) 333–3030

Lincoln Lodge,
403 West University Avenue,
(217) 367–1111

Places to Eat in Eastern Illinois

ARCOLA

Days Gone By Restaurant,
125 North County
Road 425E,
(217) 268–4106

Dutch Kitchen,
127 East Main,
(217) 268–3518

CHARLESTON

Stix Restaurant
1412 Fourth Street,
(217) 345–7849

URBANA

Kennedy's,
2560 Stone Creek
Boulevard,
(217) 384–8111

Ned Kelly's Steakhouse,
1601 North Cunningham
Avenue,
(217) 344–8201

SELECTED VISITORS BUREAUS AND CHAMBERS OF COMMERCE

Illinois Bureau of Tourism-Travel Information,
(800) 2–CONNECT

Arthur Visitor Center,
106 East Progress,
Arthur 61911,
(800) 722–6474

Champaign County Convention and Visitors Bureau,
1817 South Neil Street, Suite 201,
Champaign 61820,
(800) 554–7272

Danville Area Convention and Visitors Bureau,
100 West Main Street #146, 61832,
(217) 442–2096

OTHER ATTRACTIONS WORTH SEEING IN EASTERN ILLINOIS

William M. Staerkel Planetarium,
Champaign

Danville Stadium,
Danville

Middle Fork National Scenic River,
Oakwood

Planetarium at Parkland College,
Champaign

Central Illinois

History, Lakes, and Rivers

Illinois may be known for its cornfields, but beginning in the central part of the state, history, lakes, and rivers abound.

Vandalia was the second capital of Illinois, but it was the first capital in the state to build a statehouse from scratch.

The first Illinois statehouse was a rented building in Kaskaskia. It was the seat of state government from 1818 to 1820. When the capital was moved to Vandalia, a two-story frame building was rented and the first session of the Second General Assembly met here on December 4, 1820. On December 9, 1823, fire destroyed the building.

The State Bank Building was remodeled and repaired and became the new statehouse. In spite of the repairs, the building was still in poor condition. It was so unsound that by 1836, no one dared hold a meeting there for fear of the building collapsing.

In August 1836 Gov. Joseph Duncan authorized Auditor Levi Davis to either have the building repaired, rent an assembly hall, or build a new statehouse. It was decided to forget the old plans and build a new statehouse in the style of vernacular Federal architecture.

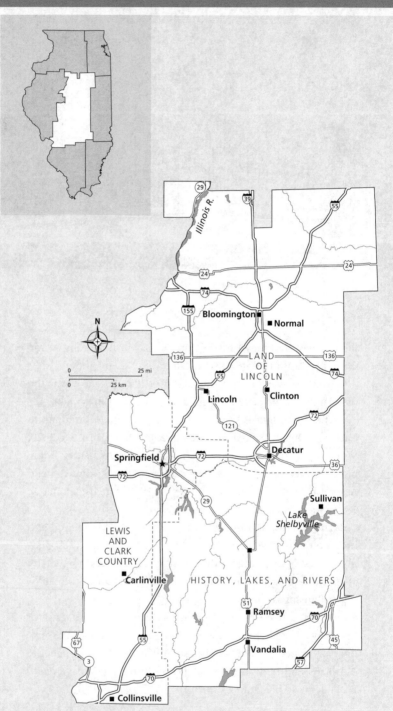

A bill of $16,378.22 was presented to the legislature for the building. The legislature appropriated $10,378.22 and Duncan drew $5,500 more from the contingency fund. The balance was contributed by individuals. The total cost of the building was $23,241.45.

Some of the important issues discussed at the *Vandalia Statehouse* were slavery and the establishment of Illinois as a free state. The first school laws of Illinois were enacted here and the controversial State Bank was debated here. The city of Chicago was also incorporated by the 1836–37 legislature, which included Stephen A. Douglas and Abraham Lincoln.

As the population shifted, proposals were made to move the capital. On February 18, 1837, the General Assembly voted to move the capital to Springfield.

In 1933 the Illinois Department of Conservation began restoration of the old statehouse. Located at 315 West Gallatin, Vandalia, it is open Wednesday through Sunday from 9:00 A.M. to 5:00 P.M. March through October, 9:00 A.M. to 4:00 P.M., Wednesday to Sunday from November through February. It is closed on most major holidays. Admission is free, donations accepted, and guided tours are available. For information call (618) 283–1161.

The area around *Ramsey Lake State Fish and Wildlife Area* was originally called Old Fox Chase Grounds and was popular with fox and raccoon hunters. It was first considered a public recreation area in the late 1920s during the administration of Gov. Len Small. In 1947 the state of Illinois purchased 815 acres for a lake site, and additional land acquisition increased the area to 1,980 acres.

Ramsey Lake is 1 mile northwest of Ramsey off U.S. Highway 51 in a rolling, wooded terrain. The lake was constructed in a valley with an elevated timbered shoreline of almost 4 miles.

Lincoln's Statehouse Days

Historians tell us that Abraham Lincoln saw Illinois' first capital, Vandalia, for the first time as his stagecoach driver "dramatically blew a horn to signal the end of the 75-mile, thirty-six-hour journey" from his home in New Salem. Lincoln roomed with the Whig floor leader during the 1834 legislative session, taking his place when the House of Representatives convened in Vandalia's old bank building's first-floor chambers.

When his first session as a state House member was completed in February 1835, Lincoln was paid $258 for his services and traveling expenses and returned to New Salem by stagecoach in subzero temperatures.

But the taste of real politics had whetted his appetite for more. When he returned to his little log cabin village, he undertook the study of law with new zeal.

AUTHOR'S TOP TEN PICKS

Springfield,
(800) 545–7300

Cahokia Mounds,
Collinsville,
(618) 346–5160

Vandalia Statehouse
State Historic Site,
Vandalia,
(618) 283–1161

Lake Shelbyville,
Findlay,
(800) 874–3529

Horseshoe Lake State Park
Edwardsville,
(618) 931–0270

Lincoln,
(217) 735–2385

Fort Crevecoeur Park,
Creve Coeur,
(309) 694–3193

Scovill Park and Zoo,
Decatur,
(217) 422–5911

Mari-Mann Herb Farm,
Decatur,
(217) 429–1404

Central Illinois Jazz Festival,
Decatur,
(217) 423–7000

Ramsey Lake has fishing, hunting, camping, picnicking, hiking, horseback riding, and snowmobiling facilities. *White Oak Campground* has ninety sites with a sanitary disposal station, electric hookups, flush toilets, and shower building. Two other campgrounds have more rugged facilities. Reservations are available from the site staff.

There are several picnic shelters, which have water, tables, and stoves. Fox Knoll, Coon Ridge, and Blackberry Fork picnic areas are small, shady, secluded knolls that overlook the lake.

Hikers will find a 1-mile designated trail and several miles of unmarked land.

The lake is stocked with largemouth bass, bluegill, red-ear sunfish, channel catfish, and black crappie. Boats can be rented, but only electric trolling motors are allowed. Fishing is also allowed in the small ponds. Check with the park office for catch and size limits on fish.

The horse trail, at the north end, is 13 miles long. A small equestrian campground is 1 mile north of the park entrance.

Dove, squirrel, quail, pheasant, and deer hunting are permitted in season, deer hunting only with a bow. Shotguns only are permitted, and no hunting is allowed inside of Lake Circle Drive.

Ice fishing, snowmobiling, cross-country skiing, sledding, and ice skating are permitted in winter.

For information and reservations contact the Site Superintendent, Ramsey Lake State Fish and Wildlife Area, P.O. Box 97, Ramsey 62080; (618) 423–2215.

Shelby County is blessed with natural resources set aside for public recreation. Within its boundaries lie Hidden Springs, Wolf Creek, and Eagle Creek State Parks; Lake Mattoon; Lake Pana; and—most importantly—*Lake Shelbyville.* This giant lake is one of the state's largest, covering 11,100 acres, with 172 miles of wooded shoreline protected from development by the U.S. Army Corps of Engineers. It reaches 20 miles from Shelbyville, the county seat in the south, to Sullivan in Moultrie County in the north.

Begun in 1963 and completed in 1970 as a flood control project, the lake contains the Kaskaskia and Okaw Rivers. Today the recreational benefits are primary on the minds of most visitors, with camping, boating, fishing, picnicking, hiking, and swimming all available to weekend adventurers. Call (217) 774–2020 for recorded lake fishing conditions. Your catch might be white or largemouth bass, walleye, crappie, channel catfish, northern pike, or any of two dozen or so varieties of fish found in the lake.

There are only three marinas on the lake—Sullivan Marina in Moultrie County and *Lithia Springs* and Findlay in Shelby County. Lithia Springs is closest to Shelbyville and boasts a modest motel, the Lithia Resort, only a short walk away. An alternative accommodation choice, however, is offered in the houseboat rental. Lithia rents spacious houseboats by the week for prices ranging from about $1,000 to $2,000; (217) 774–4121. For that you can bring six or eight people and make it a party. To reach Lithia Springs Marina, drive 3 miles east of Shelbyville on Route 16; then turn north and follow the signs.

Sailboats and fishing boats, water-skiers, and naturalists happily coexist on the lake where deep forested coves seem far away from the flat farmland that's not too distant. On shore, campers will find more than 500 campsites with electrical hookups. During the summer season Corps of Engineer personnel present a schedule of interpretive programs on a range of spiffy topics: "Family Water Safety," "Through an Insect's Eye," "Wild Edible Plants," and others. Stop at the visitors center at the *Dam East Recreation Area,* 1 mile east of Shelbyville on Route 16 (open Memorial Day through Labor Day), which offers audiovisual programs, exhibits, and an unmatched view of the dam. Tours Saturday 3:00 P.M.; Sunday 11:00 A.M. and 1:00 P.M.

Apart from the lake there's plenty to see ashore. In Shelbyville, named for Revolutionary War Gen. Isaac Shelby, drive up Washington Street to view the handsome Civil War–era homes. Downtown the French Second Empire–style *Shelbyville County Courthouse* is a local point of interest. The old, multisided *Chautauqua Auditorium* in Forest Park dates from 1903 and has played host to speakers like William Jennings Bryan and Billy Sunday.

Although farming may be the primary enterprise in Moultrie County, fishing is probably the primary pastime. Sullivan, the county seat, advertises itself as the "northern gateway to beautiful Lake Shelbyville." It shares the 11,000-acre lake with Shelby County to the south. So at the same time that the county claims first place in statewide corn-per-acre production, its production of walleye, crappie, and largemouth bass isn't bad either.

If you're camping, try **Sullivan's Marina and Campground,** south of town on Lake Shelbyville; (217) 728–7338. There are boat rentals and plenty of wooded terrain just across from the **Sullivan Recreation Area,** which has a well-maintained swimming beach.

Sullivan is situated on the Lincoln Heritage Trail. It claims to be the only town with a National Guard unit once commanded by Abraham Lincoln. Less honorably, it was also the scene of a near-riot on the day that both Lincoln and Douglas were in town to give speeches.

The **Little Theatre on the Square** is the town's pride and joy and Sullivan's claim to summer culture fame. Founded in 1957, it bills itself as the only

TOP ANNUAL FESTIVALS

Maple Syrup Time,
Springfield, February–March,
(217) 529–1111

The American Passion Play,
Bloomington, March and April,
(309) 829–3903

Bloomington Gold Corvettes USA Show,
Bloomington, mid-June,
(309) 888–4477

Illinois Shakespeare Festival,
Bloomington, late June–mid-August,
(309) 438–8110

Logan County Fair,
Lincoln, early August,
(217) 732–3311

Illinois State Fair,
Springfield, mid-August,
(217) 782–6661

Mari-Mann Herb Festival,
Decatur, late August–early September,
(217) 429–1404

Springfield Air Rendezvous,
mid-September,
(217) 789–4400

Apple 'n' Pork Festival,
Clinton, late September,
(217) 935–6066

Boo at the Scovill Zoo,
Decatur, mid-to-late October
(217) 421–7435

Christmas on Vinegar Hill,
Mt. Pulaski, mid-November,
(217) 792–3222

Victorian Splendor Light Festival,
Findlay, late November–early January,
(217) 774–2221

Holidazzle

The town of Shelbyville and its surrounds can most likely be viewed from space during its annual *Victorian Splendor Light Festival* where more than 400 displays are lit by thousands of lights. Open from late November to early January, the party begins in downtown Shelbyville on the Friday after Thanksgiving with a parade, decorated stores, tours of the candlelit courthouse, and serenades by a bell choir.

Next head to Forest Park where amazing light displays (revamped in 2006), will delight everyone. The trail passes through the Eagle Creek State Park, where lighted scenes sport a theme, such as Winter Wonderland, Winter Carnival, and Victorian Village. Consider touring by a horse-drawn carriage or a trolley.

The light festival is free, but donations are requested. Open Sunday through Thursday from dusk to 9:00 P.M., Friday and Saturday dusk to 10:00 P.M. Call the Shelbyville Chamber of Commerce for information; (217) 774–2221.

professional Equity theater between Chicago and St. Louis. And each year from early June through mid-August and at Christmas, a program of musicals and plays is presented by the Little Theatre's own company; (217) 728–7375.

On the north side of town, *Wyman Park* and *Wyman Lake* make up forty acres of recreational area offering tennis, a playground, and room for picnicking. Nearby, the *Civic Center* has an Olympic-size indoor heated pool with diving area, racquetball courts, and a gymnasium.

Before leaving town, visit the *Old School Market* at 208 West Jackson Street, where each classroom of this former elementary school is transformed into a unique shop. Buy bears, antiques, candles, and more; (217) 728–3166.

Just outside of town, east on Route 121, is *Mason Point.* Land for the home was donated before the 1900s by Mason Robert A. Miller to build a residence for Masons and their widows. The first building was dedicated in 1904. Today more than 200 retired persons reside here. Its beautiful grounds include a deer park, a landscaped lake, and a greenhouse that furnishes fresh flowers daily for the home. A small collection called *Ward's Museum* is housed in the main building. Open to the public, it includes 10,000 specimens of seashells, plus primitive furniture and other antiques. In a separate building is an old-fashioned ice-cream parlor complete with a marvelous player piano. Visitors are welcome at the home year-round; (217) 728–4394. Hours are 8:00 A.M. to 4:30 P.M. Monday through Friday, 8:00 A.M. to 4:00 P.M. Saturday and Sunday. No admission charge.

Lewis and Clark Country

Commemorating the starting point of the famous expedition to the Pacific Coast is *Lewis and Clark State Park* in Madison County. South of Wood River on Route 3, 2 miles north of Interstate 270, the monument to the expedition consists of eleven concrete pylons that form the rotunda and represent the eleven Trail States traversed by the expedition. Visit the *Lewis and Clark Interpretive Center,* at #1 Lewis and Clark Trail, Hartford; (618) 251–5811.

Cahokia Mounds in Collinsville are recognized as a World Heritage site and a U.S. National Historic Landmark. Take I–55/70 to exit 11 at Route 157, then south to U.S. Highway 40, then west to Cahokia Mounds World Heritage Site.

The most spectacular features are the sixty-five intact mounds. Originally there were approximately 120 mounds and most were ceremonial. *Monk's Mound* is the largest prehistoric mound north of Mexico. You can walk up wood-and-earthen steps to reach the top of the mound for panoramic vistas. Grounds open 8:00 A.M. to dusk. The museum is open daily from 9:00 A.M. to 5:00 P.M., mid-April to Labor Day; Wednesday to Sunday, in winter. Formal or self-guided tours available.

Edwardsville, at the center of the county, boasts seven properties listed on the National Historic Register: the *St. Louis Street Historic District* and the *LeClaire Historic District* are especially notable.

Horseshoe Lake State Park on nearly 3,000 acres on Route 111, west of Edwardsville, offers a wide variety of family fun: picnicking, boating, fishing, hunting, camping and bird-watching. The area was inhabited by Indian groups, with the earliest evidence dating from 8000 B.C. during the Archaic period. Artifacts have been found that fall into the Woodland period, 1000

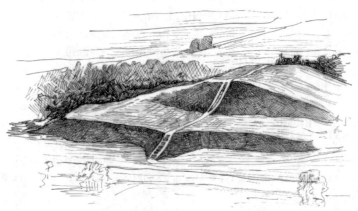

Monk's Mound at Cahokia Mounds

Without a Trace

Here's a mystery worthy of *X-Filers* Mulder and Scully.

What happened to the people who built Cahokia Mounds, the largest prehistoric Indian city north of Mexico?

They just disappeared!

That's what archaeologists can't figure out. This stretch of floodplain just 6 miles east of the Mississippi River was home to the ancient "City of the Sun," a town that was crammed with 20,000 people by A.D. 1100. Homes were arranged in rows around open plazas. More than 100 earthen-man-made mounds dotted the city. And a wooden wall about 15 feet high surrounded about 300 sacred acres of the central city.

It was an advanced civilization, scientists say. But by A.D. 1500, less than 300 years after its heyday, Cahokia was abandoned, leaving no clues about what happened to its people or where they went.

B.C. to A.D. 1000. The park is open year-round except for holidays. Contact the Site Superintendent, Horseshoe Lake State Park, 3321 Highway 111, Granite City 62040; (618) 931–0270.

Turf enthusiasts will savor the excitement at the *Fairmount Park Race Track* on Route 140 in Collinsville. Both harness and thoroughbred racing are on the bill from March through September. Call (618) 345–4300 for schedule.

For an unusual event Collinsville sponsors an annual *Horseradish Festival* each June. These homemade concoctions can set your intestines on fire, though. For more information contact the Collinsville Chamber of Commerce, 221 West Main Street, Collinsville 62234; (618) 344–2884.

Alton was the site of *Alton Prison,* the state's first penitentiary, which opened in 1833. The remnants of a cell block wall have been restored as a monument to this primitive penitentiary, which housed Confederate prisoners during the Civil War. The *Penitentiary Monument* is at the corner of Broadway and Williams Streets near downtown Alton.

The town's colorful history includes Rev. Elijah P. Lovejoy, a newspaper publisher who crusaded against slavery and was shot down by a hostile mob. He was shot on November 8, 1837, and sixty years later, a 90-foot *stone memorial to Lovejoy*—the tallest memorial in the state—was erected near his grave. In 1915 the frame of his printing press went on display in the lobby of the Alton Telegraph Building on Broadway.

Carlinville is home to the Macoupin County Courthouse, aka the *Million Dollar Courthouse,* or more affectionately, the "White Elephant." The court-

Illinois' Witch Hunt

According to my map for Illinois, a bit of the state's Mississippi River coastline is included in the section of the book I call Central Illinois. Well, just ignore this quirky geography classification, and listen to this.

In the late 1600s the French settled in what is called the Illinois French Colonial district in Cahokia, just south of St. Louis (on the Missouri side) on the Mississippi. The French also brought the first West Indian slaves into the area in the 1730s, primarily to work in the region's lead mines.

By 1732 the village of Cahokia listed 182 slaves as part of their cache; there were 106 listed as "Negro" and 76 as "Indian."

These Caribbean slaves brought their own culture with them and, in return for inhumane treatment at the hands of their French owners, poisoned some of their masters "using secret rituals of sorcery." Then, resembling a "mini-Salem" atmosphere, local authorities put several of these slaves on trial, not for murder but for "witchcraft."

Located behind Cahokia's Church of the Holy Family is a large white cross. This spot designates where some of the "poisoned" French victims were buried. Slavery was practiced in this area until the nineteenth century.

house was far beyond the needs of the county and cost much more than anticipated when construction began in 1867. Within a few months the building commissioners and the county court knew that the building would be more than double the $150,000 estimated cost.

It was two-and-a-half years before the building was finished and forty years before it was paid for. When it was finally completed, the move from the old courthouse to the new was quietly made. The eventual cost was $1,300,000.

strangebuttrue

George H. Holliday, the county clerk deemed most responsible for the massive cost overruns of the Macoupin County Courthouse, boarded a train one dark night in 1870 and disappeared without a trace.

The building is made of limestone and consists of two rectangles that cross at the center and are surmounted with a dome. The dome rises 191 feet above the street, and 40-foot columns support the roof. Every door is made of iron, and each outer door weighs more than a ton. All interior trim is of iron or stone. The judge's chair, costing $1,500, is mounted on a track behind the varicolored marble bench.

The **Macoupin County Historical Society** is located in the restored 1850s **Anderson Mansion.** It has a collection of county historical items: a music room with an old grand piano; exhibits of furniture, pottery, china, and glass; stained-glass windows from a German exhibitor at the 1893 World's Fair in Chicago; an 1890 bathroom; and memorabilia of early Macoupin County doctors. The museum celebrates three special events: a Strawberry Festival the last weekend in May, a Fall Festival the second weekend in September, and special holiday decorations for the Christmas season.

A gift shop on the premises carries postcards, county history reprints, and craft items. Hours are March through November, Wednesday 10:00 A.M. to 2:00 P.M., June through August, Wednesday 10:00 A.M. to 2:00 P.M., and Sunday 1:00 to 5:00 P.M. Donations please. The museum is on West Breckenridge Street in Carlinville; (217) 854–2850.

In Mount Olive, in the southeastern part of Macoupin County, visit the *Union Miner's Cemetery,* where a monument to Mary "Mother" Jones is erected. Here you will find a granite obelisk bearing a medallion with the likeness of Mother Jones, the septuagenarian organizer for the United Mine Workers of America and all-around agitator-extraodinaire. Flanking her obelisk are two

Ghosts R Us

The Travel Channel once named Alton the "most haunted town in the United States," even beating perennial spook capital and witch wonder, Salem, Massachusetts. There are doppelgangers in the local coffeehouse, on the waterfront, in the barber shop, at the McPike Mansion, even in the Mineral Springs Hotel.

Why Alton?

It's got some interesting history. In the 1830s Elijah Lovejoy voiced an antislavery opinion that got him killed on the waterfront, where some claim you can still hear ghosts shouting and gunshots replaying the event through time immemorial.

The barbershop ghost emits a perfume smell and seems to hold a fuzzy image of a fancy lady of the Jazz Age.

Ghostbusters claim to have filmed a ghost in a 1996 hunt at the McPike Mansion, later calling it seriously haunted. The image is said to be of a man standing in the window, wearing a striped shirt.

Alton also was the location of a Civil War Confederate prison camp where more than 1,000 troops died. It is said that soldiers wearing the distinctive garb of the Johnny Rebs haunt Mission Lodge, located on the site of the former camp.

Then there's the Mineral Springs Hotel, where nearly eighty years ago a murder occurred at the old swimming pool during a formal party. Seems a gentleman was flirting with the wrong woman and met an untimely end. Well, it seems that ghostly gal, high-topped shoes and all, is still waiting for Mr. Wonderful to return and flirt again.

larger-than-life statues of coal miners with sledgehammers. The cemetery also contains the remains of native son "General" Alexander Bradley, another UMWA organizer. To show their pride in these forward-thinking leaders, Mount Olive holds the annual *Mother Jones Festival* on the last weekend of June. Events include a gravesite memorial service, carnival rides, and parade. For more information, contact the Mount Olive City Hall at (217) 999–4261.

In nearby Lebanon, stop in at *Bumble Bees & Willow Trees,* 214 West St. Louis Street, where you'll find a wide array of handmade gift items, in addition, of course, to all the candy and fudge; (618) 537–4090.

Land of Lincoln

Local residents say, "Lincoln never lived here, but he left a lot of tracks." Abraham Lincoln gave Logan County its name, owned property here, practiced law at the Eighth Judicial Circuit Court at Mount Pulaski, and his funeral train stopped here.

Logan County was a result of Abraham Lincoln's efforts to divide Sangamon County into four smaller counties in 1839. At his suggestion one of the counties was named after Dr. John Logan, a friend of Lincoln's who was instrumental in helping persuade the legislature to move the state capital to Springfield.

The town of *Lincoln* is the only one named after him with his knowledge and consent. The honor evolved from three partners in Postville, who engaged Lincoln as a lawyer to establish joint ownership of the tract of land near Postville. The partners decided to name the town Lincoln, against the advice of Lincoln himself. He said, "Never knew anything named Lincoln that amounted to much."

Customized tours of Lincoln are available from the Abraham Lincoln Tourism Bureau of Logan County at no charge and by appointment only. Phone (217) 732–8687 (TOUR).

Other historical events involving Abraham Lincoln include his and Stephen A. Douglas's visit to the area during their senatorial campaign in the summer of 1858. On November 21, 1859, Lincoln gave a farewell address to the citizens here, and on May 3, 1865, his funeral train was greeted by mourners singing hymns and paying their last respects.

The *Lincoln Gallery,* 111 North Sangamon, has a statue of Lincoln christening the town with a watermelon! Lloyd Ostendorf's oil paintings depict Lincoln's life in Logan County, Washington, D.C., and Gettysburg. The displays are at the State Bank of Lincoln. Hours are Monday through Friday 8:30 A.M. to 5:00 P.M., and Saturday 8:30 A.M. to noon.

Lincoln College was established in 1865 with the donation of ten acres of land by John D. Gillett and Robert B. Latham, two of the college's founding fathers. The groundbreaking for *University Hall* took place on February 12, 1865, Lincoln's last living birthday. The hall is listed in the National Register of Historic Places.

> ## central illinoistrivia
>
> Logan is the geographic center of the state.
>
> There are 2,967 names on the Illinois Vietnam Veterans' Memorial in Springfield's Oak Ridge Cemetery.

The McKinstry Library, on campus, houses the *Hall of Presidents,* an outstanding collection of more than 2,500 artifacts. The **Merrill Gage Statue** showing Lincoln as a student is also on campus.

Lincoln Rustic Tavern, 412 Pulaski Street, is the site where a conspiracy developed to steal Lincoln's body from Oak Ridge Cemetery in Springfield.

The *Postville Courthouse State Historic Site,* 914 Fifth Street, is open seasonally, so call for hours; (217) 732–8930. It was here that Lincoln received his nickname "Honest Abe." The building was completed in 1840, and Lincoln served here as a member of the bar for a quarter of a century. The building was reconstructed in 1953; the original stands in Greenfield Village, Michigan.

Another site of interest in Logan County is the *Atlanta Public Library and Museum,* Race Street, Atlanta (217–648–2112). The museum contains artifacts from the area, and the building is actually Logan County's first bank. The library is listed in the National Register of Historic Places and is one of only a few octagonal-plan libraries in Illinois. Closed Sunday and Monday.

The *Middletown Stage Coach Inn* in Middletown was established in 1832 and still stands. Middletown is believed to be the oldest town in Logan County and served as a midpoint and stagecoach stop on the Peoria-Springfield Road. The *Knapp/Chestnut Building* in Middletown is the oldest brick building in Logan County.

Elkhart Cemetery in Elkhart has the *John Dean Gillett Memorial Chapel,* a charming country chapel that is privately owned and self-supporting. It was built in 1890 and erected in memory of John Dean Gillett, the "Cattle King of America."

Richard S. Oglesby, three-time governor of Illinois, is also buried in this cemetery. Oglesby was the person who nominated Lincoln for the presidency and was the first to call him the "Railsplitter." The *Lincoln Railsplitting Festival,* held the third weekend of September, is a nineteenth-century-style festival featuring a railsplitting contest, flea market, food, and entertainment. Contact

central illinoistrivia

Abe Lincoln's bronze bust, which stands at the entrance to his tomb in Springfield's Oak Ridge Cemetery, has a golden nose thanks to millions of tourists rubbing it for good luck.

the Lincoln Railsplitting Festival and Association, P.O. Box 352, Lincoln 62656; (217) 732–8687.

Mount Pulaski was named for Count Casimir Pulaski, a Polish-born soldier who joined the Continental army of George Washington in 1777. The *Mount Pulaski Courthouse* is Greek Revival architecture and one of the two surviving courthouses from Lincoln's days in the Eighth Judicial Circuit Court. It is located in the town's square and is open Tuesday through Saturday from noon to 4:00 P.M.; (217) 792–3719.

Pekin, once a major port on the Illinois River during the steamboat era, is one of the oldest settlements in Tazewell County. Like many other towns in western Illinois, it was visited by Abraham Lincoln and was used as a fort during the Black Hawk War.

Designated as the county seat of Tazewell County, Pekin takes pride in its past, and has one of the most active genealogical societies in the state. The *Tazewell County Genealogical and Historical Society* library is located at the *Ehrlicher Research Center,* 719 North Eleventh Street in Pekin. Hours are Monday 9:00 A.M. to 1:00 P.M., Tuesday 9:00 A.M. to 1:00 P.M. and 7:00 to 9:00 P.M., Wednesday 9:00 A.M. to 4:30 P.M., Thursday and Friday 9:00 A.M. to 1:00 P.M., and Sunday 2:00 to 4:30 P.M. During open hours, the library is staffed by at least two trained volunteer researchers.

The group features national speakers during its annual fall conference, and many of their services are free. If you can prove, by virtue of your genealogy research, that you are a direct descendant of an original Tazewell County settler, they will present you with a handsome certificate for your wall. For information, call (309) 477–3044.

The Pekin area lies at the boundary between the Bloomington Ridge Plain that was formed by Wisconsin glaciers nearly 22,000 years ago and the Springfield Plain formed by the Illinoisan glaciers about 200,000 years ago. The geological history of the Mississippi and Illinois Rivers can be studied through field trips sponsored by the Illinois Department of Energy and Natural Resources, State Geological Survey Division, Natural Resources Building, 615 East Peabody Drive, Champaign. Call (217) 244–2414 for information.

In mid-September Pekin holds its annual *Marigold Festival* to celebrate the flower that blooms throughout the city. A parade and art fair are part of the celebration. Contact the Pekin Area Chamber of Commerce, 402 Court Street, P.O. Box 636, Pekin 61555; (309) 346–2106, for a list of activities.

The *Spring Lake State Conservation Area*—1 mile south of Pekin on Route 29, 9 miles southwest on Manito Blacktop, and 3 miles west on Spring Lake Blacktop—is a 2,000-acre park with activities like fishing, boating, hiking, cross-country skiing, and picnicking. For information contact the Park Manager, 7982 South Park Road, Manito 61546; (309) 968–7135.

East Peoria, at the base of the bluffs on the floodplain of the Illinois River, is the home of *Fon du Lac Farm Park.* Located on Neumann Drive off Meadows Avenue at U.S. Highway 150, the park offers a timeless picture of farm life. It has duck ponds, a schoolhouse, barn, brooder, blacksmith shop, and hen-

On the Beaten Path

As the state capital, **Springfield** needs no real inclusion in this book. The site of Lincoln's home and the Illinois State Fair, its tourist draws are pretty well-known. Outside of the tourist attractions, however, you'll find Springfield a surprisingly quiet town for a state capital—or, at least, a town that keeps its excitements well hidden from the likes of me. I've been to Springfield a handful of times—mostly in the past couple of years—and have always been left to wonder, what do people do around here for fun?

Now this really shouldn't surprise me, for an old friend of mine, who grew up in Springfield, had always assured me that the town didn't have much going on. Still, some of the tales he would tell would occasionally make the place sound exciting. "We should take a trip down there sometime," I'd tell him at such moments, only to have him respond with a disdainful "Why?" Sure enough, my most recent jaunts down there for research at the Illinois State Historical Library have confirmed me in the wisdom of his attitude. There are some pleasant, casual bars and restaurants you can wander into, but nothing like an active nightlife. Outside of all the political posturing and deal making, apparently, Springfield is just not a place to go for excitement.

But what about my childhood memories of Springfield—of that time my family went to the Illinois State Fair, one of our few Illinois trips? Surely Springfield must have seemed a pretty imposing place to a lad of only eight years? Hmm, come to think of it, we were only there because my older sisters had desperately wanted to see Andy Gibb in concert. And though we visited Lincoln's house, of course, I'm afraid I have more vivid memories of the Steak 'n' Shake menu I came across, featuring a mouth-watering photo of various burgers, fries, and shakes. I'd never been to Steak 'n' Shake, you see, but from that point on—somewhere in the Cattle Pavilion or some such place—I desperately hoped to visit one as soon as possible.

So no, Springfield is not some impressive grand city pulsing with excitement and vitality that etches itself indelibly into your memory. But then it doesn't pretend to be. It's the capital and has Lincoln's home and various other tourist attractions in addition to first-rate research facilities—and that's all, thank you very much. If you want excitement too, well, I guess you'll just have to rely on the cable TV in your hotel room.

house. Animals on the farm are typical of those on many area farms and are free to roam the grounds. Visitors are allowed to pet and feed them. For information call (309) 694–2195.

The **General Store,** on the grounds of the park, offers a variety of toys, country items, and candy. The **Country Kitchen** is open to view antiques, and when a special event is scheduled, baked goods are baked in an old woodstove on the premises. Concessions as well as picnic tables are available. Summer hours are 10:00 A.M. to 3:30 P.M. Tuesday through Sunday. Closed mid-October to May 1 and weekends through May 23. Admission is $2.00 for adults, $1.50 for children.

Fon du Lac Park at Springfield and Steward Avenues in East Peoria has an extensive view of Peoria and the Illinois River Valley. Its more than 2,000 acres on the east bank of the Illinois River offer picnic areas, hiking, golf, tennis, camping, and swimming facilities. Call (309) 699–3923.

But a must-visit in these parts is **Fort Crevecoeur Park** in Creve Coeur, once the site of the explorer La Salle's outpost. The fort, established in 1680, was ill-fated. It was a proposed base for exploration and colonization of the Mississippi Valley, but when La Salle went to Quebec and left Henri Tonti in charge, the dissatisfied troops destroyed the fort and went into the wilderness with all the powder and provisions. The fort was never rebuilt. A granite marker commemorates the founding of the fort and tells the story of its desertion.

The **Fort Crevecoeur Rendezvous** is an annual event held on Memorial Day (Spring Rendezvous), and the fourth weekend in September (Fall Rendezvous). The festivities feature voyageurs with canoes, buckskin-garbed troops, flintlocks, and crafts. Contact Fort Crevecoeur Park at (309) 694–3193 for dates and information.

central illinoistrivia

It's said that Abe Lincoln started studying law books by candlelight in a room at the Onstot Cooper Shop in Lincoln's New Salem Historic Site in Petersburg, where he rented a room.

At the heart of the Illinois prairie sit the sister cities of Bloomington and Normal. The earliest records show the first white people were here around 1800—traders and trappers who made a living roaming the region bordering the Mississippi River. A local legend says that one such group hid a keg of whiskey here in a thick grove of trees, only to have it discovered by an Indian party that finished it off handily. Thus, when the first settlers arrived in 1822, the place was called Keg Grove. Seven years later, when the first post office was established, the settlement called itself Blooming Grove for the area's profusion of flowers.

McLean County was organized in 1830; a year later, Bloomington, laid out on twenty-two and a half acres donated by James Allin just north of Blooming Grove, was designated the county seat. Normal, once North Bloomington, takes its name from what was the State Normal University, now Illinois State University (founded in 1857). Bloomington's university, Illinois Wesleyan, was chartered in 1853. Apart from being university towns and a center of county government, the communities have a rich business and industrial base. For example, the home office of State Farm Insurance Company is based here.

central illinoistrivia

One of the funniest Illinois newspaper headlines ever in print occurred when a downstate publication described the wedding of a couple from different small towns; it read "Oblong Girl Weds Normal Boy."

History and politics have long been intertwined here, as well. Some say Bloomington's David Davis was the man who "made Lincoln president." A noted lawyer and member of the state legislature, Davis was elected judge of the Eighth Judicial Circuit in 1848, a position that put him in frequent contact with the lawyer Abraham Lincoln. At the 1860 Republican Convention, Davis worked behind the scenes to organize support for Illinois' favorite son. In 1862 Lincoln rewarded him with an appointment to the Supreme Court. Davis was elected to the U.S. Senate in 1877.

His mansion, ***Clover Lawn,*** at 1000 East Monroe Drive, is one of Bloomington's top attractions. A state historic site, the twenty-room Italian villa includes much of the original furnishings from the 1872 period. The house is built of yellow-faced brick with stone quoins in the corners. Its tower rises 50 feet above the ground. Inside, eight marble fireplaces decorate rooms done in high Victorian style, a fine example of upper-class life of the period. The home is open from 9:00 A.M. to 5:00 P.M. Wednesday through Sunday. Admission is free, though a $2.00 donation is suggested. Call for further details: (309) 828–1084.

Another mansion turned museum is the ***Ewing Manor Cultural Center,*** the former home of Hazel Buck Ewing, whose father was associated with William Wrigley Jr. in the foundation of the Wrigley Company of Chicago. Also known as the Ewing Castle, the 1929 estate is done in the style of a Norman castle. On the death of the wealthy philanthropist, the property became part of the Illinois State University Foundation. The home can be seen by appointment only. Emerson Street at Towanda Avenue; (309) 829–6333.

Each June through mid-August, the ***Illinois Shakespeare Festival*** presents Shakespearean plays here in repertory nightly Tuesday through Sunday.

Picnicking on the lawn of the Ewing Manor is especially popular with festival-goers; (309) 438–8110 or (309) 828–9814.

The **McLean County Historical Society Museum** catalogues the county's past with exhibits of Indian artifacts, decorative arts, military souvenirs, and crafts. Upstairs there's a neat gift shop and genealogy collection. One of the star attractions is the **"Tilbury Flash,"** a 1930s racing plane built in Bloomington, and one of the smallest piloted planes in the world. Exhibits change throughout the year. Open Monday and Wednesday through Saturday 10:00 A.M. to 5:00 P.M.; Tuesday 10:00 A.M. to 9:00 P.M.; Sunday 1:00 to 5:00 P.M. September to May; Adults $5.00 and children free. The museum is housed in the old McLean County Courthouse at 200 North Main Street; (309) 827–0428.

glacierflats

You may have read that Illinois is one of the flattest states on all the prairie. It's true. And travelers here will discover that the last great glacier, which swept through central Illinois about 10,000 years ago, leveled much of the local topography.

So, indeed, Illinois' central heartland is truly an outpost for flatlanders.

Of course, this makes it easier to get around, for all you have to do is follow roads that cut a swath through seemingly endless cornfields. Negatively speaking, it can make for some spectacularly boring driving. On the positive side, the landscape is a kind of throwback to the wide open prairie that greeted the pioneers.

At the Interstate Center in Bloomington, 2301 West Market Street, you'll find the **Third Sunday Market** is like an attic full of collectibles and antiques. Show admission is $5.00; parking is free. For information phone (309) 452–7926. The May through October event is managed by Don and Carol Raycraft, authorities and authors on country antiques.

Illinois State University provides plenty to keep a visitor busy. Stop at the university art galleries, the Funk Gem and Mineral Museum, the planetarium, the Hudelson Museum of Agriculture, or the school's historical museum. The Adlai E. Stevenson Memorial Room honors one of Bloomington's most famous citizens. And there really is an academic ivory tower here—Watterson Towers, at twenty-eight stories the world's largest college residence hall. Most campus attractions are free, and tours can be arranged. Call (309) 438–2111 for ISU information. Regular performing arts events are scheduled at Braden Auditorium; call (309) 438–2222.

Illinois Wesleyan, too, boasts a number of treasures including Evelyn Chapel, a focal point of the private school. The chapel is an example of Moravian-style architecture in Flemish patterned brick. The interior woodwork and acoustics are superb. Sheean Library holds the Indian pottery collection of Maj. John Wesley Powell, a former faculty member and first explorer of the Colorado River and Grand Canyon. Call (309) 556–1000 for campus information. McPherson Theater has a busy schedule of productions throughout the year; (309) 556–3232.

central illinoistrivia

The last Illinois buffalo roamed these parts as late as 1808—when it was promptly killed by hunters.

The Oliver Parks Telephone Museum in Springfield displays over a hundred antique telephones.

Bloomington's **Miller Park Zoo,** 1020 South Morris Avenue, is one of Illinois' best. Besides viewing rare and endangered species, you may interact with site zookeepers. Check the feeding schedule when you arrive. The **Tropical America Rainforest** features twenty species of free-flying birds; some of the other exhibits showcase sun bears, red pandas, lemurs, Galapagos tortoises, sea lions, river otters, and bald eagles. Ask about the **Junior Zookeepers** program for junior high and high school students. Open daily except Thanksgiving and Christmas day; 9:30 A.M. to 4:30 P.M.; adults $4.00, seniors and children (three to twelve) $3.00; (309) 434–2250.

A major seasonal event is Bloomington's **American Passion Play.** Since 1924 community players have enacted the life of Christ, from his Baptism to the Resurrection, in an annual spring tradition with a cast of more than 300 actors. The schedule tracks Easter, so call; Bloomington Center for the Performing Arts, 110 East Mulberry Street; (309) 829–3903.

At 901 North McLean in Bloomington, is the site of the **Adlai E. Stevenson I** home. Stevenson was vice president of the United States from 1893 to 1897. Both he and his grandson Adlai Stevenson II, former governor of Illinois, are buried at Evergreen Cemetery here. Another Illinois governor—this one a Republican—also lived in Bloomington. Joseph W. Fifer, governor of Illinois from 1889 to 1893, lived at 909 North McLean, near the Stevensons. Both homes are privately owned and not open for tours.

Southwest of the county's two major cities is historic **Funks Grove.** One of the county's first settlements, several of the original buildings still remain—the Funk Prairie Home, the 1865 Funks Grove Church, and the "sirup" factory. Here, 1,200 gallons per year of maple syrup are produced by the same family that first settled here in 1824. Visit the **Funk Gem and Mineral Museum** by appointment. To reach Funks Grove take Interstate 55 south to the Shirley exit; the town is about 10 miles southwest of Bloomington. Call (309) 874–3360 for information on spring maple tapping; store open March through August.

In Lexington stands the **Patton Cabin,** built in 1829 by John Patton, one of the county's first white settlers. Open Sunday 2:00 to 4:00 P.M., June through August. Free.

For campers **Moraine View State Park,** near rural LeRoy, offers 1,700 acres of rolling terrain plus the 160-acre Dawson Lake. Boating, fishing, camping (142 sites, most with electrical hookup), and hiking are popular activities. Call (309) 724–8032.

The center of this county, situated at the center of the state, is **Clinton Lake,** a 5,000-acre cooling lake for the Illinois Power Company's nuclear power plant. (The plant has been operating since 1987.) With 130 miles of wooded shoreline, the lake development is managed by the Illinois Department of Conservation, which has thoughtfully stocked it with largemouth and smallmouth bass, walleye, crappie, and catfish. Sailboats share the lake with fishing boats, which stop for supplies at Dockside Marina, off Route 10, about 8 miles east of Clinton. In season, hunting is allowed on the land surrounding the lake; (217) 935–8722.

central illinoistrivia

Illinois has three nicknames: Inland Empire, Land of Lincoln, and Prairie State.

Three miles southeast of Clinton is **Weldon Springs State Recreation Area,** just east of US 51. Prior to 1936 the park was privately owned and the site of a well-known chautauqua each summer. From 1901 to 1920 programs of educational, cultural, or religious interest were presented. By 1904 the yearly event drew so many people that it was necessary to build an auditorium accommodating 4,500 people. They came to hear the stars of the day: William Jennings Bryan, President William Howard Taft, Helen Keller, evangelist Billy Sunday, and temperance leader Carry Nation, among others. The park is open year-round and offers campsites (electric hookups, toilets), picnicking area, hiking trails, fishing, and boating. Weldon Springs has a special handicapped-accessible fishing dock, as well; (217) 935–2644.

The **DeWitt County Museum** is located in the **C. H. Moore Homestead** in Clinton, a restored Victorian mansion listed in the National Register of Historic Places. The 1867 Italianate residence was home to Clinton H. Moore, a former law partner of Abraham Lincoln. The architectural highlight here is a two-story library with a vaulted ceiling and an iron railing around the open upper gallery. Children will love the antique doll collection and the child's room with its child-size four-poster bed. Period rooms, a carriage collection, and the farm and railroad museum are among the exhibits. On the last weekend in September the museum sponsors an **Apple 'n' Pork Festival,** featuring stick-to-the-ribs home cooking with plenty of smoked ham, pork sandwiches, and apple cider. During the Christmas season the house is beautifully decorated in the style of the late 1800s. Candlelight tours are also available in December. The museum is open April through December, Tuesday through Saturday 10:00 A.M. to 5:00 P.M. and Sunday 1:00 to 5:00 P.M., free admission. At 219 East Woodlawn; (217) 935–6066.

A *statue of Lincoln* at the square commemorates the speech delivered in Clinton in 1848 in which Lincoln supposedly remarked, "You can fool all the people some of the time and some of the people all the time, but you cannot fool all the people all the time."

Decatur has a cornucopia of architectural styles popular from the Civil War to the Great Depression. Eighty acres of its buildings are listed in the National Register of Historic Places. In addition, the Historic and Architectural Sites Commission has published five walking tours, which take you past examples of Italianate, Second Empire, Queen Anne, Romanesque Revival, Shingle, Stick, Georgian Revival, Tudor, Art Deco, and neoclassical styles. The walking tours are free and can be obtained from the Decatur Area Convention and Visitors Bureau, 202 East North Street, Decatur 62523; (217) 423–7000.

Highlights of the tours include the *Milliken Homestead* at 125 North Pine, a Victorian mansion with fine woodwork, leaded glass, and elegant fireplaces. The *Oglesby Mansion,* 421 West Williams, is an Italianate-style building with diamond-shaped glass in its bay windows. It was the home of the former U.S. senator and three-time governor of Illinois, Richard J. Oglesby. Open June

The Milliken Homestead

Dern'd Yankees!

In the 1820s, most settlers in central Illinois were originally from Southern states like Tennessee and Kentucky. Christiana Holmes Tillson moved to the region in 1822 from Massachusetts. Her memoir, *A Woman's Story of Pioneer Illinois,* records many examples of the cultural divide between settlers from the South and those from New England. One day she offered a piece of pie to the wife of a Southern settler who rented a field from her and her husband—not just any piece of pie, mind you, but a slice of Yankee pie. The woman, according to Tillson, was taken aback, as if Tillson had just uttered a bad word.

"I didn't think you would say the like of that," the woman finally replied, "I allus knowed youens were all Yankees, but Billy said 'Don't let on that we know it, kase it'll jest make them mad.'"

Tillson told her that she was proud to be called a Yankee and that the woman didn't need to worry about using the phrase. Whereupon they discussed a few misperceptions the woman had of Yankees, such as the "nasty truck" they put in their bread—pearl ash—which the woman figured to be full of dead flies, bugs, and cricket legs.

The heartwarming net result of this talk was that the two women began to understand each other's culture a wee bit better. So remember that, my northern Illinois brethren. The next time we find our central and southern Illinoisian friends looking askance at our ways, we can pull out a big ol' slice of Yankee pie and get the dialogue a-goin'.

through August, Wednesday and Saturday 1:00 to 4:00 P.M.; March to November, open the last Sunday of the month 2:00 to 4:00 P.M.; Christmas house tours also. Free, but donation appreciated; (217) 429–9422.

The ***Scovill Children's Zoo*** is a special treat because it is designed to look as if the animals and visitors are in the same environment. The zoo encompasses ten acres and lies above the east shore of Lake Decatur. It is open 10:00 A.M. to 7:00 P.M. in the summer and on weekends, April through Labor Day, and 10:00 A.M. to 4:00 P.M. when school is in session. The zoo features rides on the ZO&O Express; admission is $3.75 for adults, $2.25 for children, and $2.75 for seniors. Tours are available by advance arrangement.

To get to Scovill Zoo, take U.S. Highway 36 east and cross Lake Decatur to 71 South Country Club Road. For information call (217) 422–7346.

The ***Macon County Historical Society Museum,*** 5580 North Fork Road, prides itself on preserving and presenting the heritage of Macon County. The museum has a collection of historic artifacts as well as examples of 1890s houses, a prairie village, and an 1860s schoolhouse. A hands-on approach is used in the displays so you can see, smell, and touch the past as well as the present. Museum hours are Tuesday through Saturday 1:00 to 4:00 P.M.; (217) 422–4919.

The *Mari-Mann Herb Farm and Gingerbread House* is at the north end of St. Louis Bridge Road. Visitors can walk among the herb beds, wildflower fields, deer trails, and formal gardens. The Gingerbread House offers herb products, Special Spoon Herbal Sauce, herbal jellies, and other herbal condiments. Teas, herbs, gourmet spices, fragrances with potpourri, and essential and fragrant oils are also sold.

The herb greenhouse carries a selection of year-round herbal plants.

The farm is open 9:00 A.M. to 5:00 P.M. Monday through Saturday and noon to 5:00 P.M. Sunday. Demonstrations, luncheons, teas, tours, and classes are available by appointment. Contact Mari-Mann Herb Company Inc., 1405 Mari-Mann Lane, Decatur 62521; (217) 429–1404.

Decatur is also the home of the *Central Illinois Jazz Festival,* which attracts thousands of jazz musicians and enthusiasts from across the nation. Admission is $8.00. For information call the Decatur Area Convention and Visitors Bureau at (217) 423–7000.

Places to Stay in Central Illinois

BLOOMINGTON-NORMAL

Best Inns of America,
1905 West Market Street,
Bloomington,
(309) 827–5333

Best Western University Inn,
6 Traders Circle,
Normal,
(309) 454–4070

Chateau Hotel,
1601 Jumer Drive,
Bloomington,
(309) 662–2020

Comfort Suites,
310B Greenbriar Drive,
Normal,
(309) 452–8588

Hampton Inn West,
906 Maple Hill Road,
Bloomington,
(309) 829–3700

Holiday Inn Express,
1715 Parkway Plaza,
Normal,
(309) 862–1600

Signature Inn,
101 South Veterans Parkway,
Normal,
(309) 454–4044

DECATUR

Country Inn and Suites Hotel,
5150 Hickory Point Frontage Road,
(217) 872–2402

Days Inn,
333 North Wyckles Road,
(217) 422–5900

Hawthorn Suites Limited,
2370 South Mt. Zion Road,
(217) 864–9311

Wingate Inn,
5170 Wingate Drive,
(217) 875–5500

PEKIN

Concorde Inn and Suites,
2801 East Court Street,
(309) 347–5533

Holiday Inn Express,
3615 Kelly Avenue,
(309) 353–3305

SHELBYVILLE

Shelbyville Inn,
816 West Main Street,
(800) 342–9978

SPRINGFIELD

Best Inns of America,
500 North First Street,
(217) 522–1100

Comfort Suites,
2620 South Dirksen Parkway,
(217) 753–4000

Courtyard by Marriott,
3462 Freedom Drive,
(217) 793-5300

Crowne Plaza Springfield,
3000 South Dirksen Parkway,
(217) 529-7777

Hilton Springfield,
700 East Adams Street,
(217) 789-1530

Holiday Inn Express,
3050 South Dirksen
Parkway,
(217) 529-7771

Mansion View Inn
and Suites,
529 South Fourth Street,
(217) 544-7411

Places to Eat in Central Illinois

BLOOMINGTON

Central Station Cafe,
220 East Front Street,
(309) 828-2323

Jim's Steak House,
2307 East Washington Street,
(309) 663-4142

COLLINSVILLE

Horseshoe Lounge,
410 St. Louis Road,
(618) 345-9350

LINCOLN

Blue Dog Inn,
111 South Sangamon Street,
(217) 735-1743

SPRINGFIELD

Maldaner's,
222 South Sixth Street,
(217) 522-4313

Saputos Twin Corner,
801 East Monroe Street,
(217) 544-2523

Sebastian's Hide-Out
221 South Fifth Street,
(217) 789-8988

SELECTED VISITORS BUREAUS AND CHAMBERS OF COMMERCE

Illinois Bureau of Tourism/Travel
Information,
(800) 2-CONNECT

Bloomington–Normal Area
Convention and Visitors Bureau,
3201 Cira Drive, Suite 201,
Bloomington, 61704
(309) 665-0033

Collinsville Convention and
Visitors Bureau,
221 West Main Street,
Collinsville, 62234
(618) 344-2884

Decatur Area Convention and
Visitors Bureau,
202 East North Street,
Decatur, 62523
(217) 423-7000

Springfield Convention and
Visitors Bureau,
109 North Seventh Street,
Springfield, 62701
(217) 789-2360

OTHER ATTRACTIONS WORTH SEEING IN CENTRAL ILLINOIS

Beer Nuts Products,
Bloomington

Miller Park Zoo,
Bloomington

Prairie Aviation Museum,
Bloomington

Children's Museum of Illinois,
Decatur

Andersen Prairie,
Pana

Dana-Thomas State Historic Site,
Springfield

Daughters of Union Veterans of the Civil War Museum,
Springfield

Illinois State Capitol,
Springfield

Illinois State Museum,
Springfield

Lincoln Memorial Garden,
Springfield

Lincoln National Home State Historic Site,
Springfield

Old State Capitol State Historic Site,
Springfield

Oliver Parks Telephone Museum,
Springfield

Washington Park Botanical Gardens,
Springfield

Western Illinois

River Towns

The most impressive feature of Quincy, a river town on the east bank of the Mississippi River, is its architecture. Stately mansions and fine old commercial buildings of Italianate, Greek Revival, Romanesque, Queen Anne, Prairie, and Moorish designs fill the town.

The *John Wood Mansion,* 425 South Twelfth Street, is an example of Greek Revival architecture. The home was built in 1835 by John Wood, founder of Quincy and a former governor of Illinois. Take an escorted tour of the restored home and see the audiovisual presentation. The *Osage Orangerie Gift Shop* is on the premises and offers handcrafted items reminiscent of the early nineteenth century.

The fourteen-room mansion is listed in the National Register of Historic Places. It was originally located across Twelfth Street, but Wood had the house moved to its present site in 1864.

On display are furnishings and many personal items of the Wood family as well as objects recalling Adams County's history. Included are a Victorian dollhouse, the first piano in Quincy, Quincy-made stoves, a table used by Abraham Lincoln,

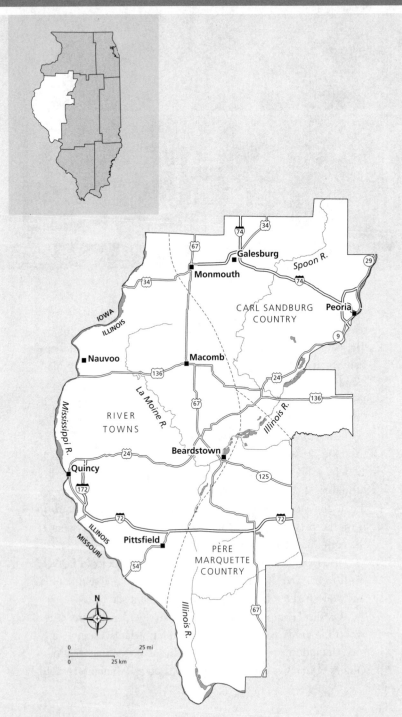

IOWA
ILLINOIS

Galesburg

Monmouth

Spoon R.

CARL SANDBURG
COUNTRY

Peoria

Nauvoo

Macomb

La Moine R.

Mississippi R.

RIVER
TOWNS

Illinois R.

Beardstown

Quincy

ILLINOIS
MISSOURI

Pittsfield

PERE
MARQUETTE
COUNTRY

Illinois R.

N

0   25 mi
0   25 km

a chandelier from a Mississippi River steamboat, and a sunstone from the Mormon Temple in Nauvoo.

Museum hours are 1:00 to 4:00 P.M. daily, April through May and September through October. Tours are conducted daily on the quarter hour. Admission is $3.00 for adults, $1.50 for students; (217) 222–1835.

The *Quincy Museum* is housed in the Newcomb Stillwell Mansion. Built in 1891, it is listed in the National Register of Historic Places. The exterior has leafy carved ornamentation and window transom bars of solid stone. Building materials of contrasting colors and textures enhance its bold facade and forceful design. It is an example typical of American architectural style of the late 1800s.

The museum is well organized. On the first floor, guests view a restored Victorian mansion. The second floor features changing exhibits and local history memorabilia. The third floor is a kid's haven, featuring dinosaurs, wildlife, and Native American artifacts and history. In May there's an old-fashioned yard and bake sale fundraiser on the museum grounds. Around Thanksgiving, the museum closes briefly, and then emerges festively decorated for Christmas. December is busy with the celebration of St. Nicolas Day and holiday open houses. The museum is located at 1601 Maine Street, Quincy; (217) 224–7669.

AUTHOR'S TOP TEN PICKS

Lincoln's New Salem State
Historic Site,
Petersburg,
(217) 632–4000

Wildlife Prairie Park,
Peoria,
(309) 676–0998

Village of Elsah,
(618) 374–1568

Père Marquette State Park,
Grafton,
(618) 786–3323

Quincy,
(800) 978–4748

Bluffdale Vacation Farm,
Eldred,
(217) 983–2854

Nauvoo,
(217) 453–6648

Carl Sandburg Birthplace
State Historic Site,
Galesburg,
(309) 342–2361

Villa Kathrine,
Quincy,
(217) 224–3688

The 1898 Duryea Motor Trap Car,
Peoria Public Library, Peoria,
(309) 497–2000

Hours are Tuesday through Sunday 1:00 to 5:00 P.M. Guided tours are available. Admission is $3.00 for adults, $2.00 for students, and free for children under five.

The *Villa Kathrine,* 532 Gardner Expressway; (217) 224–3688, is a Moorish-style castle. It is located on a bluff overlooking the Mississippi River and is listed in the National Register of Historic Places. The visitor center is manned by volunteers. Call ahead for hours. Admission is $3.00 for adults, $1.50 for children six to twelve, and free for children under six.

And the *Quincy Art Center* is located on the grounds of the *Lorenzo Bull Home,* 1515 Jersey Street. The carriage house was designed by Joseph Lyman Silsbee, a prominent Chicago architect and mentor of Frank Lloyd Wright. The center contains a permanent collection of paintings, sculpture, and graphics, and a library of art books and periodicals. It also has temporary and traveling exhibits. Hours are noon to 4:00 P.M. Tuesday through Friday, 1:00 to 4:00 P.M. Saturday and Sunday; adults $2.00, seniors, students, children $2.00; (217) 223–5900.

Quincy has a number of other museums that are worth visiting. The *Mississippi Valley Antique Auto Museum* is located in Quincy's All-American Park on the banks of the Mississippi River. Thirty antique cars and related displays make up the exhibit. The museum's collection includes a 1917 Chevrolet Royal Mail Roadster, a 1911 Little, a St. Louis–built Diana, a 1901 Columbia Electric, a Ford Roadster pickup featured in television's *Hee Haw,* and a horse-drawn hearse.

The museum is located at Front and Cedar Streets; (217) 223–1000. Hours are noon to 4:00 P.M. Sunday. Admission is $2.00 for adults, children twelve and under $1.00.

Fountain of Youth

There was a time in Illinois history when people came from all parts of the Midwest to take advantage of waters known for their alleged wonderful curative powers. The legendary medicinal value of the region's springwater was thought to cure everything from skin conditions to ulcers.

Today you can see for yourself when visiting Siloam Springs State Park, boasting 3,300 acres of pristine natural beauty, to say nothing of its "sparkling water" lake, surrounded by dense forests dotted with wildflowers in the spring.

Can these waters still cure what's ailing you? Depends. If you're looking for a natural way to reduce stress and tension, then I guess a stay at this state park and a splash in these "curative waters" will do the trick just fine. Call (217) 894–6205.

TOP ANNUAL EVENTS

Chocolate Festival,
Galesburg, early March,
(309) 343–2485

Dogwood Festival,
Quincy, early May,
(217) 223–1000

Steamboat Festival,
Peoria, June,
(309) 681–0696

Railroad Days,
Galesburg, late June,
(309) 343–2485

Taste of Peoria,
Peoria, mid-August,
(309) 681–0696

Nauvoo Grape Festival,
Nauvoo, early September,
(217) 453–6648

National Stearman Fly-In,
Galesburg, early September,
(309) 343–6409

State Corn Husking Contest,
Monmouth, early October,
(309) 734–3181

East Peoria Festival of Lights,
East Peoria, late November–December,
(309) 676–0303

The *Gardner Museum of Architecture and Design* is in the Old Public Library Building built in 1888. At Fourth and Maine Streets, it is open from 1:00 to 4:00 P.M. Wednesday through Saturday. The museum contains stained-glass windows from Quincy churches; photographs; and examples of terra-cotta, metal, fine woodwork, and other ornamentation from early Quincy homes. Admission is $3.00 for adults, $2.00 for students; (217) 224–6873.

All Wars Museum, 1707 North Twelfth Street; (217) 222–8641, displays military memorabilia with a military library and films. It is on the grounds of the Illinois Veterans Home, one of the nation's largest. Open Monday through Friday 1:00 to 4:00 P.M., weekends 9:00 A.M. to 4:00 P.M.; admission is free.

The *Lincoln-Douglas Valentine Museum,* 101 North Fourth Street; (217) 224–3355, has a unique collection of old and unusual valentines on exhibit. Open by appointment only. Donation requested.

Quincy's public square at the center of the uptown historical district was originally called John's Square, honoring the U.S. president for whom both Adams County and Quincy were named. The square became *Washington Square* in 1857. One year later it was the site of the sixth senatorial debate between Lincoln and Douglas. The spot is marked by a commemorative plaque sculpted by Lorado Taft in 1935.

Riverview Park on the northeast corner of Quincy, overlooking the Mississippi River, has a statue of George Rogers Clark. This was the site of the Black Hawk War skirmish in Quincy. Notable Quincy residents, including former Illinois governor John Wood and early pioneer John Tillson, are laid to rest in *Woodland Cemetery* on South Fifth Street. The cemetery originally contained the *Quincy National Cemetery,* a U.S. government–maintained burial plat for Civil War soldiers, before it was moved to Quincy's *Graceland Cemetery,* just one block east of Thirty-sixth and Maine Streets. Consequently, interesting Civil War–era monuments remain on the Woodland grounds. The cemeteries are open daily from dawn to dusk.

Quincy celebrates its annual *Dogwood Festival* the first week in May. Festivities include a parade, crafts fair, and military band concert along with the sight of all the dogwood trees in bloom. For a list of events and times, contact the Quincy Chamber of Commerce at (217) 222–7980.

Pittsfield, the county seat of Pike County, was a genuine transplant of New England culture when it was founded in 1833. The settlers came from Pittsfield, Massachusetts, and purchased the site from the federal government for $200.

Pork packing became the chief local industry, and Pittsfield has been nicknamed the "Pork Capital of the World," with 400,000 to 500,000 hogs marketed there annually. Pittsfield and Pike County residents celebrate *Pig Days* with a day of activities and pork sandwiches and a pork chop dinner. The festival is held during early July, and the Chamber of Commerce is happy to supply information. Write the chamber at 224 West Washington Street, Pittsfield 62363, or call (217) 285–2971.

Pittsfield also has a *Fall Festival* around Labor Day that signals the beginning of the harvest season. Again, the Chamber of Commerce has information.

olemissbliss

Anybody who travels in western Illinois soon discovers that the geography of the region is dominated by the Mississippi River. Especially in far western Illinois, the winding channels of the Mississippi and the high, tree-studded bluffs that line its shores provide great vistas for off-the-beaten-path wanderers, especially along the Great River Road, a National Scenic Byway that is marked by large green signs.

And once you head to the southern reaches of the western portion of Illinois, you start to arrive at the beginnings of the Ozark Plateau, covered with dense forests, hills that stack up to more than 1,000 feet high, and deep limestone and sandstone canyons.

But you'll learn more about this magnificent and undiscovered part of Illinois in later chapters.

There are nine Pittsfield homes still standing that boast a provenance connecting them to Abraham Lincoln. Since all but one are privately owned, a driving tour is the most suitable way to view them. Stop by the Pittsfield Chamber of Commerce or call (217) 285–2971 for a map.

The *Shastid House* at 326 East Jefferson Street was home base for Lincoln when he practiced law in Pike County. The cabin is maintained by the *Pike County Historical Society*, has been restored, and is the only historic home open for tours. Visit May through October, Thursday to Saturday 11:00 A.M. to 3:00 P.M.; free admission.

Two of Lincoln's personal presidential secretaries, John G. Nicolay and John Hay, lived in Pittsfield: Nicolay's boyhood home, called the *Garbutt House* (the name of his foster parents), stands at 500 East Washington Street, and the *Hay House* is at 322 West Washington Street. These men also collaborated on a ten-volume biography of Lincoln after his assassination.

western illinoistrivia

Oquawka's claim to fame might be the Allaman Covered Bridge; built in 1866. It is listed on the National Register of Historic Places. The structure is 104 feet long and spans Henderson Creek in Henderson County.

Although no students currently matriculate at the *Old East School* at 400 East Jefferson Street, the converted school remains busy since it is home to an interesting collection of Pike County artifacts and the Pike County Historical Society. The building was designed by architect John Mills Van Osdel, and is one of just two remaining examples of his work. It is protected by the designation of the National Register of Historic Places. Changing exhibits include china and dishware, furniture, vintage wedding gowns, a dray wagon, and a printing press. There are also photographs and a genealogy library for researchers. Open from May to October 31, Thursday through Saturday 11:00 A.M. to 3:00 P.M. and for special holiday and summer events. Admission is free.

The *Pittsfield Theatre Guild* presents its plays on the second-floor stage of the old school. Contact the Chamber of Commerce for show schedule at (217) 285–2971.

Another site to visit is the old *Pike County Courthouse.* Architect Henry Elliot created a remarkable structure that has been called one of the most beautiful courthouse buildings in Illinois. Featuring an octagonal footprint, the chiseled exterior stonework is a prime example of stonemason Robert Franklin's craftsmanship. Open during regular business hours, 9:00 A.M. to 4:00 P.M. Visitors are welcome to view the courthouse interior, which features stained-glass windows, balcony, and curved staircases.

Pine Lakes Camping and Fishing Resort, 1½ miles north of U.S. Highway 36 near Pittsfield, has camping facilities that include water and electric hookups, laundromat, camp store, recreation room, paddleboat rental, rowboats, bathhouse, and snack bar. Enjoy swimming with attendants on duty, fishing in a forty-five-acre lake, horseshoe pits, hayrides, and a playground.

Besides campgrounds, cottages and cabins are available for rent. Contact Pine Lakes Resort, 1405 Lakeview Heights, Pittsfield 62363; (217) 285–6719.

Pike County has its share of natural beauty. Bound by the Mississippi River on the west and the Illinois River on the east, it has rolling countryside and majestic bluffs. Streams, ponds, and small lakes abound for fishing, boating, and swimming. Hunting and camping grounds, including privately owned camps, are also plentiful.

Now a trading center for coal mining and a grain- and fruit-growing region, Rushville began as a tiny wilderness village of twelve families in 1825. It was named for a famous Philadelphia surgeon, Dr. Benjamin Rush. It has stayed a small town with only 3,212 residents. As the county seat of Schuyler County, the community is rich in nineteenth-century history. During the Black Hawk War, Abraham Lincoln and his troops camped near Rushville. It is believed that in 1844 Governor Ford left Springfield with a company of militia and camped overnight in the town square. A tablet in the center of the town square reads, ABRAHAM LINCOLN ADDRESSED THE PEOPLE OF RUSHVILLE ON OCTOBER 20TH, 1858. The event was memorable as Lincoln was jeered by townspeople sympathetic to the Democratic Party. Lincoln also practiced law in the county courthouse that once stood on this spot.

When Stephen A. Douglas came to Rushville to speak in the senatorial campaign of 1858, his followers arranged a welcome that would be remembered in the town's history. They borrowed a cannon from the nearby community of Beardston, brought it over to the town square, and loaded it with a heavy charge of powder and wet scraps of leather. When the salute to Douglas was fired, the cannon was blown into pieces; miraculously, no one was hurt.

The *Schuyler County Courthouse* dates back to 1881. The building is open for visitors from 8:00 A.M. to 4:00 P.M. and questions can be answered at (217) 322–4734. It is a two-story building of faded brick and topped with a square clock tower. The cornerstone is dated according to the Masonic calendar and reads JUNE 24 A.L. 5881. The first county building was a log cabin on the north side of the square. In 1829 it was replaced by a plain unornamented brick building, which served until the present courthouse was built on the corner of Lafayette and Congress Streets.

The *Schuyler-Brown County Historical Society* at 200 South Congress, 62681 (on U.S. Highway 24, just a block from the courthouse corner) displays genealogical materials and the history of Schuyler and Brown Counties. The center of the building is an old jailhouse. A collection of undertakers' sticks, used to measure the deceased for custom-built coffins, is on display. The society's museum is open weekdays 1:00 to 5:00 P.M. March through November, and on Sunday the rest of the year.

At the same location is the *Jail Museum*, open daily 1:00 to 5:00 P.M. April 1 to November 1. Winter hours are Saturday and Sunday 1:00 to 5:00 P.M. Admission is free. The museum is open at other times by appointment only. Special exhibits change monthly. Call (217) 322–6975 for more information about these museums.

strangebuttrue

Norma Jean, a 30-year old circus elephant, was chained to the only tree in the Oquawka town square on the morning of July 17, 1972, when a sudden storm blew in. Her trainer rushed to undo her chain and bring her into shelter, but at that moment the tree was struck by lightning, and the 6,500-pound elephant died on the spot. She is now buried where she fell, with a monument marking the site.

Tasty souvenirs are to be found at *Bartlow Brothers Meats;* (217) 322–3365. The retail store at South Liberty sells heavenly honey-cured hams, bacon, sausages, and a local specialty, Korn Top Wieners.

Scripps Park was formerly the eighty-acre farm of Edward Wyllis Scripps, founder of the Scripps-Howard newspaper chain. The park was given to the town in 1922 by Scripps and his two sisters, Virginia and Ellen Browning Scripps. The latter contributed the $100,000 to build the Community House that marks the site of the Scripps homestead, the birthplace of Edward Wyllis Scripps. The park is located outside of Rushville, southwest of the junction of US 67 and US 24; (217) 322–4444.

Founded in 1899, *Western Illinois University,* 1 University Circle, is an important landmark in Macomb and throughout the western part of the state; (309) 298–1414. Over 11,000 students attend the institution.

The *Western Illinois Museum* is located at 201 South Lafayette, in Macomb. Its collections feature Civil War memorabilia, Native American costumes, antique farm implements, and historical materials from the region. Exhibits are rotating and special events are held seasonally. Open Tuesday through Saturday, 10:00 A.M. to 4:00 P.M.; (309) 833–1315.

If you've got a green thumb, or need to develop one, you'll enjoy the *WIU Biological Sciences Botany Greenhouse* at 316 Waggoner Hall on campus;

(309) 298–1004. The 4,500-square-foot space houses an international collection of plants used in classroom analysis.

The university's *Leslie F. Malpass Library* is one of five campus libraries. Its unique pinwheel-like architecture, with balconies and long hallways, creates a fascinating structure. The atrium opens six stories and seating is arranged to accommodate 2,500 students. And while on campus, visit the *Hainline Theatre*, which produces top-notch plays and musical events; (309) 298–2900.

On the square in downtown Macomb, the stately *old brick courthouse* is worth a visit, too. Built in the summer of 1879 at a cost of $155,370, the renovated building still serves as the center of government. For that matter, there's plenty of history in Macomb. To begin with, the city, founded in 1830, is itself named after Gen. Alexander Macomb, a hero of the War of 1812.

The *Clarence Watson/Wiley Schoolhouse Museum*, 301 West Calhoun, is a restored 1877 one-room schoolhouse, evocative of the days of pigtails and inkwells. Open 8:30 A.M. to 4:30 P.M. Monday through Friday. It's on the grounds of the United Way. Call (309) 837–9180.

Home of the McDonough County Preservation Society is the *Old Bailey House,* an 1887 Eastlake-style residence at 100 South Campbell, built by the founder of Macomb's Union National Bank. Open Monday through Friday, 9:00 A.M. to 5:00 P.M., and weekends by appointment. Call (309) 833–1727 for more information.

Argyle Lake State Park, 7 miles west of Macomb and 2 miles north of Colchester off US 136, has 700 acres of recreational land within its boundaries, including the ninety-three-acre Argyle Lake. Interestingly, the State Department of Conservation in 1970 showed a remarkable sense of doing a job right when, after twenty years of poor fishing, the department simply drained the whole lake to remove undesirable species and restocked it with the fish the department wanted. The park takes its name from a group of early settlers of Scottish descent, who called the area Argyle Hollow. The old Galena-to-Beardstown stagecoach passed through here in the early 1800s. Today the park offers visitors picnicking, boating, fishing (for bluegill, largemouth bass, crappie, and channel catfish), camping (electrical hookups available), hiking, and a summer interpretive program. Boats and canoes can be rented. The park is open year-round, and winter brings cross-country skiing, snowmobiling, ice-skating, and sledding. Contact the Site Superintendent, 640 Argyle Park Road, Colchester 62326; (309) 776–3422.

Hancock County, at the western edge of the state where the Mississippi turns and bends its way around Illinois' bulging middle, has a rich and colorful history inextricably linked with the Mormon religion. It was here, at Nauvoo and Carthage, that some of the most significant—and tragic—chapters of Mormon history were written.

What was once the site of Sauk and Fox Indian villages, had come by the 1830s to be a sleepy river village known as Commerce. After being driven out of Missouri in the spring of 1839, church founder Joseph Smith brought his followers here, to the place he called Nauvoo, to create a homeland for his people. By special negotiation with the Illinois legislature, the group obtained a charter that allowed its members extraordinary powers—their own courts, militia, university—and any other authority not prohibited by the United States or Illinois constitutions. Nauvoo became virtually an autonomous state. With Mormon converts arriving from across the country and from overseas, the town grew to be Illinois' second largest city, with a population of 12,000 by 1845.

Discontent with the leaders' power grew within and outside of the church. When a group of dissidents published an antiestablishment newspaper with views critical of the leadership, the paper was shut down. For that, Joseph Smith and his brother Hyrum were jailed at the county seat, Carthage. An anti-Mormon mob stormed the jail and murdered the two churchmen. Brigham Young took control of the group and led it west to Utah in 1846.

Nauvoo was abandoned until 1849, when a group of French communalists, the Icarians, arrived from Texas to practice their own brand of philosophy

Barn-a-Rama

It's impossible not to notice the many farms dotting the countryside as you pass through areas like Macomb and McDonough Counties. The Macomb Area Convention and Visitors Bureau has turned antique barn watching into a sport, providing a map and detailed descriptions for those enthusiasts eager to locate all things Gambrel, hipped, stick, or batten. The driving tour is broken into four county segments: north, central, southwest, and southeast. Thirty barns, from seventy to nearly one hundred and forty years old, await your admiration. Just remember to view these from your car, since all barns stand on private property.

Old Illinois barns were commonly built in the cross-gable style, meaning there is a gable on each of the four sides. But that's not the only type you'll find on this trip.

A rare "true round" barn, called the **Kleinkopf Barn,** was built in 1914, and is listed on the National Register of Historic Places. Most round barns are actually polygonal, whereas a "true round" is absent of all straight lines. The **Kipling Barn** is a three-story 1920s specimen, complete with an internal grain elevator. An example of a square barn is the **Ausbury Barn,** circa 1918. Supposedly the owner celebrated its construction with a rowdy barn dance.

Contact the Macomb Area Convention and Visitors Bureau, 201 South Lafayette, Macomb 61455; (309) 833–1315.

under their leader, Etienne Cabet. Their experiment lasted until 1856. During their tenancy, however, they began the production of wine and cheese.

Today groups associated with branches of the Mormon church have extensively restored Nauvoo and the old Carthage jail. The **Nauvoo Visitors Center,** at Young and Main Streets, includes a historical exhibit and a short film on the early days of the community. Admission is free. Call (217) 453–2237 for hours.

Just outside the center is a sculpture garden, the **Monument to Women.**

western illinoistrivia

In Nauvoo, site of the historic Mormon settlement in western Illinois, you'll find millers still grinding wheat and corn for baking; there is a 140-year-old vineyard still producing wine; and the area remains famous for its homemade blue cheese.

Some of the historic homes and shops open to visit in Nauvoo are the **Brigham Young Home;** the Mormon newspaper office of the *Times and Seasons;* the Joseph Smith Mansion; Jonathan Browning's gunsmith shop; and the Clark store. Many have guides and period craft demonstrations. The historic homes are open Monday through Saturday from 9:00 A.M. to 9:00 P.M., Sunday 10:30 A.M. to 6:00 P.M. in the summer, and Monday through Saturday from 9:00 A.M. to 5:00 P.M., Sunday 12:30 to 5:00 P.M. in the winter. Visit between early July and early August to enjoy the annual **Nauvoo Pageant**—a free outdoor musical event, handsomely costumed and well performed; call (800) 453–0022, extension 315.

Also in Nauvoo be sure to visit the **Joseph Smith Historic Site,** on Water Street off Route 96. Here there is a film, a history of the town, and a walking tour to the log cabin homestead where Smith first lived and the family cemetery. Admission is $2.00; (217) 453–2246.

On the hill overlooking the river plain is the **Nauvoo Temple** at 50 North Wells. Dedicated in 2002, this temple stands in place of the original, which was destroyed more than one hundred years ago by arson and a tornado. Stop by the **Nauvoo Temple Visitors Center** for information. The interior is not open for tours; (217) 453–6252.

Nearby, **Nauvoo State Park** features a museum operated by the Nauvoo Historical Society. Camping, a playground, a picnic area, and a stocked fishing lake are also available at the park. For more information contact the Site Superintendent, Nauvoo State Park, P.O. Box 426, Nauvoo 62354; (217) 453–2512.

Labor Day weekend marks the annual **Nauvoo Grape Festival** (217–453–6648), with tastings of the local blue cheese and wine, some of the area's best souvenirs. Stop by **Baxter's Winery,** at 2010 East Parley Street, (217)

453–2528, for tours and tastings. Open 9:00 A.M. to 5:00 P.M. Monday through Saturday, and 10:00 A.M. to 5:00 P.M. Sunday. Throughout the year, some delightful tastes come from the kitchen of the *Hotel Nauvoo.* The hotel, once a private home, dates from the Mormon period around 1840. In addition to the restaurant, where dinner prices range from $10 to $20, there are a limited number of overnight accommodations; a double costs $78 and up. At 1290 Mulholland; (217) 453–2211. Call for reservations.

In Carthage the old jail, which once held Joseph and Hyrum Smith, is at 307 Walnut Street. Free admission; (217) 357–2989.

Also of interest is the *Hancock County Courthouse,* a Greek Revival structure that's one of the prettiest in the state. It was here, on October 22, 1858, that Abraham Lincoln addressed a crowd of 6,000 in his senatorial campaign against Stephen A. Douglas. A stone marker commemorates the event.

The *Kibbe-Hancock Museum,* across from the old jail on Walnut Street, is the personal collection of a former biology professor at the now-closed Carthage College. In addition area residents have contributed their treasures. The collection includes Civil War relics, World War II memorabilia, Indian artifacts, fossils and rocks, and a natural history exhibit. Free. Open Monday, Wednesday, and Friday through Sunday 1:00 to 4:00 P.M.; (217) 357–3119.

Along the western edge of the county, the *Great River Road* runs next to the Mississippi, providing dramatic views and scenic photographic opportunities. In the winter months, from early November through early March, scores of bald eagles roost in the vicinity. January is the best time for observation around the open waters below Lock and Dam No. 19 near Hamilton. From sunrise to around 10:00 A.M. is the best time to catch the eagles feeding. The *Alice Kibbe Life Science Field Station* of Western Illinois University on the Hamilton-Warsaw Road is open for nature observation and hiking at most times of the year. The resident manager of the station is available by appointment from 8:00 A.M. to 5:00 P.M. to explain the eagle's natural environment. Call (217) 256–4519.

Carl Sandburg Country

Galesburg is a city that retains the flavor of the nineteenth century through its architecture. The city is so proud of its treasures that it has published six walking tours, thirty to forty-five minutes each, that take you through the historic districts, pointing out buildings and telling tales of Galesburg's history. Walking tours are available through the Illinois Department of Tourism or from the Galesburg Area Convention and Visitors Bureau, 2163 East Main Street, 61401; (309) 343–2485.

In the mid-1830s George Washington Gale, Galesburg's founding father, came to the area to create a labor collective similar to the Oneida Institute of

Science and Industry, a collective he founded in New York. Galesburg began as a religious colony under Gale's leadership, and in June 1836, 560 acres were allocated for the town and 104 acres for a college. By the end of the first year, forty families were established in Galesburg.

Railroads were the mainstay of the town. In 1854 the first train, called Reindeer, came to Galesburg. The railroads allowed for area produce to be shipped to other markets and employed a major portion of the town's workforce. By 1880 the town had quadrupled in size and had grown in prosperity as evidenced by the many large Victorian homes here.

western illinoistrivia

G. W. Gale Ferris, who built the world's largest entertainment ride (which still bears his name) for the 1893 World's Columbian Exposition in Chicago, lived in Galesburg.

Galesburg's public square was the starting point for commerce in the town. The first general store was established at the northwest corner of Broad and Main Streets. The square was traversed by trolley tracks and was proposed as the site of the courthouse or post office. But, after 140 years the square still remains an open, grassy area.

Galeburg's most prominent citizen was Carl Sandburg, noted poet, socialist, biographer, historian, minstrel, and lover of humanity. He lived in Galesburg until he was twenty-four years old. *Carl Sandburg's birthplace,* 331 East Third Street, the second house east of the Chicago, Burlington, and Quincy Railroad tracks, is now a state historic site. The house is a three-room cottage bought by August Sandburg, Carl's father, in the fall of 1873. A neighboring house is open as a visitor center housing Sandburg exhibits and memorabilia. Sandburg is the only author to win the Pulitzer Prize in two categories: history and poetry.

Carl Sandburg Park is located behind the birthplace. Legend says that Sandburg was so taken with the spot's beauty that he requested it be his final resting place.

In 1966 a memorial named *Remembrance Rock,* after Sandburg's only novel, was erected here. The memorial is a large, red granite boulder unearthed during highway construction northeast of Galesburg. It is a glacial remnant and product of the prairie.

Sandburg's ashes were placed beneath Remembrance Rock in 1967. Ten years later his wife, Lilian Paula Sandburg, was buried beside him.

The house is located in the southwest section of Galesburg. Enter Galesburg via the Main Street off Interstate 74 and follow directional signs through the town. For more information or group appointments, call (309) 342–2361.

Museum hours are 9:00 A.M. to 5:00 P.M. Wednesday through Sunday; closed major holidays.

Another worthwhile side-trip is the *Galesburg Railroad Museum* at South Seminary and Mulberry Streets. The museum houses a Pullman parlor car, locomotive #3006, and caboose #13501 among other railroad memorabilia. The museum was once the Burlington Northern Depot. Open April through November, Tuesday through Saturday, 10:00 A.M. to 4:00 P.M., or by appointment.

Carl Sandburg's Birthplace

Galesburg holds an annual national *Stearman Fly-In* in early September. Stearmans are the biplane trainers that gave wings to more military pilots than any other aircraft series in the world. The celebration lasts five days with commercial exhibits, miniair shows, Stearman contests, aerobatic competition, short-field takeoff, flour-bombing, spot landing, and formation flying contests. For information call the National Stearman Fly-In office at (309) 343–6409.

Railroad Days is another yearly event in Galesburg. Railroad memorabilia, a street fair, and a carnival are part of the festivities. There are also tours of Galesburg's historic sites. Railroad Days is always the fourth weekend in June. For more information contact the Galesburg Area Convention and Visitors Bureau, 2163 East Main Street, Galesburg 61401; (309) 343–2485.

The Seminary Street Historic Commercial District on Seminary Street in downtown Galesburg is three blocks of restored, turn-of-the-century buildings that house specialty shops and restaurants. For information call the Seminary Street Historic Commerical District at (309) 342–1000.

And yet another Galesburg annual event is the *Galesburg Heritage Days Festival* in August. A tram tour through the historic district features shops with "ghosts" from the past. Also featured are old-time craft demonstrations, entertainment, and a Civil War battle reenactment; (309) 343–2485.

The *Orpheum Theater,* 57 South Kellogg Street, first opened in 1916 as William J. Olson's vision to raise the public's perception of the meaning of the word *theater* to a level never imagined by local builders and audiences of the time. Employing the Chicago architectural firm of C. W. & George L. Rapp, whose philosophy was that a theater should be "a shrine to democracy where the wealthy rub elbows with the poor," Olson created a perfect microcosm of nineteenth-century eclectic architecture. The Orpheum was billed as a vaudeville house and hosted such stars as Jack Benny, George Burns, Houdini, and Fanny Brice. Converted to a movie theater by the late 1970s, the Orpheum was forced to close down in 1982 due to high operating costs. The theater is now renovated and is a not-for-profit community performing arts center. For a schedule of events, call (309) 342–2299.

Knox College, Cherry and South Streets, (309) 341–7000, was founded in 1837 and has been described as "a monument to the vision of the founding fathers of both the college and city." *Old Main,* the administration building, was restored and stabilized during the 1930s. It is registered as a National Historic Landmark and is an example of American Gothic Revival architecture. Old Main is the only building left standing where Lincoln and Douglas debated in 1858. Hours are 8:00 A.M. to 4:30 P.M., Monday through Friday, May through September.

Knox County Scenic Drive through the Spoon River Valley is a perfect self-guided driving tour when the surrounding countryside is transformed by Mother Nature's autumn palette into a kaleidoscope of colors. The first two full weekends in October are a festival with music, flea markets, arts and crafts, exhibits, and good country cooking. For information call the Galesburg Area Convention and Visitors Bureau; (217) 342–1000.

For fans of old TV westerns, the most important sightseeing stop in the county is surely the house at 406 South Third Street in Monmouth where Wyatt Earp was born in 1848. Known for the 1881 O.K. Corral gunfight in Tombstone, Arizona, Earp is feted as America's most heroic lawman-gunslinger. The privately owned homestead is sometimes open for special events. A memorial to Earp stands in *Monmouth Park.* Although he found a final resting place in California, many of his relatives are buried in Monmouth's *Pioneer Cemetery* at 200 North Sixth Street. In fact a walk around the old cemetery gives you some historical perspective on the town, which was founded in 1833.

A county landmark is *Monmouth College,* established in 1853 by a group of Scottish Presbyterians who pioneered the settlement of this part of the state. The campus has many attractive brick buildings in the Greek Revival style. The white-framed *Holt House,* at 402 East First Avenue, is the birthplace of Pi Beta Phi sorority. Architecture buffs will also enjoy a drive down *East Broadway,* where the homes bring memories of a more gracious period. Historic district status for the area is being pursued.

In front of the castlelike 1895 "Richardsonian Romanesque" county courthouse in Monmouth stands a *statue of Gen. Abner C. Harding,* a hero at the second battle of Fort Donaldson during the Civil War.

Cruisin' with My Baby

It's only one night a year, and yet it probably draws more people to Warren County than any other annual event: it's **Cruise Night,** a mammoth car show that celebrates American's love affair with automobiles. The event is sponsored by the **Maple City Street Machines** club, and remarkably, there is no entry fee to show your car, and no admission fee to see the cars.

Recent shows featured over 1,600 autos, ranging from new Corvettes to pristine Model Ts. Eager entrants often breeze in before the city streets are closed at 8:00 A.M. Cars are parked as they arrive, around the town square and north and south along city blocks.

It's estimated that over 25,000 people attend this gathering. The official hours are from 5:00 to 10:00 P.M. That's when live music and the smell of great cooking fill the air. During the evening, there are drawings for prizes, and a 50/50 raffle is held to benefit a worthy local charity. Contact the Monmouth Chamber of Commerce for more information; (309) 734–3181.

And though Dixon claims the title as Ronald Reagan's boyhood home, Monmouth, too, shares the honor, for the family lived here briefly during the former president's early years, at 218 South Seventh Street (now a private residence).

The **Western Stoneware Company** employed Monmouth area potters for generations, but just shy of its one-hundredth anniversary in 2006, the company closed. However, in true American spirit, three employees reopened the enterprise shortly afterward under the name **W. S. Incorporated of Monmouth.**

Today, the revitalized business maintains its long tradition of quality by creating all-handmade pottery. The phrase "mass production" is not in this company's vocabulary. See for yourself! Stop by the **Pottery Store** at 1201 North Main Street; open Tuesday through Saturday 10:00 A.M. to 5:00 P.M.; Sunday noon to 5:00 P.M.; (309) 734–6809.

Each year right after Labor Day, the **Warren County Prime Beef Festival** is held in Monmouth. There are livestock shows, parades, a demolition derby, and a carnival. Call (309) 734–3181 for more information.

For recreation during the warmer months, the eighteen holes of **Gibson Woods Golf Course** are open to the public. The course is adjacent to Monmouth Park on US 34 immediately northeast of Monmouth; (309) 734–9968.

Monmouth Airport, northeast of town on US 34, is the oldest continually operating airport in the state; (309) 734–3411.

Out in the rural part of the county, visit the **Warren County Historical Museum** in Roseville at 210 East Penn Avenue.

If old bones, skulls, and Indian burial grounds grab your interest, Fulton County is the place you should visit. It is one of the richest archaeological areas in the Midwest. There are 800 mounds in Fulton centered at the junction of the Spoon and Illinois Rivers. The most famous is the **Dickson Mound** near Lewiston.

The Dickson Mound is on a high bluff overlooking the two rivers. It was originally crescent shaped with the points facing east. It measures 550 feet along its outer curve and is 35 feet high. A reproduction of one of the burials is exhibited at the Field Museum of Natural History in Chicago. The **ISM Dickson Mound Museum** itself offers an outstanding collection of Native American artifacts and exhibits. It also hosts a number of special programs throughout the year. Call (309) 547–3721. The mound is located off Route 97 and Route 78 near Havana, 5 miles south of Lewistown. Open daily year-round 8:30 A.M. to 5:00 P.M.; free admission.

For the literary-minded, Edgar Lee Masters immortalized the Spoon River Country and particularly Lewistown in his *Spoon River Anthology*. Masters's home was in Lewistown, and **Oak Hill Cemetery** on North Main Street shows many names identical to characters in the anthology. The area is also filled with interesting buildings, historic markers, and antiques shops.

The **Ross Mansion,** 409 East Milton Avenue, was the inspiration for the McNeely Mansion in the anthology. The mansion was modeled after a home on the Hudson River that Col. Lewis W. Ross admired. The New England–style home has seventeen rooms and is made of stone from the Spoon River Valley.

Maj. Newton Walker's house had the honor of having Abraham Lincoln as a guest. The home was built in 1833 and is located at 1127 North Main Street. Unfortunately, it is not open to the public.

Other places of interest in Lewiston are the **Phelps Store,** Main and Washington Streets (originally an Indian trading post), and the **Church of St. James,** at Broadway and Illinois Streets, an example of Victorian Gothic architecture.

In the nearby town of Ellisville is an opera house from the nineteenth century, and in London Mills is the **Ross Hotel,** an authentically restored hotel.

The **Spoon River Scenic Drive,** especially dramatic in the color-filled fall, takes you through 60 miles of woodland and towns. To obtain a map from the Spoon River Scenic Drive Associates, write to them at Box 525, Canton 61520, or call (309) 647–8980. Special signs mark the drive.

No matter the season, Fulton County is a lovely area for a drive. Pause to watch the water pouring over the spillway at the dam in **Bernadotte,** or stop for ice cream at any one of the other quaint little towns along the route.

Some of the greatest concentrations of wild ducks and geese in the nation are to be found in the **Illinois River Wildlife and Fish Refuge** in Mason

County. These feathered creatures contribute to the area's reputation as a hunting and fishing paradise.

The refuge is a vital link in the chain of resting, feeding, and wintering areas for migratory birds along the Mississippi Flyway. During the annual migration ducks and geese are often so numerous their masses darken the sky.

The refuge has 4,500 acres of land and water where wild ducks and geese can be observed each fall and winter. The average peak concentration during early winter exceeds 100,000 ducks and up to 40,000 Canada, blue, and snow geese. Mallards make up most of the duck population, with smaller numbers of wood ducks, pintail, widgeon, black duck, blue-winged teal, scaup, shoveler, gadwall, goldeneye, and mergansers.

The wood duck is the most common nester in the refuge. Wood ducks normally rest in natural cavities in hardwood timber, but they have adapted to nesting boxes erected in the refuge.

Bald eagles winter in several concentrated groups here. More than 240 eagles have been counted along the river. Eagles usually arrive in October and stay until the ice disappears in the spring.

More than 275 species of birds reside in the refuge. Great blue herons, green herons, great egrets, and black-crowned night herons are generally summer residents. Marsh, water, and shorebirds are common during the spring and fall, and their migration is spectacular during August and early September.

The refuge is open to the public, and an interpretive foot trail is located in the headquarters. Roads next to portions of the refuge offer opportunities for viewing wildlife without disturbing them.

Fishing, mushroom and berry picking, and hiking are permitted. *Lake Chautauqua* is known for its bluegill, crappie, and catfish fishing, especially during April, May, and early June.

Waterfowl hunting is permitted in the Liverpool section, located outside Lake Chautauqua.

For additional information contact the Refuge Manager, Illinois River Wildlife and Fish Refuge, 19031 East County Road 2110N, Havana 62644; (309) 535–2290. The refuge is 8 miles northeast of Havana on the Manito Blacktop. A sign marks the entrance.

The *Jake Wolf Memorial Fish Hatchery,* 5 miles west of Manito on Oil Well Road, has 160 acres within the Sand Ridge State Forest. The hatchery is named after the late Jacob John "Jake" Wolf, who was once deputy director of the Department of Conservation for the State of Illinois. Wolf is remembered as a friend of the outdoor sportsman and sportswoman. During Wolf's career as a state legislator and a member of the Department of Conservation, numerous conservation bills were passed that benefited hunting and fishing enthusiasts statewide.

The complex includes a 36,000-square-foot hatchery building, fifty-six indoor rearing tanks, spawning and egg incubation facilities, modern fish harvest, and distribution and feeding systems. Outside is a twenty-two acre solar pond that uses energy from the sun to heat water for fish production, twenty-eight rearing raceways, and seven brood raceways.

Specialties of the hatchery are chinook, coho salmon, rainbow and brown trout, walleye, muskellunge, northern pike, striped bass, bluegill, channel catfish, and large- and smallmouth bass. The fish produced at the hatchery are used to stock Lake Michigan, private farm ponds, state-owned lakes, reservoirs, streams, and rivers. Anticipated production at the hatchery is forty-two million fish a year.

Tours are on a self-guided basis, although employee-guided tours can be scheduled for large groups. Visiting hours are 8:30 A.M. to 3:30 P.M. daily; (309) 968–7531.

New Salem State Historic Site, located 2 miles south of the county seat, Petersburg, on Route 97, is a reconstruction of the village in which Lincoln lived from 1831 to 1837. Admission to the park is free, though a donation of $2.00 for adults, $1.00 for children is suggested.

Here homes, shops, and taverns take you back to the time when Lincoln was just beginning his political career. He served here as postmaster and deputy surveyor and was defeated for election to the Illinois General Assembly in 1832, then elected two years later.

The 1835 ***Onstot Cooper Shop*** is the only original building on the site, and it was here that Lincoln studied law books late in the night. The ***Lincoln-Berry store*** is an authentic re-creation of the general store in which Lincoln was a partner. At the ***Rutledge Tavern*** lived his first love, Ann Rutledge (who is buried in Oakland Cemetery in Petersburg).

Costumed interpreters run the shops and exhibits, so you may encounter a blacksmith at a forge, a baker taking freshly baked bread from the oven, or a candlemaker working with tallow. Oxen and other farm animals are part of the scene. Inside the park flowers and plants have been planted for historic authenticity. Vegetable gardens and herb gardens are tucked behind the cabins and wild plum, blackberry, gooseberry, and other trees and shrubs add to the look of the 1830s village.

western illinoistrivia

Abe Lincoln's "lost love," Ann Rutledge, is buried in a cemetery just outside Petersburg.

And the park's outdoor amphitheater, surrounded by tall trees, features a special Lincoln production every summer.

The park has camping facilities available on the grounds (200 campsites, with showers and electric hookups available). Open Wednesday through Sunday, 9:00 A.M. to 5:00 P.M. March 1 to April 15, and daily from 9:00 A.M. to 5:00 P.M., April 16 to Labor Day. Call for winter hours; (217) 632–4000.

In Petersburg at Jackson and Eighth Streets, is the **Edgar Lee Masters Memorial Home.** The poet and author of *Spoon River Anthology* lived here as a boy. Much of his work reflects the feeling of this part of Illinois. Restored to its 1875 period, the home holds memorabilia of the family and his work. Open Memorial Day through Labor Day, on Tuesdays, and Thursday through Saturday 10:00 A.M. to noon and 1:00 to 3:00 P.M.; (217) 632–7363. Admission is free. Masters is buried in the town's **Oakland Cemetery.**

They used to ask, "Will it play in Peoria?" These days it decidedly does. Named one of the country's "All-American" cities, and called an "in" place to live by *BusinessWeek* magazine, Peoria's a hit.

The **George L. Luthy Memorial Botanical Gardens,** 2218 North Prospect Road; (309) 686–3362, has a rose garden with more than 800 all-American award-winning selections. The All-Seasons Garden has plants selected for their unique characteristics that provide beauty year-round. The herb garden has plants that are pleasant to smell and add zest to culinary arts.

The conservatory is the permanent home of a collection of tropical plants and fragile specimens and the biocenter has education programs, workshops, films, and seminars. Conservatory admission is $2.00 for adults.

Admission to the gardens is free, and they are open from 8:30 A.M. to dusk. The conservatory and gift and plant shop are open Tuesday through Saturday 10:00 A.M. to 5:00 P.M., Sunday noon to 5:00 P.M.; call for special winter hours.

The **Lakeview Museum of Arts and Sciences** is the largest private museum in Illinois outside of Chicago. It is also one of only fifty U.S. museums that feature exhibits in both the arts and sciences. The art gallery contains an extensive permanent collection of folk art, Illinois quilts, and Illinois River decoys. Science exhibits tackle astronomy, geology, anthropology, and Illinois wildlife. A Children's Discovery Center provides hands-on experiences for all ages. A laser light show is presented in the planetarium. There is always something new here, as traveling exhibits are featured throughout the year. Located at 1125 West Lake Avenue, Peoria; hours are Tuesday, Thursday, Friday, and Saturday 10:00 A.M. to 5:00 P.M., Wednesday 10:00 A.M. to 8:00 P.M., Sunday noon to 5:00 P.M. Admission is $6.00 for adults, $4.00 for children; planetarium is $4.00 for adults, $3.50 for children ages four to seventeen; a combination

Man versus Nature

Wildlife Prairie Park is a great place to bring toddlers, for though the animals are in "natural" environments, they cannot escape detection and hide from the gaze of paying customers. Thus even the most unfocused toddler can usually spot them, even if he seems more interested in the chain-link fence enclosing the animals—no matter how much you try to redirect his attention to the dad-blamed animals! Yes, my little family's first sojourn in Wildlife Prairie Park became a contest of wills between myself and my sixteen-month-old son—a foretaste, no doubt, of many battles to come.

It started out fine enough. We headed directly to the wolf enclosure, for I'd made my son familiar with wolves through picture books. As we approached, a wolf trotted right up to the gate and kept following us along the perimeter of the enclosure. My son had shown appropriate interest and delight in the wolf, so I wasn't all that concerned when he focused on rattling the chain-link fence of the buffalo viewing area rather than observing the animals.

A pattern soon developed. Sure, my son would point with interest at each new animal, but then he would immediately become fascinated with the fence. It was only when we reached the bridge over the cougar enclosure that I started getting agitated, for though there were two cougars slumbering in plain view right below us, he simply refused to glance their way no matter how many times I held him up and pointed.

"Look, cougars," I would state with increasing emphasis, but he would immediately begin wiggling and kicking to be let down and go back to fiddling with the fence, unmindful of the magnificent animals only a glance away—a glance he refused to take!

Now I guess I wouldn't have been as adamant about the whole thing if it hadn't been for what had happened earlier that morning. After entering the visitor center, he spotted a stuffed, mounted cougar above a stairwell and instantly pointed at it with a grin, making a growling sound. That told me how excited he would get if he could see the real thing—if only I could get him to glance at them!

My wife was starting to get a bit annoyed by now. "He's not interested," she told me, "it's no big deal."

admission fee for both the museum and the planetarium is available; (309) 686–7000.

But Peoria's Showplace might be **Wildlife Prairie Park,** which began as a project of the Forest Park Foundation. The theme was native North American animals living in natural habitat enclosures, with other areas of the park portraying Illinois' natural history. You can watch wolves roam the park, see a buffalo herd grazing on the prairie, and watch elk saunter through the grasses.

"He is interested," I testily replied, "he just doesn't realize it!"

Suddenly I thought we had a breakthrough. He finally spotted the plaque along the fence featuring a drawing of a cougar and a list of its attributes and habits, and his response was exactly the same as it had been to the stuffed cougar in the visitor center.

"You see," I told my wife, "he is interested!"

Unfortunately, my attempts to get him to look continued to meet with failure. He was no longer intrigued by the fence but now ran to the end of the bridge and tried to slip off the path into the woods. He cried each time I brought him back, only to wiggle and kick and tear off for the woods again as soon as I put him down. But although he had refused to notice the cougars, they had certainly noticed him. He had woken them up, and they were watching his every movement with interest probably reflecting on what a tasty snack he would make.

The folly might have continued indefinitely had my wife not finally asked my son where the cougars were. Sure enough, he pointed quickly and dismissively at the very spot, then made another dash for the woods.

"But, I don't understand . . ." I muttered, following my wife in defeat. So he had known all along they were there but had simply not been interested? How was that possible? Since when did he develop the capacity to be uninterested in something I felt he should be excited about?! Then I remembered my own father's attempts to get me enthusiastic about working on cars or—of even less interest to me—skinning and butchering the deer he brought home from hunting trips. So is this what having a child comes to? They just develop their own interests and passions? What's the point of even having 'em!

Ah well, though I acted like more of a baby than my son that day, I do believe I've come to terms with this issue and will be better able to deal with it when it develops more fully in the future. And yes, Wildlife Prairie Park played an instrumental role in this even if it taught me more about human nature than animal nature.

Better yet, rent the Cabin in the Woods for a night's stay at the preserve and listen to the wolves howl at the moon.

The park offers special events that include the Illinois Art League show, tree-planting parties, and Pops on the Prairie Concerts with the Peoria Symphony Orchestra.

From March 1 to April 30 hours are 9:00 A.M. to 4:30 P.M. From May to Labor Day hours are 8:00 A.M. to 6:30 P.M. Through September hours are 9:00 A.M. to

wannabet?

If you're willing to take a gamble, head to nearby East Peoria's Par-a-Dice, the state's big daddy of big payoffs. Its Big Hit slot machines start with a jackpot of $100,000 and increase until someone gets a . . . big hit. Like David Riddle, the current big-hit record holder who broke the bank on these very slots, winning almost $500,000 on a $1.00 wager.

Of course, there are lots more slots, video poker games, keno, blackjack, roulette, and craps on this floating casino. Call (309) 699-7711.

6:30 P.M., and October through mid-December, 9:00 A.M. to 4:30 P.M. A 24-inch-gauge railroad system travels through the park. A gift shop and country store are on the grounds.

The park is located 10 miles west of downtown Peoria, off I–74 via exit 82 on Taylor Road. Admission is $5.50 for adults, $3.50 for children ages four through twelve, and free for children under four. Call (309) 676–0998.

The *Peoria Historical Society* offers four riding tours of Peoria: the River City Historical, the All-American City, Old Peoria and Judge Tour, and the Springdale Cemetery Tour. Although the society operates from 611 South West Washington Street, the tours have different starting points, so clarify where you pick up the trolley. Price range for tours is $8.00–$12.00. The society also runs nine historic walking tours. Call (309) 674–1921. The *Pettengill-Morron House* is also available for viewing. Call (309) 674–1921 to arrange a tour.

Père Marquette Country

Father Jacques Marquette, a French Jesuit missionary, and explorer Louis Joliet were the first Europeans to come to this area in 1673. The history of the area, however, is traceable back some 200 million years when movements of the earth resulted in dislocation of rocks, producing the Lincoln Fold in Père Marquette State Park.

Père Marquette State Park lies 5 miles west of Grafton on Route 100 in Jersey County. The 8,000-acre park, lying on bluffs that overlook the confluence of the Mississippi and Illinois Rivers, is the largest state park in Illinois.

Another trace of prehistoric times is *McAdams Peak,* where twin springs flow from Ordovician-Silurian rocks that were deposited in the sea more than 350 million years ago. All the ridges have loess (pronounced *less*) on them. Loess is windblown dust laid down a million years ago during the Great Ice Age. The river's banks of yellow clay are composed of loess and capped with black topsoil that supports the forest.

Prehistoric people also left their mark here. There are eighteen sites indicating their presence, and a village once stood where the park lodge now stands. Nomadic hunters and fishers lived in the Illinois Valley around the beginning of the Christian era, and Stone Age people left remnants of arrowheads and coarse, heavy pottery.

When the French came to this region, the tribes of Illinois, Potawatomi, and Kickapoo Indians remained near their ancestral cemeteries and burial mounds. Their houses and village sites dotted the Illinois Valley and are still visible throughout the park.

The *Père Marquette Lodge,* located in the park (618–786–2331) has been wonderfully remodeled. It boasts fifty rooms and twenty-two cabins, plus an indoor swimming pool. There is a dining room and a 700-ton stone fireplace in the lobby. The park also has what is believed to be the world's largest chess set. The board is 12 feet square and has figures bigger than the average six year old.

Within the grounds is an amphitheater with a movie screen. The theater seats about 200 people. There are also facilities for boating, camping, fishing, and picnicking, and more than 15 miles of hiking trails and horseback riding. Watch for American bald eagles in the bluffs throughout the area.

The visitor center displays the history of the park, and a park interpreter is available for assisting bus tours, hikes, and demonstrations. The visitor center is open Monday through Saturday 9:00 A.M. to 3:30 P.M., and Sunday 10:00 A.M. to 3:30 P.M. year-round. For reservations with the interpreter, call (618) 786–3323 or write Park Interpreter, Père Marquette State Park, Box 158, Grafton 62037.

Just downriver away from Grafton is the quaint *Village of Elsah,* the first entire community to be listed on the National Register of Historic Places. On the Great River Road, this Mississippi River town seems more like a New England village. Plan a stay at the charming *Corner Nest Bed and Breakfast,* 3 Elm Street. The 1883 French-American mansion overlooks the river with an inviting screened porch. Each of the four rooms is decorated with antiques. Phone (618) 374–1892.

Greene County lies in the west-central part of the state about 20 miles from the mouth of the Illinois River. Primarily an agricultural region, the terrain

western illinoistrivia

The little Mississippi River hamlet of Elsah, looking unchanged since its riverboating days, was the first entire town to be placed on the National Register of Historic Places.

is marked by broken, hilly land as its western edge along the river bluffs. Here fruit cultivation is an important industry.

A number of historic sites are found throughout the county: In Carrollton, the county seat, the *Hodges Building* on the northwest corner of the town square houses the Greene County Historical Society. The *County Courthouse,* along with the entire square, is listed in the National Register of Historic Places. On the west side of the town square is the former *home of Maj. Marcus Reno,* who fought with Custer in the Battle of Little Big Horn.

The *Henry T. Rainey Home* is ½ mile east of Carrollton on Route 108. The three-story brick house faced with columns holds a wealth of historical artifacts. Rainey was the Speaker of the House in the Seventy-third Congress. In *Rainey Memorial Park,* on the north edge of town, a bronze statue honors the legislator who served in every session except one from 1903 until his death in 1934.

One of the few working farm vacations in the state can be had at *Bluffdale Vacation Farm,* 4 miles north of Eldred on the Bluff blacktop road. It's good old-fashioned fun with plenty of outdoor activity. The farm holiday includes lodging, truly memorable meals, horseback riding, boating, hayrides, and swimming—as well as a chance to lend a hand with farm chores, like collecting eggs, feeding animals, baling hay, and more. The historic 1828 *John Russell House* is situated on the property as well. For reservations call (217) 983–2854.

Other recreational opportunities are available at *Greenfield City Lake,* 1½ miles east of Greenfield, and *Roodhouse Reservoir,* 2 miles east of Roodhouse. Both offer camping, fishing, and boating. But, of course, the *Illinois River* is the major body of water in these parts. Try water-skiing downstream or take a free ferry from the terminus of Route 108, west of Eldred, across to Calhoun County.

For golfers there is the *Lone Oak Golf Course,* 3 miles east of Carrollton on Route 108, then right 1¼ miles on the country road. The nine-hole course is situated in a beautiful rural setting; (217) 942–6166.

Farm Follies

Bluffdale, a 320-acre farm run by the same family since 1828, is one of the best country-time getaways for city folks—or any other kind of folks.

I mean, where else can you help feed the chickens and pigs, gather eggs, move geese, bottle-feed calves, pick fresh blackberries, and harvest vegetables from a two-acre garden—and have loads of fun doing it?

Or enjoy horseback riding up in the nearby bluffs, take daylong canoe trips, go arrowhead hunting, take a hayride, stomp your feet during square dancing, or just hang out at the outdoor heated pool?

Everybody loves Bluffdale—even Charles Dickens, who visited the farm in the 1840s. So if you want a farm vacation that's filled with history and loaded with all kinds of great activities, point the nose of your car to Eldred right now, and put the pedal to the metal.

In White Hall, which is in the northern part of the county, the *Annie Louise Keller Memorial* is a sculpture by the famous artist, Lorado Taft, dedicated to a schoolteacher who lost her life rescuing her pupils during a tornado in 1927. Here, too, is the *grave of the Little Drummer Boy of Shiloh*.

Plan a drive along the river bluffs from Eldred to Hillview. It's especially beautiful in the fall.

Places to Stay in Western Illinois

ELSAH

Green Tree Inn,
15 Mill Street,
(618) 374–2821

Maple Leaf Cottage Inn,
12 Selma Street,
(618) 374–1684

GALESBURG

Comfort Inn,
907 West Carl Sandburg Drive,
(309) 344–5445

Country Inns and Suites,
2284 Promenade Court,
(309) 344–4444

Holiday Inn Express,
2285 Washington Street,
(309) 343–7100

Ramada Inn,
29 Public Square,
(309) 343–9161

Vista Lodge,
565 West Main Street,
(309) 343–3191

GRAFTON

Père Marquette Lodge,
Route 100,
(618) 786–2331

LEWISTOWN

Cottonwood Motel,
805 South Main Street,
(309) 547–3733

MACOMB

Amerihost Inn,
1646 North Lafayette,
(309) 837–2220

Days Inn,
1400 North Lafayette,
(309) 833–5511

Holiday Inn Express,
1655 East Jackson,
(309) 836–6700

Olson Conference Center,
Western Illinois University Campus,
(309) 298–3500

NAUVOO

Hotel Nauvoo,
1290 Mulholland Street,
(217) 453–2211

Mississippi Memories,
1 Riverview Heights,
(217) 453–2771

Nauvoo Family Inn,
1875 Mulholland Street,
(217) 453–6527

NEW SALEM

Thomas Benton Gray House,
R.R. 1, Box 30,
(217) 285–2230

PEORIA

Baymont Inn and Suites,
2002 West War Memorial Drive,
(309) 686–7600

Best Western Signature Inn,
4112 North Brandywine,
(309) 685–2556

Comfort Suites,
1812 West North War Memorial Drive,
(309) 688–3800

Holiday Inn City Center,
500 Hamilton Boulevard,
(309) 674–2500

Hotel Père Marquette,
501 Main Street,
(309) 637–6500

Mark Twain Hotel,
225 N.E. Adams Street,
(309) 676–3600

Radisson Hotel Peoria,
117 North Western Avenue,
(309) 673–8040

Red Roof Inn,
1822 West War Memorial Drive,
(309) 685–3911

SELECTED VISITORS BUREAUS AND CHAMBERS OF COMMERCE

Illinois Bureau of Tourism-
Travel Information,
(800) 2–CONNECT

Greater Alton/Twin Rivers Convention
and Visitors Bureau,
200 Piasa Street, 62002
(618) 465–6676

Galesburg Chamber of Commerce,
311 East Water Street, 61401
(309) 343–1194

Macomb Area Convention and
Visitors Bureau,
201 South Lafayette Street, 61455
(309) 833–1315

Peoria Area Convention and
Visitors Bureau,
456 Fulton Street, Suite 300, 61602
(309) 676–0303

Quincy Convention and
Visitors Bureau,
300 Civic Center Plaza, Suite 237,
62301
(800) 978–4748

PETERSBURG

The Oaks,
510 West Sheridan,
(217) 632–5444

PITTSFIELD

Green Acres Motel,
625 West Washington Street,
(217) 285–2166

QUINCY

Fairfield Inn by Marriott,
4315 Broadway Street,
(217) 223–5922

Holiday Inn,
201 South Third Street,
(217) 222–2666

Places to Eat in Western Illinois

GALESBURG

Chez Willy's,
41 South Seminary Street,
(309) 341–4141

Jumer's Continental Inn,
260 South Soangetha Road,
(309) 343–7151

Landmark Cafe,
62 South Seminary Street,
(309) 343–5376

Packinghouse Dining
Company,
441 Mulberry,
(309) 342–6868

The Steak House,
951 North Henderson,
(309) 343–9994

GRAFTON

Père Marquette Lodge,
Route 100,
(618) 786–2331

MACOMB

Dillons,
538 North Lafayette Street,
(309) 836–3647

NAUVOO

Grandpa John's,
1255 Mulholland Street,
(217) 453–2310

Hotel Nauvoo,
1290 Mulholland Street,
(217) 453–2211

PEORIA

Jumer's Bar at Radisson Hotel Peoria,
117 North Western Avenue,
(309) 673–8040

Kelleher's Irish Pub and Eatery,
619 South West Water Street,
(309) 673–6000

Spirit of Peoria,
100 Northeast Water Street,
(309) 636–6169

OTHER ATTRACTIONS WORTH SEEING IN WESTERN ILLINOIS

Old Carthage Jail and Visitor Center,
Carthage

Par-a-Dice Riverboat Casino,
East Peoria

Central Congregational Church,
Galesburg

Illinois Citizen Soldier Museum,
Galesburg

Lake Storey Recreational Area,
Galesburg

Seminary Street Historic Commercial District,
Galesburg

Historic Barn Tours,
Macomb

Metamora Courthouse State Historic Site,
Metamora

African-American Museum Hall of Fame,
Peoria

Glen Oak Zoo,
Peoria

Peoria Chiefs,
Peoria

Bradley University,
Peoria

Southeastern Illinois

Red Hills Country

One mile northeast of Sumner in Lawrence County is *Red Hills State Park,* a 948-acre preserve of high wooded hills, deep ravines, meadows, and year-round springs. Hickory, oak, sycamore, maple, gum, crab, walnut, and apple trees grow in abundance in this area. Squirrels, doves, woodcock, quail, and rabbit live and multiply in this haven for nature lovers and sports enthusiasts.

U.S. Highway 50 divides the park into two sections, and the park itself is a historical crossroad, the westernmost edge being the first land in Illinois ceded by Indians to the U.S. government. The borderline runs through the park from southwest to northeast and was set by a treaty made in 1795 at Greenville, Ohio, by Gen. Anthony Wayne and Native American tribes. The Indians relinquished all claims to the land northwest of the Ohio River and east of a specified line. The area was called the Vincennes Tract.

The name Red Hill comes from the peak by the same name, which is the highest point along the Baltimore and Ohio Railroad between Cincinnati and St. Louis. Red Hill is topped

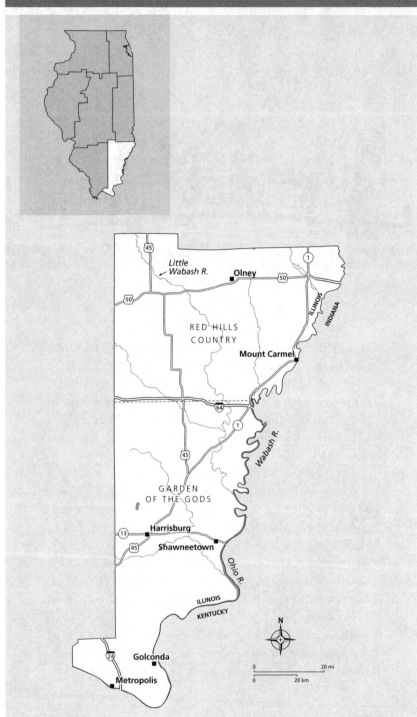

by a tower and cross, constructed and financed by residents cooperating in an interdenominational council.

The park has picnicking, fishing, boating, camping, and hunting facilities. A park interpreter conducts summer recreation programs. There is a trail through the woods, and other areas are suitable for hiking. Ice fishing and ice-skating are permitted in season. The park is open from sunrise to 10:00 P.M. daily. For more details contact Red Hills State Park, R.R. 2, Box 252A, Sumner 62466; (618) 936–2469.

Lawrence County residents like to celebrate, and there are four festivals of note: **Bridgeport SummerFest,** the first week in July; **Sumner Fall Festival,** the first weekend after Labor Day; **St. Francisville Chestnut Festival,** the first weekend in October; and the **Lawrenceville Fall Festival,** the second weekend in September. For exact dates and a list of activities contact the Lawrence County Chamber of Commerce, 619 Twelfth Street, Lawrenceville 62439; (618) 943–3516.

For nature buffs **Beall Woods Nature Preserve and State Park,** 6 miles south of Mount Carmel in Wabash County, is the largest tract of original decid-uous forest remaining in the United States and is relatively untouched by human beings. Sixty-four species of trees have been identified in the forest, and there is reason to believe that more will be discovered. Approximately 300 trees with trunks greater than 30 inches in circumference at chest height are in the park.

The tract of land that is now the park was under the ownership of the Beall family for more than 102 years. After the death of Laura Beall, the property was sold to a man who intended to clear the land and farm it. Conservation-minded individuals and groups helped to create the original acquisition by the state of Illinois in 1965 by invoking the law of eminent domain in order to preserve the virgin woodland for posterity.

AUTHOR'S TOP FIVE PICKS

Garden of the Gods,
(618) 287–2201

Superman's Metropolis,
(618) 524–2714

Cave-in-Rock,
(618) 289–4325

Rim Rock National Recreation Trail,
(618) 287–2201

Fort Massac Encampment,
(618) 524–4712

TOP ANNUAL EVENTS

Annual Superman Celebration,
Metropolis, early June,
(618) 524-2714

Golconda Fall Festival,
Golconda, October,
(618) 683-6246

Fort Massac Encampment,
Fort Massac State Park,
Metropolis, mid-October,
(618) 524-4712

**Olney Community Christmas
Light Display,**
Olney, late November–December,
(618) 395-1473

Annual Tour of Homes,
Metropolis, early December,
(618) 524-2714

Beall Woods is a registered landmark and is listed as the "Forest of the Wabash." The woods are made up of 270 acres of primeval woodland that borders the Wabash River, and the area was dedicated as an Illinois nature preserve to ensure that the forest will remain in its natural condition.

Beall Woods is sometimes referred to as the "University of the Trees" because it is a living forest community with a natural ecological system containing native plant and animal life. Hikers can view red fox, deer, raccoon, and pileated woodpeckers, and the forest floor supports a variety of interesting flowers.

There are plenty of hiking trails for those interested. The trails begin at the visitor center, where informative displays explain the early natural history of the area. Ask the park interpreter about nature programs that run from April to October. Hours are 8:00 A.M. to 4:00 P.M. daily.

There are also facilities for picnicking and a playground. The park is open year-round except for Christmas and New Year's Day. For information contact the Site Superintendent, 9285 Beall Woods Avenue, Mount Carmel 62863; (618) 298-2442. Beall Woods is near Keensburg off Route 1, about 6 miles south of Mount Carmel.

Edwards County is known as the Chowder Capital of the World. The aroma of this fragrant dish can be detected around the county anytime from June through September.

There is no exact information on when chowder became popular here, but records from the time of the Civil War indicate that it was enjoyed as early as the 1860s.

Chowder is generally cooked in large black kettles ranging in size from twenty to seventy gallons. A variety of ingredients, including tomatoes, are added to boiling water; chowder time traditionally starts when the tomatoes ripen and closes with the first heavy frost.

The *Albion Pagoda* in Albion was erected in 1914 and is the town's pride. The first pagoda was built around the mineral-water well in 1890. The waters were said to cure rheumatism, kidney and urinary troubles, "derangements of the stomach and bowels," and many other afflictions. When the original pagoda deteriorated, a second one was built in the same location; then in 1906 the current two-story structure replaced the two previous ones. The third pagoda was designed by architect W. E. Felix of Fairfield and constructed as a community program by the Albion Women's Beautifying Club.

The pagoda is octagonal with eight brick columns. The roof is made of red clay, resembling the roofs of the pagodas in East Asia.

Olney is the home of the white albino squirrel. Local legend says that the white squirrel first appeared here in 1902. A hunter captured two squirrels, a male and a female, and put them on display in a town saloon.

Another townsman heard about the squirrels and sent his son over to get the animals and release them in the woods. As soon as the squirrels were freed, a large fox squirrel jumped down from a tree and killed the male. The son shot the fox squirrel as he tried to attack the female. Weeks later baby white albino squirrels were seen, and the population has increased to hundreds of albino squirrels.

A city ordinance has been enacted to protect these special citizens. A white squirrel has the right of way on any street in Olney, and a motorist is fined $25 for running over one. Anyone caught taking one out of town will also be fined.

Believe It!

It is worthwhile to visit West Salem (yes, it is located east of the town of Salem, and just south of Olney) to soak up a bit of both history and oddity. This little settlement was home to the only Moravian congregation in Illinois. These utopian pioneers, who believed in God, hard work, and communal living, first settled in Salem, North Carolina, to escape religious persecution in nineteenth-century Europe.

Here in West Salem's little cemetery, you can see the only real remnants left of that historic community. Note that men and women are buried in separate plots. And a headstone reported to be the "smallest in the world" by *Ripley's Believe It or Not* is here, too. Can you find it? Call (618) 548–3010 for information.

Olney residents are also protective of their bird population. At Bird Haven in the **Robert Ridgway Memorial Arboretum and Bird Sanctuary,** you can walk and observe nature. Robert Ridgway, a naturalist, scientist, artist, and author, is famous for his books *Birds of Middle and North America* and *Color Stands and Color Nomenclature.* He was associated with the Smithsonian Institution and was a zoologist for the Survey of the Fortieth Parallel. He was also an authority in the field of ornithology.

Ridgway purchased the eighteen acres of Bird Haven in 1906. By the 1920s the arboretum and bird sanctuary was said to have had the second-largest number of plant species of any arboretum, second to a larger tract in Japan.

southeastern illinoistrivia

This section of Illinois is often called the "empty quarter," holding the state's least populous counties.

The Ridgway summer cottage once stood on the grounds, and a replica of the front porch has been reproduced on the cottage site. Dr. Ridgway's grave is on the grounds and is marked by a granite boulder with a bronze plaque with birds sculpted on it.

Bird Haven's hours are from dusk to dawn. For more information contact Olney City Hall, 300 South Whittle Avenue, Olney 62450; (618) 395–7302. Bird Haven is a half mile northeast of Olney on East Fork Lake Road.

Olney holds an annual **Arts and Crafts Festival** on the last Saturday of September. The event features performing arts and a juried art show. There's plenty of great food, too. For information or entry forms, contact City Hall at 300 South Whittle Avenue, Olney 62450; (618) 395–7302.

Garden of the Gods

In the southeast corner of the county, where Saline, Gallatin, and Hardin Counties triangulate into the **Shawnee National Forest,** is the **Garden of the Gods,** one of the state's most dramatic natural attractions. Created more than 200 million years ago from geologic uplifting, spectacular rock outcroppings have been formed through the action of water and wind. The unusual rock formations have been given names by imaginative explorers—Camel Rock, Noah's Ark, Mushroom Rock, Fat Man's Squeeze, and Tower of Babel are some of the more colorful ones.

One mile of well-maintained trails and 5 miles of semideveloped trails allow hikers to trek through the low mountainous region. Part of the Shawnee National Forest, which runs across the width of southern Illinois, the Garden of the Gods is a perfect spot for camping. For information on the Garden of the Gods, contact the Shawnee National Forest Headquarters at (618) 253–7114. Just north is the Saline County Conservation Area with its Glen O. Jones Lake.

Harrisburg, the county seat, was at one time a major center for tobacco growing and, later, coal mining. Here the *Saline County Area Museum,* 1600 Feazel Street, is a popular attraction. Set in a parklike setting are a handful of furnished historic buildings, moved here from around the area. You can visit a nineteenth-century one-room schoolhouse, an old Moravian church, a log cabin, general store, post office, and barn with its original threshing floor. The museum is open limited hours Tuesday through Sunday in summer, and weekends in winter. Call for specific appointment; (618) 253–7342. Admission is $3.00 for adults, $1.00 for children.

The prize of McLeansboro, the Hamilton County seat, is the *McCoy Memorial Library,* on the west side of the public square. The Cloud family built this handsome brick Victorian mansion, with a central tower and unique roofline, in 1884. It is listed in the National Register of Historic Places. Along with an 8,000-volume collection, the library boasts countless antiques on display for visitors. A central feature of the home is the number of noteworthy fireplaces throughout the structure—nine. On the second floor, the *Hamilton County Historical Society Museum* exhibits souvenirs of the area's past. Open Monday through Saturday 1:00 to 4:00 P.M. The library is open every day but Sunday; (618) 643–2125.

Next to the library building and once a residence is the *People's National Bank,* built by the same family, the Clouds, and also listed in the National Register.

Rocky Rim Rendezvous

The Rock Rim Trail in the Garden of the Gods region is perhaps the most unusual spot in the Shawnee National Forest—maybe even in all of Illinois.

Here you can hike over flagstone paths meandering through spectacular rock formations that have eroded and uplifted over more than 200 million years into a jumble of shapes and forms. But it is on the way back to Golconda that you can experience a perfect southeastern Illinois moment. Stop at Indian Kitchen, a tall rock shelf with a panoramic view of Lusk Creek Canyon. This is some of Illinois' most rugged (and unexpected) terrain.

And the narrow trail that leads up to the top of the precipice is a must for experienced trekkers.

Before leaving McLeansboro, retreat to the ***Innstead Bed and Breakfast,*** 400 South Washington Avenue, for a peaceful sleep. A full country breakfast in the morning will make you glad you stayed in town. For reservations call (618) 643–2038.

Although today we can get in our cars and speed hundreds of miles over broad, smoothly paved interstate highways, travelers in the first part of the nineteenth century turned to rivers and riverboats for efficient travel. And of those rivers, the Ohio was one of the longest and most frequently chosen routes, an interstate expressway from Pennsylvania all the way to the Mississippi River. Thus, the importance of Gallatin County and its seat, Shawneetown, is clearly understood in terms of a river port. Today one of the world's longest-span cantilever bridges crosses the Ohio at Shawneetown.

Shawnee Indians had a village here in the mid-1700s, and burial mounds can be seen throughout the area. The earliest white settlers arrived around 1800. In 1810 the federal government laid out Shawneetown on the river, and it quickly became a major port and gateway for immigrants into the new frontier. In 1814 it became the first incorporated town in Illinois. A ferry service, crossing the river into Kentucky, was begun. Four years later the U.S. Land Office for southeastern Illinois opened at Shawneetown. Adding to the economic growth of the community were the nearby saltworks at Equality, which supplied an important pioneer commodity and shipped salt throughout the region. Thus, Shawneetown became an important financial center in the American westward movement. One early resident was Gen. Thomas Posey, a member of George Washington's staff who was present for the British surrender at Yorktown. He is buried 2 miles north of the town in ***Westwood Cemetery.***

The first bank in the territory opened here in 1816. Known as the ***John Marshall Bank*** for the early merchant who began it in his house, the brick structure has been reconstructed by the local historical society and is open for tours by appointment. There are also walking tours available that take in a number of sites in the historic town.

anewillinois

Now that you have made it past the cornfields, past the sea of prairies, and past the glacier's drift, you'll discover a new kind of Illinois. One with dense forests, 200-million-year-old sandstone cliffs and outcroppings of spectacular shapes and sizes, deep ravines, and incredible river bluff vistas.

Your travels might be slower here due to the local geography. There are fewer big roads, but more backcountry beauty. Relax and enjoy, ease your pace. Follow the contours of the land to new adventures—the kind you never dreamed that you'd discover in Illinois.

A second bank, the 1839 *First State Bank,* is a handsome Greek Revival building with Doric columns supporting a portico. (It's now listed in the National Register of Historic Places.) For its construction, sandstone was floated down the Ohio by flatboat from quarries in the East. A favorite local story is of the time when businessmen from the tiny village of Chicago rode to Shawnee-town to ask bankers there for a loan. They were refused on the grounds that Chicago was much too far from Shawneetown to ever prosper.

The Ohio River proved a blessing and a curse for the community. Major floods struck the town in 1884, 1898, 1913, and 1937. In 1937 residents rebuilt their community in the hills 3 miles inland. In Old Shawneetown, the original settlement, many of the old landmarks are part of *Shawneetown State Memorial Park,* on the banks of the river.

The most famous visitor of all to come to Shawneetown was Marquis de Lafayette. The Revolutionary War hero was honored here at a reception at the Rawlings Hotel on May 7, 1825. Gov. Edward Coles greeted the soldier at the waterfront. The hotel burned in 1904 and was later rebuilt.

Equality, at the west side of the county near Route 142 and Route 13, was the site for the United States Salines, salty springs first discovered by the Indians. Later, French and American settlers made salt at the site. As an important early industry, the springs became the property of first the federal, then the state government. Andrew Jackson, before becoming president, attempted to lease these springs. Today only some crumbling foundations remain. A mural in the *Gallatin County Courthouse* depicts these salt-making operations.

At the northwest border of the county, at New Haven, once stood the mill of Jonathan Boone, who was the brother of Daniel Boone. Jonathan Boone died here in 1808. A state historical marker records the spot today.

Two miles off Route 1 and 11 miles south of Cave-in-Rock is Pounds Hollow, an especially scenic recreation area. A twenty-two-acre lake is nestled under steep bluffs. Follow Rim Rock Trail around the lake to the prehistoric *Pounds Wall,* a 7,000-year-old Indian structure. It is uncertain whether this Pounds Wall, once 8 to 10 feet high, was used as a fortification or for killing buffalo. Most experts guess the latter use because a buffalo wallow is nearby. Buffalo would have been rounded up against the wall and slaughtered.

southeastern illinoistrivia

Marion's Illinois Centre Mall, spread over more than 200 acres, is Southern Illinois' largest shopping mall.

At the southeastern tip of Illinois, on the Ohio River, Hardin County has long been a stopping place for restless pioneers moving west. One of the first

Cave-in-Rock Rocks

Let me set up the Cave-in-Rock scene for you in *How the West Was Won,* a blockbuster movie starring a roll call of Hollywood stars of the 1960s, including John Wayne, Jimmy Stewart, Debbie Reynolds, and George Peppard. Debbie Reynolds's family is traveling down the Ohio on a river raft when they are lured to the shore by "merchants" advertising all kinds of needed goods from a perch in a cavern set high in a bluff overlooking the river.

Of course, the "merchants" are nothing more than river pirates set on looting the westward settlers, killing the men, and stealing the women. And they would have, too, if not for the intervention of scout Jimmy Stewart, who comes to their rescue.

But go rent the movie at your nearest video store—not necessarily for the film itself (it's an okay flick). However, the photography at Cave-in-Rock, which was used for the location shoot for this segment of the movie, is spectacular. And once you get a glimpse of the beauty of southeastern Illinois country, you'll want to visit it even more.

was Samuel Mason, an officer of the Continental Army and renegade son of an important Virginia family, who came to Illinois territory in 1797. Discovering a deep cavern on the bluff overlooking the river, Mason set himself up in business, advertising over the arched cavern opening, LIQUOR VAULT AND HOUSE OF ENTERTAINMENT. His business, though, was not innkeeping, but rather piracy, and he handily plundered gullible travelers and flatboat crews. When his notoriety caught up with him, he fled, leaving the cave to a long line of fellow thieves. It has gained further fame since being used as a locale for the movie *How the West Was Won* and the two television series about Davy Crockett and Daniel Boone.

Today *Cave-in-Rock* is part of a state park of the same name, with facilities for picnicking, hiking, boating, fishing, and camping (sixty sites, thirty-four with electric hookups). It's off Route 1 and open year-round, Box 338, Cave-in-Rock 62919; (618) 289–4325.

From the little town here runs the only ferry on the Ohio River that shuttles cars and passengers. It operates 6:00 A.M. to 6:00 P.M. daily. On the third weekend in mid-September each year, Cave-in-Rock holds *Frontier Days* to commemorate its historic past. The event features a parade, beauty pageant, carnival, square dancing, and craft exhibits.

Four miles north of Rosiclare near the junction of Route 34 and Route 146 is the *Old Illinois Iron Furnace,* the first in Illinois. It began in 1837 on colorfully named Hog Thief Creek, eventually supporting one hundred families. Some of its production was used at the Mound City Naval Shipyards to clad gunboats during the Civil War. The furnace was abandoned in 1883. There are two interpretive trails at the site along with an inviting "swimming hole" in Big Creek.

At Elizabethtown on Route 146 at the Ohio River is the **River Rose Inn** (618–287–8811), a bed-and-breakfast housed in a Greek Revival building. The River Rose Inn specializes in gourmet breakfasts.

Seven miles west from Cave-in-Rock and about 4 miles south of Route 146 is **Tower Rock**

Old Illinois Iron Furnace

Park Recreation Area, where the scenery is a fine example of that found throughout the Shawnee National Forest, which covers the county. The Ohio River runs along the southern edge of the park, providing opportunities for fishing and boating. Camping and picnicking are also available at Tower Rock. Ranger's Office: (618) 287–2201.

The people of Metropolis will swear to you that Superman really exists. Metropolis claims to be the hometown of the fictional movie and cartoon character Superman. A billboard of Superman welcoming visitors to Metropolis

City of Festivals

Metropolis may be best known as the "home of the Man of Steel." Why not? It is the only town in the entire United States named Metropolis. And who's going to argue with Superman, anyway?

But Metropolis offers much more for wanderers to this extreme southern outpost of Illinois. In fact, it might even be called a city of festivals, because it seems as if some kind of celebration is slated virtually every month.

So besides the annual Superman celebration in June, don't miss German Fest in April; the Rotary Car Show in June; Labor Day Celebration, Arts in the Parks, and Superman Jet Rally in September; the Fort Massac Encampment in October; the Home Town Christmas (at Fort Massac) in November and December; and the Old Tyme Christmas Celebration in December.

If you can't find something special to do in Metropolis, then you aren't trying. Call the Metropolis Chamber of Commerce at (618) 524-2714.

Legendary Nonsense

A legend has persisted that the ground upon which Fort Massac is built was the site of a massacre of French troops by Indians in the early eighteenth century. Thus, when the French built a fort here, they named it Fort Massacre, which later became shortened by Americans to Massac.

Most legends have a kernel of truth about them, but not this one. The fort was actually named Massiac, after a French minister of colonial affairs, and it did come under attack once by a large force of Cherokee, but the garrison repulsed them. After the French and Indian War, the fort was abandoned, and a band of Chickasaws promptly burned it to the ground. So in a way, yes, a massacre did take place here—but it was a massacre of lice and vermin, not humans.

greets you as you enter the town, and another portrait of their hero adorns the water tower. The Chamber of Commerce boasts the only official Superman phone booth, where you can actually speak with the Man of Steel. And just for the sake of continuity, the local newspaper is called the *Daily Planet*.

An annual **Superman Celebration** usually falls on the second weekend in June, runs for two days, and includes a beauty pageant, style show, arts and crafts show, street dance, flea market, and Superman Run.

Massac County is home to Fort Massac. One of five former French forts in the Illinois park system, it borders the Ohio River at the southern tip of the state. Indians were believed to have first used the site because of its strategic location on the river. In the early 1540s Spanish explorer Hernando de Soto and his soldiers constructed a fortification here for protection from hostile Indians.

In the eighteenth century the French constructed Fort Massiac, later anglicized to Massac. Reconstruction of the fort and an accompanying museum was completed in 1973. Three of the buildings were originally used as living quarters for enlisted men and as means of defense, with loopholes through which muskets were shot.

The **Fort Massac Museum** houses a miniature replica of the fort, artifacts, and a history of the fort. It is open year-round Wednesday through Sunday 9:30 A.M. to 4:30 P.M. Guided tours are available. Call (618) 524–9321 for an appointment.

Fort Massac State Park is open daily. The replica of the fort is open daily from April 1 to October 30, 10:00 A.M. to 5:30 P.M. The park offers picnicking, fishing, boating, and camping facilities, and two self-guided trails for hiking. Hunting is allowed in season. For information contact the Site Superintendent, 1308 East Fifth Street, Metropolis 62960; (618) 524–9321.

The *Fort Massac Encampment* is an annual festival recreating the atmosphere of a military encampment in the Illinois country in the 1700s. It is traditionally held the third weekend in October. Contact the park office for events and times.

Fort Massac State Park is located 2½ miles west of Metropolis off Interstate 24 on Route 45. The museum and encampment are on the grounds.

Kitch-mus-ke-nee-be, or the Great Medicine Waters, was the Shawnee name for the area known as *Dixon Springs State Park.* Spanning over 800 acres, the park is perched high upon a bed of rock and offers staggering views of hills and vales. The spring rains create waterfalls surging down the cliffs. The area is rich in native species of trees and fauna, and populated with an abundance of forest animals from squirrels and deer to red fox. Despite its natural beauty and excellent hunting grounds, the park has been a draw for centuries because of the seven mineral springs that percolate from beneath the ground.

William Dixon claimed the land for himself as the area's first white settler in 1848. A small settlement grew here and when word of the springs bubbled out to the general public, Dixon Springs became host to a rush of visitors, some from as far away as Indiana and Kentucky, who traveled great distances to secure the mineral-rich brew. Others arrived by riverboat to partake in what has been called a "nineteenth-century health spa."

Today, it's the expansive views of ancient giant trees and breathtaking rock formations that continue to draw visitors.

Picnicking, camping, biking, and hiking are permitted. Enjoy the self-guided 1.7-mile nature trail or the modern swimming pool supplied by spring water, with lifeguard and bathhouse facilities. A concession stand is located near the pool as well as picnic shelters, playgrounds, and drinking water.

History Lesson

To discover an interesting slice of little-known southeastern Illinois history, put on your hiking boots—because you are going to need them. No doubt you'll have to slosh through some muck while visiting Miller Grove Cemetery in Golconda. It is said to be the last vestige of an early African American settlement that some historians claim was the first such community in Illinois.

The town of Miller Grove is thought to have been established before the Civil War began. Free black families came to live here in the 1830s, and some burial sites in the cemetery date back to 1865. However, people deserted the town by 1925, and the cemetery is all that is left of this historic locale.

The park is open year-round except for holidays. For information contact the Site Superintendent, Dixon Springs State Park, R.R. 2, Box 178, Route 146, Golconda 62938; (618) 949–3394.

The Mansion in Golconda is a Victorian-style house converted into a bed-and-breakfast and restaurant; several Illinois governors have enjoyed the home-cooked meals here; 515 Columbus, Golconda; (618) 683–4400. Full breakfast is included in the fare, and the restaurant is open to the public.

Places to Stay in Southeastern Illinois

ALBION

Albion Hotel,
Route 15 West,
(618) 445–2311

ELDORADO

Neal Motel,
1014 Highway 45 North,
(618) 273–8146

GOLCONDA

The Mansion,
515 Columbus Street,
(618) 683–4400

METROPOLIS

Best Western
Metropolis Inn,
2119 East Fifth Street,
(618) 524–3723

Comfort Inn of Metropolis,
2118 East Fifth Street,
(618) 524–7227

Days Inn,
1415 East Fifth Street,
(618) 524–9341

OTHER ATTRACTIONS WORTH SEEING IN SOUTHEASTERN ILLINOIS

Albion Public Library,
Albion

The Chocolate Factory,
Dixon Springs

Lake Glendale Recreation Area,
Dixon Springs

Smithland Pool,
Golconda

Ohio River Recreation Area,
Golconda

Lincoln Heritage Trail State Monument,
Lawrenceville

Super Museum,
Metropolis

Major Elijah P. Curtis Home and Museum,
Metropolis

Merv Griffin's Theater,
Metropolis

Harrah's Metropolis Casino,
Metropolis

Olney Animal Sanctuary,
Olney

Lake Thunderhawk,
Ozark

Teutopolis Monastery Museum,
Teutopolis

Moravian Church and Cemetery,
West Salem

SELECTED VISITORS BUREAUS AND CHAMBERS OF COMMERCE

Southernmost Illinois Tourism and
Convention Bureau,
Anna, 62906
(800) 248–4373

Illinois Bureau of Tourism–Travel,
(800) 2–CONNECT

MT. CARMEL

Shamrock Hotel,
Route 1 North,
1303 North Cherry,
(618) 262–4169

Town and Country Motel,
1515 West Third Street,
(618) 262–4171

OLNEY

Royal Inn Motel,
1001 West Main Street,
(618) 395–8581

Shady Timbers Lodge,
5569 North Sugar Creek,
(618) 393–4900

Travelers Inn Motel,
1801 East Main Street,
(618) 393–2186

Places to Eat in
Southeastern Illinois

CAVE-IN-ROCK

Cave-in-Rock State Park
Lodge and Restaurant,
1 New State Park Road,
(618) 289–4545

GOLCONDA

The Mansion,
515 Columbus Street,
(618) 683–4400

METROPOLIS

Harrah's Metropolis
Casino,
100 East Front Street,
(618) 524–2628

Southwestern Illinois

The Lake Region

Carlyle Lake, the largest inland lake in Illinois, lies primarily within the borders of Clinton County. Created in 1967 by damming the Kaskaskia River, its area covers some 26,000 acres with 83 miles of shoreline. The U.S. Army Corps of Engineers, which maintains the reservoir, estimates that almost one million visitors enjoy the lake each year. Its primary attractions are fishing (for white bass, crappie, largemouth bass, channel catfish, and bluegill), sailing, boating, and hunting, in season. With two state parks on its shore—*Eldon Hazlet State Park* and *South Shore State Park*—camping is readily available. More than 400 sites (336 with electric hookups) can be found in the state parks alone. Additional campsites are available at lake recreation areas and at commercial campgrounds. Eldon Hazlet State Park is off Route 127, 6 miles north of Carlyle. South Shore State Park is off U.S. Highway 50, 2 miles east of Carlyle. The parks have the same phone number: (618) 594–3015.

A good place to begin a visit is the *Carlyle Visitor Center,* operated by the U.S. Army Corps of Engineers. The center displays a model of the lake and dam, showing how the reservoir was created. Exhibits of the area's natural history are

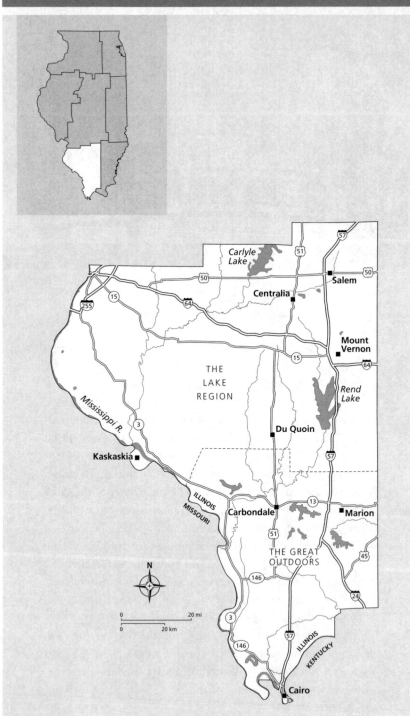

Carlyle
Lake

Salem

Centralia

Mount
Vernon

THE
LAKE
REGION

Rend
Lake

Mississippi R.

Du Quoin

Kaskaskia

ILLINOIS
MISSOURI

Carbondale

Marion

THE GREAT
OUTDOORS

N

0   20 mi
0   20 km

ILLINOIS
KENTUCKY

Cairo

especially informative. On weekends the center schedules worthwhile interpretive programs such as nature walks, discussions of area Indian history, and
water safety seminars. Open Memorial Day through Labor Day 10:00 A.M. to
6:00 P.M. every day. Open weekends only in April and October; (618) 594–5253.
The Carlyle Visitor Center is located at the Dam West recreation area, immediately west of the main dam 1 mile north of Carlyle off Route 127.

The *Carlyle West Access Marina* supplies services to the lake's boaters—
docking and fuel, motorboats, Hobie Cats, sailboards, and cabin sailboats for
rent. The proprietor can be reached at (618) 594–2461. The marina is immediately west of the main dam, off Route 127 north of Carlyle.

Just south of the main dam, off Route 127, is a one-and-a-half-acre plot of
natural prairie. In 1974 park rangers seeded the land with grasses and wildflowers indigenous to the Illinois prairie of 150 years ago. A 1-mile trail leads
through the prairie. Pick up a walking guide that explains the various plants at
the Carlyle Visitor Center.

Carlyle even has its own entry in the National Register of Historic Places—
the 1859 *General Dean suspension bridge,* the only suspension bridge in
the state. Built to span the Kaskaskia River on the east side of town, the bridge
was a link in the old St. Louis–Vincennes Trail. Stone towers 35 feet tall support a 280-foot span. The bridge was restored in 1977 for use as a pedestrian
crossing. On the east side of the bridge is a recreation area with picnic tables and
grills and a boat ramp. The bridge was named for William F. Dean, a Carlyle
native and hero of the Korean War.

Illinois residents don't dwell much on the topic of earthquakes, since they
are a rare occurrence in the Midwest. However, in 1811 a shaker along the
New Madrid fault started a domino effect of migration away from the borders
of Missouri and Illinois. One such pioneer looking for more stable ground was

AUTHOR'S TOP FIVE PICKS

Giant City State Park and Lodge,
(618) 457–4836

Fort de Chartres,
Prairie du Rocher,
(618) 284–7230

Du Quoin State Fair,
Du Quoin,
(618) 542–1515

Kaskaskia State Historic
Site and Island,
Ellis Grove,
(618) 859–3741

Rend Lake,
Benton,
(618) 435–8138

The Town the Train Built

Illinois Central Gulf Railroad founded the town of Centralia, just southeast of Carlyle Lake. It's an interesting spot to visit for lots of reasons, but here are two.

The rail company had car shops on the south edge of town and at one time held deeds to almost all the land in the central business district. So this proud old railroad town displays one of the last great classic steam engines made here: Engine 2500, now located in Fairview Park. Volunteers had to lay more than 1 mile of temporary track to get this behemoth here from its former location.

Also in Centralia's central business district stands the Centralia Carillon, a huge tower boasting sixty-five bells, the largest of which weighs almost six tons. Local carilloneurs (that's what the musicians who play this instrument are called) must huff and puff up 173 steps (that's fourteen stories) to address a keyboard that's almost 8 feet long. The instrument can produce any kind of music, from pop and classical to marches and college fight songs. But music written specifically for the carillon is preferred by these specialized music wizards, who produce such dulcet tones from this mammoth instrument. Call (618) 533–4381.

Captain Samuel Young. Young ended up building his homestead in Marion County, on what is now the courthouse lawn of the Salem square.

Salem became a stagecoach stop on the Vincennes Trail, and the arrival of the railroads from 1850 to 1860 produced Salem's first boom. In the early 1900s oil brought another boom to the town, and in 1939 Salem was the nation's second-largest oil field.

Salem also has some prominent history in its veins. William Jennings Bryan, called the Silver-Tongued Orator and The Great Commoner, was born here. He was the U.S. secretary of state, 1913–15, and a three-time presidential candidate.

Salem's American Legion Post played an important role in producing the GI Bill of Rights. It took seven months and eight days from the time the Salem Legionnaires collaborated on the plan before it was approved by Congress in 1944.

Salem is full of historic architecture, and the Chamber of Commerce, 615 West Main Street, Salem 62881; (618) 548–3010, has published a walking tour that highlights the sites. The tour begins at the west end of the IGA parking lot on East Main and takes you past many notable landmarks. A statue of favorite son, William Jennings Bryan is a must-see, as it was sculpted by Gutzon Borglum, the artist best known for creating the faces on Mount Rushmore. The statue was originally dedicated in 1936 by President Theodore Roosevelt in

Washington, D.C. It was moved to its current spot across from the Bryan Memorial Park in 1961. Bryan earned national recognition after successfully prosecuting another former Salem resident, John Thomas Scopes, for teaching the theory of evolution in his classes. The contest was called the "Scopes Monkey Trial."

The *birthplace of William Jennings Bryan,* at 408 South Broadway, is on the National Register of Historic Places and is open for tours on all days but Thursday from 1:00 to 5:00 P.M.; (618) 548–3010 or (618) 548–2222.

There are several Salem properties that warrant a drive-by. The *Badollet House,* circa 1854, sits at 310 North Washington. It was here that John Thomas Scopes stayed while attending high school. Ironically, Bryan was the keynote speaker at Scopes' graduation from Salem High School in 1919, and the two were friends, despite the trial. Supposedly, Bryan offered to pay the $100 judgment that the court levied on Scopes.

The *Lemen-Frakes House,* at 321 South Franklin, has a long history of famous guests from foreign royalty to American royalty in the form of Abraham Lincoln.

The *Halfway Tavern,* 10 miles east of Salem on US 50 East, was built in 1818 and served as a stagecoach stop until 1861. It was built on the trail across Illinois that Capt. George Rogers Clark had used in 1799, and Abraham Lincoln later used it as a stopover.

Oil was first discovered near Salem in 1909, but the oil boom came in 1938. The Salem Oil Field ranked seventeenth in the nation in volume of oil production. It currently produces more than three million barrels a year. Pumps can be seen at the field 6 miles southwest of Salem.

The *Stephen A. Forbes State Fish and Wildlife Area,* 15 miles northeast of Salem, has outdoor recreation including fishing, hunting, boating, picnicking, waterskiing, swimming, camping, hiking, and horseback riding. The *Sam Parr Biological Station Research Center* conducts aquatic biology and fisheries experiments. The center is open to visitors Monday through Friday. Tours can be arranged by calling (618) 245–6348.

For information about the park, contact the Site Superintendent, Stephen A. Forbes State Fish and Wildlife Area, 6924 Omega Road, Kinmundy; (618) 547–3381.

Jefferson County is filled with southern hospitality brought over the state line from Dixie. Mount Vernon, the county seat, was settled by southerners and remains peopled by the descendants of southern families.

Mount Vernon is also known as "The King City" because it "crowns southern Illinois."

A variety of activities awaits tourists, ranging from cultural activities to historic sites, to sweet corn and watermelon festivals.

The *Mitchell Museum at Cedarhurst,* a ninety-acre estate, features an 8,000-square-foot exhibit gallery, a smaller lecture gallery, and storage for its extensive collection of nineteenth- and twentieth-century American art acquired by the late John R. and Eleanor Mitchell.

Cedarhurst's permanent collection contains work from world-renowned artists such as American master Mary Cassatt. The gallery also rotates exhibits, making each visit a unique one for guests. A children's gallery displays colorful creative works and features an annual scholastic competition and exhibition. Children will also enjoy educational but entertaining shows by Cedarhurst's *School of Performing Arts.* A chamber music concert series and annual craft show has wide appeal.

Possibly the most fascinating way to spend the day is to walk the paths along the extensive *Sculpture Garden.* Here you can ponder the craft of major artisans such as Martha Enzmann and Dennis Oppenheim. There are sixty large-scale works presented along the trails of the ninety-acre estate, around the pond and through the meadow, providing a satisfying blending of art combined with the natural world.

TOP ANNUAL EVENTS

Fruehlingfest (Springfest),
Maeystown, early May,
(618) 458–6660

Fort du Chartres Kids Day,
Prairie du Rocher, mid-May,
(618) 284–7230

Fort de Chartres Annual Rendezvous,
Prairie du Rocher, early June,
(618) 284–7230

Grape Stomp,
Cobden, mid-June,
(618) 893–2557

Archaeology Day,
Kampsville, late June,
(618) 653–4316

Annual Popeye Picnic,
Chester, mid-September,
(618) 826–4567

Murphysboro Apple Festival,
Murphysboro, mid-September,
(800) 406–8774

Applebutter Festival,
Maystown, late September,
(618) 458–6660

Riverboat Days,
Cairo, late September–early October,
(618) 734–2737

Oktoberfest,
Maeystown, mid-October,
(618) 458–6660

Fort de Chartres Winter Rendezvous,
Prairie du Rocher, early November,
(618) 284–7230

Open Tuesday through Saturday 10:00 A.M. to 5:00 P.M.; Sunday 1:00 to 5:00 P.M.; closed holidays and Mondays. Free admission except on special programs. Located at Richview Road in Mount Vernon; (618) 242–1236.

The *Veterans Memorial Walkway* is a memorial to all Jefferson County soldiers killed in war. A special bronze plaque is mounted on granite for each soldier, and these granite stones border the County Courthouse at Route 37 and Main Street in downtown Mount Vernon. An 8-foot-tall black Carmelian granite monolith lists the wars in which Jefferson County citizens participated.

And the *Appellate Courthouse* has plenty of history within its walls. Abraham Lincoln successfully argued a famous tax case here in 1859, and Clara Barton used the building as a hospital in 1888. It is now the Fifth District Appellate Court and law library. Tours of the building are available when the court is not in session. It is located at Main and Fourteenth Streets. Hours are Monday through Friday 8:30 A.M. to 4:30 P.M. Call (618) 242–3120 for information.

The newly remodeled *Brehm Memorial Library* houses historical documents regarding local history and genealogy. It is located at 101 South Seventh Street, and its hours are Monday through Thursday 9:00 A.M. to 8:00 P.M., Friday 9:00 A.M. to 5:00 P.M., Saturday 10:00 A.M. to 4:00 P.M., and Sunday 1:00 to 5:00 P.M., closed Sunday June through August; (618) 242–6322.

The *Illinois Sweet Corn and Watermelon Festival* is held the third week in August. A week of activities includes sweet corn and watermelon served in the town square. Contact the Mount Vernon Convention and Visitors Bureau, P.O. Box 1708, Mount Vernon 62864; (618) 242–3151.

As well as providing nine to eleven million gallons of water daily for the area, *Rend Lake* offers a recreational retreat. The lake is surrounded by rolling-hill prairie country and has excellent crappie fishing. Waterfowl are hunted here as well as deer, rabbit, dove, quail, pheasant, and squirrel.

Picnic grounds for both small and large groups are adjacent to the lake, and the *Dale Miller Youth Area* is designed for the handicapped and youth groups. Advance reservations are necessary for that area.

Beaches are located at the *South Sandusky Recreation Area* and *North Marcum Recreation Area.* There are many boat launching facilities for sailboats and motorboats, and a marina is located on the west side of the lake. An eighteen-hole golf course, tennis courts, pro shop, trap shooting, restaurant, and meeting rooms are also available to tourists.

Observation of geese and ducks, eagles, osprey, loon, swans, heron, and songbirds on the Mississippi Flyway is a special treat for bird-watchers.

For information contact the U.S. Army Corps of Engineers, Rend Lake Management Office, 12220 Rend City Road, Benton; (618) 724–2493; or Rend Lake Conservancy District, 17738 Conservation Lane, Whittington; (618) 629–2368.

Lodge Luxuries

Rend Lake Resort is more than just your typical state park overnight accommodation. This multigabled waterside getaway, which sits on the edge of the 18,900-acre Rend Lake, is one of the state's finest first-class resorts in one of the region's top recreational areas—Wayne Fitzgerrell State Park.

This stylish lodge creates an elegant atmosphere in the midst of natural wonders, with all 105 guest chambers (resort rooms and cabins) boasting balconies and decks. (Ask for one of the rooms featuring a lakefront view.) There are also full private baths, television for kids who can't live without it, telephone, and more.

Some special accommodations offer sleeping lofts and spas with whirlpools, too.

Let's not forget to mention the resort's premier restaurant, Windows on Rend. Whether you choose to dine inside or on the outdoor deck, you'll enjoy great food—including the restaurant's specialty: pork chops and catfish (though not necessarily together!).

And when you're ready to work off that meal, choose from a twenty-seven-hole golf course, fishing, pontoon boat rentals, hiking, swimming, tennis, even bird-watching (blue herons and bald eagles are plentiful here). Call (800) 633–3341.

Franklin County shares its greatest natural resource, Rend Lake, with its neighbor, Jefferson County, to the north. Second largest in the state, the 18,900-acre lake has 162 miles of rugged shoreline, next to which is the 3,300-acre **Wayne Fitzgerrell State Park.** The park has 243 campsites, most with electric hookups, and offers a broad variety of recreational activities. For information contact the Site Superintendent, Wayne Fitzgerrell State Park, 11094 Ranger Road, Whittington; (618) 629–2320. The park is open year-round.

The Rend Lake Reservoir was created by damming the Big Muddy and Casey Fork Rivers, giving it its unusual Y shape. The Army Corps of Engineers is responsible for the administration of the lake and its visitor center.

Crappie, bass, and catfish are the most-caught species here. In season, hunting is available for all types of waterfowl, quail, pheasant, rabbit, deer, and squirrel.

Families will enjoy the picnic areas scattered throughout the lake's recreation areas. Swimming beaches are located at the South Sandusky and North Marcum recreation areas. The one marina on the west side of the lake has boat rentals available.

On the east side of the lake, the **Rend Lake Golf Course** is a twenty-seven-hole PGA facility with especially scenic terrain. Tennis courts, a restaurant, and a lighted driving range are part of the club. Bird-watching is excellent here, as the lake is situated on the Mississippi Flyway, allowing the observer to view great migrations of geese and ducks and offering sightings of eagles, ospreys, loons, herons, and other birds. In Wayne Fitzgerrell State Park, dog field-trial grounds are host to regional and national championships. For information contact the lake management office; (618) 724–2493. Located on the lake in the state park is **Rend Lake Resort;** (618) 629–2211 or (800) 633–3341. This new state facility has cabins and "boatel" suites.

In early May each year the **Rend Lake Water Festival** features parades, a carnival, craft exhibits, and entertainment. Call (618) 438–2121.

For all of us who love days off, Franklin County's seat, Benton, is where Memorial Day was first established. Here John A. Logan, a Civil War major general, U.S. representative and senator, and candidate for vice president in 1884, proposed the holiday in 1868, as commander of the Grand Army of the Republic. A historical marker designates his home site at 204 South Main Street.

At the southern edge of the county is the town of West Frankfort, where the government is seeking ways to protect its historic buildings. One successful example of recycling an older structure is the home of the **Frankfort Area Historical Museum,** which operates from the former Logan School at 2000 East St. Louis Street. The space is used cleverly: classrooms are full-scale vignettes showing aspects of prairie life. The tea room serves lunch and a gift shop is open on Wednesday and Thursday 11:00 A.M. to 1:00 P.M. The museum is open 9:00 A.M. to 3:00 P.M. Wednesday and Thursday or by appointment. Free admission; (618) 932–6159.

West Frankfort hosts the **Old King Coal Festival** the third week of September annually. There's a coronation of a king and queen, a midway, contests, and plenty of food; (618) 932–6562.

Du Quoin got its start as a stopping point on the old Shawneetown-to-Kaskaskia Road, where there was a crossing at the Little Muddy River. The town took its name from Kaskaskia Indian Chief Jean Baptiste Ducoigne, who came to the aid of George Rogers Clark after the fall of Kaskaskia and later served in the Revolutionary Army under Lafayette in Virginia. His tribe camped near the spot of the first white settlement, which took his name. When the railroad came to town in 1853, the town site moved a short distance to its present location.

Today the area is an important center for agriculture and mining and is the largest coal-producing county in Illinois. Numerous strip mines are found throughout the region. Du Quoin's major annual event is the **Du Quoin State Fair,** which begins in late August and runs through Labor Day. Over 200,000 visitors are attracted to the more-than-sixty-year-old event. Name entertainment, championship auto racing, and world-class harness racing headline the fair. The fairground's dirt track is called the "Magic Mile" for the number of speed records that have been set here. Tractor pulls and livestock shows round out the schedule. Throughout the year other events are staged at the fairgrounds, including camping rallies and a rodeo. Contact the Du Quoin State Fair offices at 655 Executive Drive, Du Quoin; (618) 542-1515.

southwestern illinoistrivia

Kaskaskia was the capital of the old Illinois Territory; government leaders rented a two-story brick building for $4.00 per day, making that the first state capitol.

Randolph is one of the most historically and geographically unique counties in all of Illinois. A tiny appendage protruding into the main body of Missouri, Kaskaskia Island is the only part of the state lying west of the Mississippi River.

Kaskaskia is the second-oldest settlement (after Cahokia) in the state, founded as a Jesuit mission in 1703. Thus, the area's French heritage is rich. Fort Kaskaskia was erected in the village and served as an outpost in the French and Indian War (1754–63). After the Treaty of Paris in 1763, the region came under British control. In 1778 George Rogers Clark captured the settlement for America, and it became a county of Virginia. It became part of the new Northwest Territory in 1787, part of the Indiana Territory in 1800, the capital of the Illinois Territory in 1809, and the first state capital in 1818 (until 1820 when the capital moved to Vandalia).

Kaskaskia declined in importance, and Mississippi floods around 1885 eventually destroyed the old settlement, cutting a new channel for the Mississippi through the heart of the town and creating Kaskaskia Island on the western side.

What remained on the eastern side of the river is now *Fort Kaskaskia State Historic Site* (618–859–3741). The park is an especially scenic area with places for picnicking among the trees. Situated on a hill, it overlooks the Mississippi River and Kaskaskia Island.

Three Flags

Kaskaskia reminds us that the territory known as Illinois, now the heartland of the United States, belonged to the French in the early 1700s. And that as part of the Treaty of Paris, which ended the French and Indian War in 1763, a large part of France's North American possessions—including Illinois—were awarded to Great Britian. It wasn't until George Rogers Clark captured Kaskaskia from the Brits in 1778 that an American flag flew here.

Just below the park, at the foot of the hill, between Chester and Ellis Grove, off Route 3, is the **Pierre Menard Home,** now a state memorial. Built in 1802 in French Colonial style, with a wide gallery porch and a low, hipped roof, this was the residence of the first lieutenant governor of Illinois, one of the most important men in the history of the territory. The house has been restored and furnished with pieces of the period. Open daily from May 29 to Labor Day 8:00 A.M. to 4:00 P.M.; limited winter hours; (618) 859–3031. The museum is free to the public though a donation of $2.00 is suggested.

On **Kaskaskia Island** is the **Liberty Bell of the West.** A gift from Louis XV of France, the bell was towed upriver from New Orleans by men pulling it on a barge. Today it's a state memorial. To reach the island cross the Chester toll bridge at Route 51 and travel 12 miles to St. Mary's, Missouri, then follow the directional signs to the island.

Chester, the county seat of Randolph County, has fostered a wide array of notable characters, both real and fictional.

Chester is home to Popeye, the lovable sailorman. His creator, Elzie Crisler Segar, was born here in 1894 and it is believed that he based the cartoon troupe on several of Chester's unwitting and colorful residents. In 1977 a **statue of Popeye** was erected in Segar Memorial Park. A **Popeye Picnic and Parade** are usually held the weekend after Labor Day.

North of Chester on Route 3 are large orchards with peaches, apples, and strawberries for sale. At the **Guten Tag Orchard,** you can view apple cider being pressed; (618) 826–3300.

Seven miles east of Chester on Route 150 between Chester and Bremen is the **Mary's River Covered**

southwestern illinoistrivia

The Kaskaskia Indians, unlike most tribes and bands in the region, took no part in the War of 1812 against the United States. Because of the enmity this aroused among other Indian groups, they were unable to hunt for fear of retaliation, so the government was forced to support and protect them over the length of the conflict. But it wasn't only other Indians the government had to protect them from. As one of Governor Ninian Edwards's subordinates stated, they were in more danger from "our own citizens, who neither can nor will discriminate between friends and foes when they meet an Indian in the woods."

southwestern illinoistrivia

During the Revolutionary War, Illinois became part of Virginia when George Rogers Clark captured Kaskaskia and Cahokia from the English in 1778.

Mary's River Covered Bridge

Bridge. One of the few such structures in the state, the 98-foot single-span bridge of hand-hewn native oak was erected in 1854.

North of Chester and Fort Kaskaskia are Prairie du Rocher (field of rock) and Fort de Chartres. No missionary is responsible for the settlement here. Instead credit goes to an early entrepreneur who set the stage for a long line of American land speculators to follow. John Law was a Scotch businessman who obtained a charter from the French government to colonize the region. His Company of the West brought in immigrants from France, Italy, Switzerland, and Germany. Law promised speculators great profits, but his "Mississippi Bubble" burst in 1720, leaving the settlers stranded.

Most stayed, under the protection of Pierre Duque, Sieur de Boisbriant, commandant of the Illinois country. By 1720 he completed the construction of **Fort de Chartres,** named for the Duc de Chartres, son of the French regent. The fort was rebuilt three times, and in its final form, which was stone, it was considered one of the strongest in North America.

Today parts of the old fort have been reconstructed and are part of a state park. Each year in June the **Fort de Chartres Rendezvous** re-creates life in the French era with volunteers in militia uniforms, a fife and drum corps, much firing of cannon, and French Colonial cooking. In early October there is an exciting **French and Indian War Encampment.** Fort de Chartres is open year-round, except major holidays, 9:00 A.M. to 5:00 P.M. Admission is free; (618) 284–7230.

In the northwest corner of the county, at Sparta, is the **Charter Oak School,** one of only a few octagonal schoolhouses remaining in the United States. Built in 1873, it served its public purpose until 1953.

From Chester, *U.S. Bicycle Route 76* leads east to Shiloh Hill and the county line, along scenic back roads. The paved bikeway is also referred to as the TransAmerica Bike Route. The trail continues across the United States and ends on the eastern coast of Virginia.

Perhaps one of the most unusual hotels in the state is the *Original Mineral Springs Hotel and Bath House* in Okawville, just off I–64 in the northwest part of the county. Built in 1892, the forty-room hostelry is listed in the National Register of Historic Places. For more than a hundred years, guests have been coming for the relaxing mineral water baths. Book a Swedish massage and a therapeutic soak when you visit. Open year-round; (618) 243-5458.

Preserved rather than restored, the *Heritage House Museum of Okawville,* also called the *Schlosser Home,* is located at 114 West Walnut Street. Open Saturday and Sunday noon to 4:00 P.M. *Dr. Poo's Home and Medical Museum,* at 202 North Front Street, is the former Victorian home of Dr. Poo. Open by appointment. Donations requested; (618) 243-5694.

Nashville is the Washington County seat, and was named after the hometown of the first area settlers from Tennessee. In the northeast part of the city, on thirty-seven acres of rolling wooded land, *Nashville Memorial Park* is a center for outdoor recreational activity. A swimming complex with separate areas for diving, toddlers, and intermediate swimmers was completed in 1981. The pool can accommodate 371 on a busy summer day. The park's other facilities include four baseball diamonds, tennis courts, a playground, picnic areas, and even a challenging par 36 nine-hole municipal golf course.

In town the *First Presbyterian Church,* 419 West St. Louis Street, is one of the oldest churches in Illinois. Organized in 1832, the present church building dates from 1884.

southwestern illinoistrivia

After Illinois came under U.S. control following the Revolutionary War, many of the French inhabitants of the region, unimpressed with the American lifestyle, left for Spanish Louisiana,. A French traveler in southwestern Illinois in the 1790s observed this phenomenon among his North American brethren, noting the large number of abandoned homes in what had once been French villages. He chalked this up to the rather negative traits his countrymen had acquired in this strange land, which made them unfit for a proper livelihood—hence their exodus. "The French of the Illinois country", he remarked, "have been brought up in and accustomed to the Fur Trade with the savages, and have thus become the laziest and most ignorant of all men. They live and the majority of them are clothed in the manner of the Savages."

magicwaters

For more than 150 years, visitors have flocked to a haven of health in the village of Okawville. The Original Springs Hotel and Bath House, which was renovated in 2004 and is recognized on the National Register of Historic Places, is the last natural mineral springs resort still operating in the state.

In the late 1800s Okawville weathered competition from Dixon, Illinois, which touted its own hotel "health spa" and seven mineral springs. Eventually, the Dixon enterprise fell into disrepair and in the 1940s the land and mineral springs were incorporated in to Dixon Springs State Park.

The *Washington County Historical Society Museum,* 300 South Kaskaskia Street, houses artifacts and exhibits relative to the history of the area. The museum is open Sunday 1:30 to 3:30 P.M. or by appointment. The historical society also maintains the nearby historic *McKelvey one-room schoolhouse* just west of town (open by appointment only).

Or plan a visit on the third week in September when Nashville holds its yearly *Fall Festival Days* on the courthouse square, complete with music, food, and crafts. Call (618) 327–3700.

Four miles south of Nashville, off Route 127, is the *Washington County Conservation Area,* a 1,440-acre preserve set in rolling wooded hills. A central part of the area is a 248-acre lake with 13 miles of shoreline. Bass, bluegill, crappie, and catfish are the most frequently caught species. The lake, which has a ten-horsepower limit, has launch ramps and a marina that rents boats and motors and sells tackle, bait, and snacks. A 7-mile trail winds through the woods of the conservation area. Campers, too, can enjoy the habitat, with campsites for tent camping and others with electric hookups and showers. The park is accessible year-round; (618) 327–3137.

The Great Outdoors

Carbondale, with a population of 21,000, is the largest city in Jackson County and home to *Southern Illinois University* (founded in 1869). The college, with 22,000 students, is known for its sports teams, the Salukis, especially in basketball, which is played at SIU Arena, and football, at McAndrew Stadium. If you're in town during the season, be sure to catch a game with all its Southern Illinois enthusiasm. For tickets contact the Soluki Ticket Office, SIU; (618) 453–2000. The university's *Faner Museum and Art Galleries* have changing exhibits and works of special interest to southern Illinois. Open Tuesday through Friday, 10:00 A.M. to 4:00 P.M., Saturday and Sunday, 1:00 to 4:00 P.M. Call (618) 453–5388.

With the city having a name like Carbondale, one might guess that a primary industry hereabouts is coal mining. On the banks of the Big Muddy River, which flows to the west of Carbondale, was the first coal-mining operation in Illinois. As early as 1810 the river bluffs supplied coal for local needs and to ship downriver to New Orleans. The beauty of the landscape, however, is largely undisturbed, with the Shawnee National Forest beginning just miles to the south and rivers and lakes all around.

Giant City State Park, with 4,000 acres of recreational area, is located in the southeast corner of the county, 12 miles south of Carbondale off U.S. Highway 51 and Route 13. The park takes its name from the huge and dramatic sandstone formations here, such as the dramatic Devil's Stand-table, just west of the park's *Visitor Center.* The center has trained staff who will explain the various natural features of the park and offers *Illinois Junior Naturalist* programs and a Discovery Center.

One unusual man-made structure here is the *Stone Fort,* which sits atop a 50-foot sandstone cliff. The *Stone Fort Trail* will take you to the stone wall, which today is probably a fraction of its original height, and is thought to be the work of Native Americans. This is one of ten examples of such forts in southern Illinois, which may have been used for defense or ceremonial purposes.

civilwar memories

Once you stretch toward the southernmost points of Illinois, especially in the foothills-of-the-Ozarks country, you start to notice more mentions of the Civil War. When in Carbondale, take a brief sidetrip to Woodlawn Cemetery, which is listed on the National Register of Historic Places.

It was here in 1866 that the first unofficial Memorial Day service was observed honoring our fighting men who died in battle. Wander the tranquil grounds, and you'll discover more than sixty graves of Civil War soldiers.

Other evidence of prehistoric people in the region is found in rock shelters, whose roofs are presumably smoke stained from campfires. During the Civil War these shelters were used by deserters from both sides.

A surprisingly modern construction in the park is the award-winning design of the park's 100,000-gallon spherical water tank. Eighty-two feet high, the tower has an observation platform with excellent views of the park. Some 50 feet up, the platform is reached by a spiral steel staircase.

Within the park is the 170-acre *Fern Rocks Nature Preserve,* where such rare plants as French's shooting star and large flowering mint may be found. Hiking is allowed only on the preserve's well-marked trail. Spring may

Chateau Carbondale

When you think of fine wine country, you might think of France, or in the United States, the Sonoma Valley in California. Now add Carbondale to that list.

Okay, so Carbondale might not be on a par with those renown wine-producing regions of the world. But it is the heart of Illinois' wine country, with at least three vineyards that have coaxed award-winning vintages out of the heartland soil.

See (and taste) for yourself at Carbondale's Alto Vineyards (618–893–4898), Blue Sky Vineyard (618–995–9463), and Starview Vineyards (618–893–9463).

be the best time to visit the park, for it is abloom with more than one-hundred different types of ferns and flowering plants. Birds abound in the park as well, and they make for excellent bird-watching.

Fishing is offered at *Little Grassy Lake,* adjacent to the park, and picnicking and camping are available, too (161 sites, 117 with electric hookups). For information on Giant City State Park, contact the Site Superintendent, 235 Giant City Road, Makanda; (618) 457–4836. You will receive a brochure that includes a short discussion of Little Grassy Lake. For a complete list of regulations governing the use of boats on this lake, however, write: Refuge Manager, Crab Orchard National Wildlife Refuge, Marion 62958 or call (618) 997–3344.

Noncampers might opt for the *Giant City Lodge and Cottages*—thirty-four rustic cabins built of native stone in the state park. The dining room serves hearty meals around a handsome fireplace. There's a swimming pool here, too. Open February to December. Call (618) 457–4921.

Jackson County's second major city is Murphysboro, the county seat. The apple is king here, with more than thirty-one commercial orchards in the vicinity. In fact, mid-September ushers in the annual *Apple Festival,* with pie-baking, apple-peeling and apple-butter contests, a beauty pageant, and a parade led by Captain Applesauce. For dates and events, call the Chamber of Commerce at (618) 684–6421. Historically, Murphysboro is the birthplace of Gen. John A. Logan, Civil War leader and United States senator.

Kincaid Lake, northwest of Murphysboro, was created in 1968 by the state as a recreation area and water supply for the region. Its 2,750 acres, with 82 miles of timbered shoreline, serve those purposes admirably. Fishing, camping, boating, swimming, and hunting in season are offered. Bass fishing is best during the months of April and May in this deep reservoir, bottoming out at 68 feet near the dam. Kincaid Lake is bounded by Route 149, Route 3, and Route 127 and is located approximately 5 miles northwest of Murphysboro.

Two marinas service the boating public. One of them, *Kincaid Lake Marina,* not only sells bait and tackle but also has boat rentals, a restaurant, and campground; (618) 687–4914. To get there travel west from Murphysboro on Route 149 approximately 8 miles to a blacktop road marked Kincaid Lake.

Lake Murphysboro State Park is situated about 1 mile west of Murphysboro off Route 149. The 1,000-acre park offers a number of recreational possibilities, from fishing to woodland hikes. An unusual feature of the park is the patches of native wild orchids. Nine varieties grow here. Camping includes sites with electric hookups (seventy-seven sites total). Contact Site Superintendent, 52 Cinder Hill Drive, Murphysboro; (618) 684–2867.

Cedar Lake, in the southern part of the county, is a 1,750-acre body of water about 4 miles southwest of Carbondale on Route 51. For more information call (618) 549–8441.

Crab Orchard National Wildlife Refuge was officially established by the Department of the Interior in 1947 and now covers 43,000 acres. The area includes three lakes, twelve natural areas, and a 4,000-acre wilderness area.

Forest, prairie, and wetland plants and animals live harmoniously in Crab Orchard. Wildlife management is centered on providing winter feeding and resting areas for Canada geese, and the refuge's goose flock may build up to 200,000 birds by December. Many species of ducks and bald eagles can be seen in the trees overlooking the goose flock.

Spring brings most of the migratory waterfowl, and eagles, whitetail deer (common year-round), coyote, beaver, muskrat, opossum, and raccoon also inhabit the area. A bird list is available at the refuge headquarters.

Land of the Giants

This might be one of the most beautiful natural areas in the entire state. Giant City is nestled in the dense hills of the sprawling 260,000-acre Shawnee National Forest. It got its name from early settlers who thought that the unusual sandstone rock formations, formed more than 200 million years ago, resembled the streets of a city built for a giant.

That's what I thought, too, the first time I ventured down to this extreme southern portion of the state. But the long drive from Chicago was well worth it. And if you don't want to camp in a leaky tent, you'll find overnighting at the Giant City State Park Lodge a night well spent. Built in 1930 by members of the government's Civilian Conservation Corps, the lodge is located in the midst of nearly 4,000 acres of sandstone bluffs and woods. Both the park and the lodge are listed on the National Register of Historic Places.

Wildlife-oriented recreation is encouraged, and the opportunities for wildlife observation are excellent. For hikers there is the self-guided ***Chamnesstown School Trail.*** The trail explores a reconstructed schoolhouse and ventures out along old fire trails in open areas of the refuge. Observation towers are wonderful lookouts for watching geese, and there are picnicking areas by ***Crab Orchard Lake.***

Hunting and fishing are allowed, and there are a concession-operated campground and marina as well as swimming.

The refuge is located between Carbondale and Marion, accessible from Interstate 57. Visitors are permitted only in designated areas. The visitor center is open 8:00 A.M. to 4:30 P.M. Monday through Friday. For information contact the Refuge Manager, Crab Orchard National Wildlife Refuge, 8588 Route 148, Marion; (618) 997–3344.

Little Grassy Fish Hatchery, downstream of Little Grassy Lake, is a 115-acre hatchery with a visitors' observation area where you can view rearing, spawning, and egg incubation tanks.

more surprises

Giant City, Fern Rocks, Buffalo Rock, Rainbow Arch . . . these names can't possibly describe stunning geographical features in the prairie state of Illinois, right?

Wrong. The surpassing terrain, at least surprising to visitors who haven't ventured to the far reaches of southern Illinois, is one of the great revelations of this region, one filled with rock formations and landforms that took more than 200 million years to develop into fantastical shapes. Then there's the Shawnee National Forest, another of Mother Nature's treasures. And what about those craggy, tree-studded bluffs hugging the shores of the Mississippi and Ohio Rivers?

Surprises are endless for travelers here, so take your time (actually, you have no choice due to geography and resultant road patterns) and enjoy nature's handiwork.

The warm-water hatchery combines two methods of fish rearing: intensive and extensive culture. Intensive culture uses a high water exchange through a rearing unit for environmental control and allows rearing of large numbers of fish per unit. Extensive culture uses earthen ponds, an extension of nature, but with some control as to the number of fish per pond and the food organisms available.

The original hatchery was built in 1959, and expansion and modernization began in July 1979, as a result of a state study of projected demands for fish stocking. Largemouth bass, bluegill, red-ear sunfish, and channel catfish are reared here as well as some smallmouth bass, walleye, muskellunge, northern pike, and striped bass.

The hatchery is south of Carbondale and accessible via Little Grassy Road. It is within the boundaries of Crab Orchard Wildlife Refuge. Visitor tours are on a self-guided basis, though employee-guided tours can be scheduled for large groups. Hours are 8:00 A.M. to 3:30 P.M. daily; (618) 529–4100.

Johnson County is a paradise for those interested in Indian history and nature.

Buffalo Rock, 3 miles northeast of Simpson off Route 147 toward Reynoldsburg, has the outline of a buffalo etched into the side of a sandstone cliff. Native Americans are said to be the artists responsible for this drawing. The trail leading to the site is filled with lovely beech and sugar maple trees, and dozens of colorful wildflowers carpet the forest floor in spring.

The **Milestone Bluff,** north off Route 147 at Robbs, is an ancient Indian dwelling and burial site. The bluff has a prehistoric stone wall and Indian grave sites. The Mississippi Indians are believed to have inhabited the area from A.D. 1000 to 1500. The hiking trail to the bluff begins at the parking lot.

Rainbow Arch, less than 1 mile west of Cypress off Route 37, is a bridge of sandstone rock surrounded by beautiful white and red oak trees and wild black cherries. One of the largest natural bridges in southern Illinois, it is 66 feet long, 3 ½ feet wide, and 7 feet high at its peak.

The **River-to-River Trail,** east off U.S. Highway 45, 3 ½ miles north of I–24 at Vienna, is a dirt trail stretching nearly halfway around the entire southern tip

Where Am I?

For my money, southwestern Illinois and the Shawnee National Forest are the most intriguing places in the state. I feel this way, I suppose, because they are so unlike the Illinois I'm used to. On my first trip down here, many were the times when I momentarily believed I was in some other state, only to remind myself with a jolt that I was indeed in Illinois.

My first night was spent camping in Turkey Bayou, which reminded me of Louisiana. The next day I hiked and drove along the backroads, which at times had me convinced I was in Kentucky or Tennessee—especially when I had to drive around two old hound dogs asleep in the middle of the street in front of a shack selling cigarettes and beer.

My campsite in Giant City State Park had a path leading to a rocky bluff where I sat and watched the hawks circling over the ridges and valleys—a vista very similar to what you find in the mountains of Virginia.

For a northern Illinois flatlander like myself, it was indeed a truly dislocating experience.

of Illinois. Three connecting trails make it more than 170 miles long. Plans are being made to extend the trail over the entire southern end of Illinois.

The peaceful *Tunnel Hill State Trail* follows the former Norfolk Southern railroad bed, sans the tracks. In fact, the surface of compacted limestone makes the 45-mile trail popular with bicyclists and hikers. The 543-foot-long tunnel is a highlight, taking explorers from daylight to an eerie darkness, and back to daylight. The *Breeden Trestle* is the tallest of the twenty-one still remaining. Information kiosks, rustic bathroom facilities, and drinking water are along the way. Start at the trail headquarters in Vienna, on the north side of Illinois Route 146. Open daily, dawn to dusk; (618) 658–2168.

southwestern illinoistrivia

In 1925 a deadly tornado ripped through Murphysboro, killing 700 after it swept through Illinois, Missouri, and Indiana. Its path was 220 miles long and 1 mile wide.

Little Black Slough Natural Area, half a mile east of Route 37 and Route 146, boasts some of the most unusual and spectacular terrain in all of Illinois— and is one of its best-kept secrets. The area is a mixture of primeval tupelo and cypress swamps, rich floodplain forest, and upland woods, with small patches of limestone prairie glades. Some of the oldest living trees east of the Mississippi River are here, and a boardwalk allows access to the heart of the swamp. Nine miles of hiking trails wind through Little Black Slough.

Ferne Clyffe State Park, 1 mile south of Goreville, is another natural eye-opener. It has almost 2,500 acres of the largest bluffs and caves in the area. A sixteen-acre fishing lake is within the park. The preserve has a central valley from which radiate gorges and canyons. Shady dells, natural cathedrals, domes, brooks, cascades, and rills have formed here. Several so-called caves are not really caves but great protruding ledges of rock that make an arched roof.

Hawks Cave is a sheer cliff of stone so hewn by wind and water that an excavation has been made at its base at least 150 feet long and as many feet high. The cave has a natural pulpit and excellent acoustics. Park facilities include picnicking, fishing, camping, and horseback-riding trails.

For information about both Ferne Clyffe State Park and Little Black Slough Natural Area, contact the Site Superintendent, Ferne Clyffe State Park, P.O. Box 10, Goreville 62939; (618) 995–2411.

Vienna can't live up to the expectations of its name, but it does have some attractions worth seeing. The *Vienna Times Building* is beautifully preserved. It was built around 1890 as a bank, and in 1915 the *Vienna Times* newspaper took it over. It is at the Vienna public square 4 blocks west of the junction of

Route 146W and US 45 at the corner of East Main and Fourth Streets. It is open to the public during business hours.

The *Paul Powell Home and Museum,* also 4 blocks west of this junction at 404 Vine Street, is the home of former Illinois secretary of state and Illinois representative Paul Powell. The Johnson County Historical Society is located in the house, which is open Tuesday and Friday 10:00 A.M. to 4:00 P.M., and Saturday 8:00 A.M. to noon; by appointment in winter; (618) 995–2068.

Cairo, the county seat of Alexander County, is where the magnolia vies with the mimosa. The southernmost city in Illinois, it stands on the tip of a narrow peninsula where the Mississippi and Ohio Rivers join on their journey to the Gulf of Mexico.

This area, known as Little Egypt, has many attractions for tourists to explore. A notable bronze statue titled **The Hewer** stands prominently in Halliday Park. Created by artist George Grey Barnard, the work was commissioned by the wife and children of former local resident Captain Halliday and was presented to the city in 1906. The inscription on the base reads: A VISION OF MEN LABORING ON THE SHORE OF A FLOOD HEWING AND DRAGGING WOOD TO SAVE THE PEOPLE FROM DEATH AND DESTRUCTION. Lorado Taft said *The Hewer* was one of the two finest nudes produced in America.

The *Cairo Public Library* contains several fine works of art. The building itself is an example of Queen Anne architecture. The leaded stained-glass windows are original. In two niches at the entrance stand statues of *Clio,* the Greek muse, and *Concordia,* the Roman goddess of peace. A bronze fountain entitled **Fishing Boys** is the work of American sculptor Janet Scudder.

In the library reference room is a replica of the steamboat **City of Cairo** carved by a river pilot, Capt. Henry T. Ashton, in 1876. On the first landing is a rare Tiffany grandfather's clock, one of only four of its type made by Tiffany.

Other artifacts are a chandelier that originally hung in the Cairo Opera House, a desk belonging to President Andrew Jackson, Cybis porcelains, and a collection of fine paintings. Hours are Monday 10:00 A.M. to 8:00 P.M., Tuesday and Wednesday 10:00 A.M. to 5:00 P.M., Thursday 2:00 to 8:00 P.M., Saturday 9:00 A.M. to noon; 1609 Washington Avenue; (618) 734–1840.

southwestern illinoistrivia

Steamboat pilots called the section of the Mississippi River between Cairo and St. Louis "the graveyard" because more than 300 boats had sunk in that stretch of water by 1867.

The *U.S. Customs House* at Washington Avenue and Fifteenth Street is a rare example of a Palazzo or Commercial Italianate–style stone building, and it is on the National Register of Historic Places. Inside you'll find a museum featuring local and Civil War history, as well as Lewis and Clark exhibits. Open 10:00 A.M. to noon and 1:00 to 3:00 P.M. Monday through Friday; (618) 734–1019.

Magnolia Manor, 2700 Washington Avenue, is a Victorian mansion and museum. It is open Monday through Saturday 9:00 A.M. to 4:30 P.M. and Sunday from 1:00 to 4:30 P.M.; (618) 734–0201. Admission is $5.00. The house is a four-story redbrick mansion of Italianate architecture. Large magnolia trees grace its lawn. There are fourteen rooms and a bed that Gen. Ulysses S. Grant slept in.

Grant also attended a lavish party given in his honor here. Especially suited for celebrations, the home sparkles during the holidays. Christmas open houses are Sunday 1:00 to 4:00 P.M., but dates fluctuate, so call for schedule; (618) 734–0201.

southwestern illinoistrivia

Collinsville boasts the "world's tallest catsup bottle," which is actually a 170-foot water tank.

Now a park, *Fort Defiance,* at Cairo Point, was a strategic site for settlement and fortification as early as 1673, when it was first sighted by explorers Jacques Marquette and Robert La Salle.

Where the Mississippi and Ohio Rivers meet, there is a single piece of mounted artillery. Starting in 1848 the cannon was used to greet arriving boats.

Fort Defiance State Park has facilities for picnicking and fishing on its thirty-eight acres. The *Boatmen's Memorial* is a triple-decked building resembling a boat. The first deck is a sheltered picnic area with tables. The second and third decks provide outlooks; the second also supports the flagpole. For information call (618) 734–4127.

Mound City National Cemetery, 4 miles from the park, is a Civil War cemetery with 27 identified Confederate soldiers and 2,759 unknown ones.

Also interesting is the *Thebes Historical Courthouse* in Thebes, west of Route 3 at Thebes Spur. It is a brick-and-stone courthouse set precariously near the edge of a limestone bluff overlooking the town of Thebes and the Mississippi River. The courthouse was known as the "Courthouse on the Bluff." Here Dred Scott was imprisoned and Abraham Lincoln practiced law. It is an example of Greek Revival architecture and made of local materials.

Between mid-December 1838 and early March 1839, over 8,000 Cherokee were forced to travel 800 miles from their home in the Great Smoky Mountains to a reservation in present-day Oklahoma. The exiled Cherokees stopped in southern Illinois because of floating ice on the Mississippi and made camp. The camp provided little shelter against the unusually severe winter that year and many died. The Cherokees' westward journey became known as the "Trail of Tears."

Trail of Tears State Forest, formerly Union State Forest, is northwest of Jonesboro near the Mississippi River. It lies within the beautiful Shawnee Hill country and is a preserve to protect native tree species of Illinois. Approximately 120 acres are devoted to the Union State Tree Nursery, and nearly all species of trees in southern Illinois are found here.

The park has picnicking facilities, approximately forty-four trails totaling more than 36 miles, hunting, and tent camping. You can reach the park by taking Route 3 to Wolf Lake; then drive east for 5 miles. For information call (618) 833–4910.

The **Union County Conservation Area** is in the Lower Mississippi River Bottomlands Division of Illinois. It is a haven for wildlife; most prominent for five months of the year is the flock of Canada geese and other waterfowl that winter in the area. Hunting is allowed on the south end of the site, but there are no overnight or day-use facilities. This conservation area is southwest of Jonesboro off Route 3 near Reynoldsville. For information contact the Union County Conservation Area, 2755 Refuge Road, Jonesboro; (618) 833–5175.

Finally, last, but not least, the town of Cobden is proudly nicknamed the Appleknocker Town after the school's mascot. In June 2006, the **Union County Illinois Historical and Genealogy Society Museum** opened its doors after more than thirty years in the planning. The new home is in the 1892 H. A. Dubois building which is a monument in itself, being a fine example of a metal-front Mesker Brothers building. Part of the collection on display is that of the former Cobden Museum, which was formed in 1961. This new museum is a labor of community love, as many of the displays contain treasures donated by area citizens. Hours are Saturday and Sunday 1:00 to 5:00 P.M., or call for an appointment. Closed holidays. Free admission; (618) 893–2865.

southwestern illinoistrivia

The late Robert Pershing Wadlow, "the world's tallest man" at 8'11", was born in Alton.

Kaskaskia Island is the only part of Illinois that lies west of the Mississippi River.

southwestern illinoistrivia

The Bald Knob Cross in Alto Pass, a 111-foot-tall cross of steel and white porcelain, is one of the largest Christian monuments in North America.

Places to Stay in Southwestern Illinois

CARBONDALE

America's Best Inn and Suites,
1345 East Main Street,
(618) 529–4801

Giant City Lodge,
460 Giant City Lodge Road,
(618) 457–4921

Horizon Inn,
800 East Main Street,
(618) 529–1100

Quality Inn,
1415 East Main Street,
(618) 549–4244

Ramada Inn,
801 North Giant City Road,
(618) 351–6611

Touch of Nature Environmental Center Lodge
at Southern Illinois University,
Makanda,
(618) 453–1121

DU QUOIN

Budget Inn,
1266 South Washington,
(618) 542–5014

Francie's Bed and Breakfast Inn,
104 South Line Street,
(618) 542–6686

FAIRVIEW HEIGHTS

Drury Inn,
12 Ludwig Drive,
(618) 398–8530

Fairfield Inn,
140 Ludwig Drive,
(618) 398–7124

Four Points Sheraton,
319 Fountains Parkway,
(618) 622–9500

Hampton Inn,
150 Ludwig Drive,
(618) 397–9705

MARION

Comfort Inn,
2600 West Main Street,
(618) 993–6221

Drury Inn,
2706 West DeYoung Street,
(618) 997–9600

Hampton Inn,
2710 West De Young Street,
(618) 998–9900

OKAWVILLE

Original Springs Hotel,
506 North Hanover,
(618) 243–5458

SELECTED VISITORS BUREAUS AND CHAMBERS OF COMMERCE

Southwestern Illinois Tourism and Convention Bureau,
10950 Lincoln Trail,
Fairview Heights 62208
(800) 442–1488

Carbondale Convention and Visitors Bureau,
1245 East Main Street,
Carbondale 62901
(800) 526–1500

Williamson County Tourism Board,
1602 Sioux Drive,
Marion 62959
(800) 433–7399

OTHER ATTRACTIONS WORTH SEEING IN SOUTHWESTERN ILLINOIS

U.S. Custom House,
Cairo

West Walnut Historic District,
Cairo

Hundley House,
Cairo

Southern Illinois University Touch of Nature Environment Center,
Carbondale

Chester Riverfront Mural,
Chester

Owl Creek Vineyard and Winery,
Cobden

Maeystown National Historic Site,
Maeystown

Little Grand Canyon,
Murphysboro

Rainbow Ranch,
Nashville

Dr. Poo's Museum,
Okawville

Places to Eat in Southwestern Illinois

CARBONDALE

Larry's Pit BBQ,
1181 Rendleman Road,
(618) 549-1599

Mary Lou's Grill,
114 South Illinois Avenue,
(618) 457-5084

Tres Hombres,
119 North
Washington Street,
(618) 457-3308

DU QUOIN

To Perfection,
1664 South Washington
Street,
(618) 542-2002

MARION

Hideout Steakhouse,
2606 West Main Street,
(618) 997-8325

Sao Asian Bistro,
2800 Seventeenth Street,
(618) 993-2828

Indexes

Entries for Festivals and Museums appear in the special index beginning on page 225

FESTIVALS

MUSEUMS

About the Authors

Bob Puhala is an award-winning writer who has authored more than thirty books. He also wrote a syndicated travel column for the *Chicago Sun-Times* for fifteen years. His work has apeared in national magazines, and he has been a frequent expert guest on television and radio talk shows. Bob's travels have taken him extensively through America's heartland, as well as the rest of North America.

Lyndee Jobe Henderson has been digging up history, literally, ever since she was a little girl accompanying her father on archaeological digs. As a freelance writer and lifelong student of Pennsylvania and Illinois history, she has authored several books on her favorite subjects including *Johnstown, Pennsylvania,* and *More than Petticoats: Remarkable Illinois Women.*